A RACE TOO FAR

A RACE TOO FAR

Chris Eakin

EBURY
PRESS

1 3 5 7 9 10 8 6 4 2

Published in 2009 by Ebury Press, an imprint of Ebury Publishing
A Random House Group Company

The Random House Group Limited Reg. No. 954009

Addresses for companies within the Random House Group can be
found at www.randomhouse.co.uk

A CIP catalogue record for this book is available from
the British Library

The Random House Group Limited supports The Forest Stewardship
Council (FSC), the leading international forest certification
organisation. All our titles that are printed on Greenpeace approved
FSC certified paper carry the FSC logo. Our paper procurement
policy can be found at www.rbooks.co.uk/environment

Mixed Sources
Product group from well-managed
forests and other controlled sources
www.fsc.org   Cert no. TT-COC-2139
© 1996 Forest Stewardship Council
FSC

Printed in the UK by CPI Mackays, Chatham, ME5 8TD

ISBN 9780091932596

All photos © The *Sunday Times*/NI Syndication except for the following:
Belongings on *Victress*; Tetley self portraits; Eve Tetley at reunion –
all courtesy of Eve Tetley.
Knox-Johnston approaching Falmouth © Mirrorpix

To buy books by your favourite authors and register for offers visit
www.rbooks.co.uk

CONTENTS

In memory of my mother,
Valerie Eakin (1933 to 2008)

ACKNOWLEDGEMENTS

This book could not have been written without the time and co-operation given so generously by the people involved in the story. Eve Tetley, Clare Crowhurst and Francoise Moitessier all welcomed me into their homes and tolerated persistent and, at times, intense questioning. Thank you.

Likewise, Simon Crowhurst.

The book would have been incomplete without Sir Robin Knox-Johnston and less colourful without Chay Blyth, both famous and busy men.

Bill King and daughter Leonie laid on an entertaining and fascinating weekend in their Galway castle. Loïck Fougeron and Alex Carozzo were gentlemen.

Craig Rich, in his Plymouth study, was an immense help in sorting fact from fiction. Glin Bennet, the Bristol psychiatrist, showed me material old and new.

Many people helped me around French and Italian language difficulties. Kathy Harcombe, a journalist colleague at the BBC, used her own time to read Francoise's autobiography and translate key sections, and was the telephone contact with Francoise. Grainne Harrington in Paris found Francoise Lecat, my excellent translator for the south of France visit. Emanuel

Richelmy, an Italian sailing journalist at Fare Vela, was invaluable in helping track down Alex Carozzo at the eleventh hour.

Staff at the British Newspaper Library in north London helped direct long days of research on the race. Likewise, the local library in Dover.

Many of the photographs in this book have been seen rarely, if at all. The *Sunday Times* archive staff in Wapping tolerated my presence over two days. Thanks especially to Chris Whalley, Sinead Porter and Mick Bone. Also, the film director Jerry Rothwell was generous in giving me access to existing photo scans.

Literary agent John Pawsey understood the strength of the story instantly. Likewise, thanks to the Ebury team, led by Andrew Goodfellow and Ali Nightingale.

My brother Mike was invaluable for reading, correcting and lobbying hard in the interests of non sailors.

My wife, Debbie, put up with long periods of obsessive behaviour and, most importantly, was the single biggest influence on the text. Her repeated proof readings were forensic and unforgiving and this book is much the better for it.

Finally, my mother, for being embarrassingly enthusiastic about the book but who passed away unexpectedly before having the chance to read it.

Golden Globe yacht race of 1968 - world route

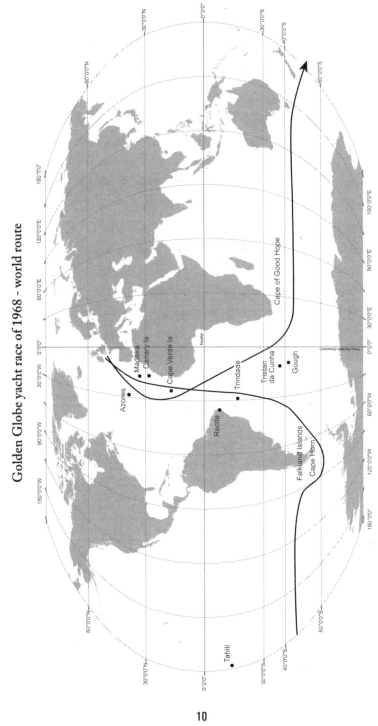

1 : THREE WIDOWS

All three women were dressed up in fine winter coats to keep out a cold, New Year wind on the River Thames. Each was poised and elegant, knowing that, for now, they were the story. The press photographer took no risks, manoeuvring his inexperienced subjects into a variety of poses. The women showed only the slight apprehension of those unfamiliar with a photo shoot. They were in the prime of their lives and were enjoying the attention brought to them by their husbands' race at sea. By now, the race had been under way for seven months and probably had another six to go. Already there had been chaos. Storm-force winds at the bottom of Africa had knocked some boats out. Others suffered structural damage, their battered skippers left with potentially life-or-death decisions: should they carry on beyond the point of no return, into the vast and wild Southern Ocean, or should they give up? Those who continued were in unknown territory; no one had ever achieved what each was striving for, to be the first person to sail around the world single-handed without stopping.

Out of nine starters, there were only four left. A young officer in the merchant navy, Robin Knox-Johnston, had separated from his wife well before leaving. In the superficial world of newspaper stunts, therefore, he did not count on the occasion of this photo shoot. The three remaining entrants, to the relief of newspaper editors, did have wives: Clare Crowhurst, Francoise Moitessier and Eve Tetley. On this January day in 1969, they were ushered around the deck of a tall ship, *Discovery*, stopping at every conceivable backdrop to smile for the camera. They chatted nervously, always wary of the fact that their husbands were rivals. Above all, they did what was asked of them. In an age when some of the boats racing round the world did not have radios and their dramatic stories went unheard for months, the three women were helping a newspaper industry that was having a terrible time filling in long, blank spaces between the relatively rare moments of real news. If they had realised how contrived the day's story was going to be they might have been less willing. The headline beneath the chosen photograph shouted *'The Sea Widows They Left Behind'*. It was disposable nonsense at the time, but it was to become eerily prophetic: two of the women would become widows for real and the third a widow in all but name.

The photo shoot in London was to be the first and only time all three women would meet, even though their stories would become entwined. They would each endure a personal tragedy with one thing in common – publicity. Once the media interest was turned on, it could not be turned off. The women's grief would be played out on the front pages. Two, Clare Crowhurst and Eve Tetley, would spend the next 40 years barely speaking of their suffering – even to friends and family – and it is only four decades on that all three women have spoken frankly.

Eve Tetley was a tall, vivacious newly-wed, living her life in something of a whirlwind. She had been married to Lieutenant Commander Nigel Tetley for only two years, having known him for all of a month before walking down the aisle. They were introduced to each other at a meeting set up by friends in a Plymouth pub. It is a moment still etched on her mind. 'I even remember exactly what I was wearing, a beautiful little Jaeger, twill cotton suit. The Mary Quant look with a short skirt, and of course long hair,' she says, guffawing with laughter. She was then a 27-year-old geography teacher far from her home in the north east of England, which she left to go to university in the south west. He was an older man, every inch the chisel-jawed Royal Navy commander looking forward to retirement in a couple of years' time at the age of 45. 'I looked across and it was just, you know … You read about it and you think what a load of rubbish. What a load of rubbish, and that was it. It was a love-at-first-sight job. A month later I sent my parents a telegram saying "Arranged wedding". We were married in Durham, literally a month after we met.' Eve's father, a detective chief superintendent and head of Durham CID, looked up the name and rank of Lieutenant Commander Nigel Tetley in the Royal Navy list to check the man his daughter was marrying was real. In fact, Nigel was from rather good stock or, as Eve puts it now, from a 'très snob' English family of British Empire days. His mother was the daughter of a judge in southern Africa where Nigel himself was born and where his father was in the British Army.

The newly-weds were nonconformist from the start. Eve rejected the logical route of officers' married quarters and instead they set up home on board Nigel's boat, a 40-foot-long trimaran berthed in Plymouth's industrial docks. His two sons from his previous marriage, teenagers Philip and Mark, lived with them when they were not away at boarding school.

It was the same boat, *Victress*, on which Nigel was now racing around the world in competition with eight other men. Like so many of the other competitors, Nigel had tried and failed to raise sponsorship money for a purpose-built boat. As a result, he ended up leaving Britain's shores in the family home.

At the photo shoot on the Thames, Eve Tetley was getting on considerably better with Francoise Moitessier than she was with Clare Crowhurst. When Eve mentioned her own unpaid bills, like £150 for a self-steering device for her husband's boat, she felt Clare was upstaging her with talk of bills for thousands. 'I just didn't like her,' says Eve laughing loudly, forty years on. 'It isn't often I don't like people. I don't think she liked me. We met just that once. Never since. Never talked. No communication.'

Clare Crowhurst remembers that meeting and remembers putting to Eve that their two husbands were perceived as specific rivals before they had even started. They were the only two to be sailing trimarans, a relatively new type of boat seen as fast but potentially dangerous for such a voyage. 'There was that comment before they went,' says Clare. 'Nigel Tetley said the one person I am not going to allow to beat me is Donald Crowhurst. When I met Eve in London she brushed that comment off.'

It would be remarkable if the two women's memories of each other had not been influenced by the terrible events yet to unfold. Eve would go on to blame her rival's husband for the downfall of her own.

Clare Crowhurst and Eve Tetley had one thing in common. Just as Eve had moved from Durham to Plymouth, so Clare had moved hundreds of miles from home as a young woman. She had grown up in Killarney in the west of Ireland where her Anglo-Irish mother had settled with an Irish farmer, converting to Catholicism in the process. Clare was barely out of her teens when she moved with her sister to England in what were the post-war years of the early 1950s. She worked in the BBC monitoring station at Caversham in Berkshire, where she typed up listening reports for Downing Street and the Oval Office. The two sisters shared a flat in Reading, and it was at one of their parties that Clare met Donald. He was in his mid 20s and had a growing reputation. Not only had he been an officer in both the RAF and the army, he had been thrown out of both for a series of largely drunken exploits, including trying to steal a car, being found under a bed in a compromising position with a brigadier's daughter and crashing a car into a bus, for which he lost his licence. Without a car but undefeated, Donald wooed Clare with trips on a tandem. 'It was great fun,' she says. 'We used to ride everywhere. He was different. He was a very different person.' By the time of the Golden Globe, they had four children. In that respect, Clare Crowhurst had more in common with the oldest of the three women, Francoise Moitessier.

At the time of the three women's meeting, Francoise was a fortnight from her 40th birthday. Unlike the other two, she was an established ocean-going sailor in her own right but was now concentrating on bringing up her three teenaged children. Francoise had married as soon as she left a Catholic boarding school at the age of 18. Three children in three years were followed closely by divorce, which for a young Catholic mother in 1950s France was not easy. The unpredictable Bernard Moitessier soon came into her life but with less of the chance with which Clare Crowhurst and Eve Tetley had met their men. Francoise's family had been close to Bernard's for two generations. Their fathers had gone to the same school in Marseilles, and their grandfathers had gone to the same *polytechnique*. She remembers childhood holidays with the two families together. Somehow it felt natural that Bernard should, one Sunday morning in the spring of 1958, turn up on her doorstep.

There was nothing ordinary about Bernard. His upbringing had been unorthodox. His parents had moved to Hanoi, the capital of French Indochina, just before he was born there in 1925. His father quickly made money out of colonial trading with an import/export business. Bernard grew up for 20 years in what is now Vietnam, living in something of a dream world – he failed to impress at least one teacher who called him an anarchist and a lazy dunce who would never amount to anything – a world in which he would often walk the riverbanks, watching sailing junks plying their trade. When, years later, he pitched up at Francoise's front door, near Marseilles, he was in the middle of writing a book called *The Vagabond of the Sea*, based on a series of haphazard voyages that began with sailing away from Indochina in, to no one's surprise, a junk. This man liked his freedom.

The relationship was predictably odd from the start. It was Bernard's idea to marry but only because Francoise had announced she was going to move to Brussels where she had accepted a job offer in health management. The evening before the wedding he seized up with doubt, and they talked about it all night before deciding in the morning to go ahead with the ceremony. Quite why Bernard was so worried about his freedom is a mystery, as he clearly never intended to give up much of it. By the time the three Golden Globe women were being photographed in London, Francoise had grown used to tolerating an ever-growing string of affairs. 'I knew he was with other women,' she says. 'But I knew our relationship was strong, so it didn't matter. It was a good marriage. We were happy.'

Bernard's upbringing and wayward lifestyle would eventually go some way to explaining his bizarre behaviour in the Golden Globe.

For now, Robin Knox-Johnston and the three husbands, Nigel Tetley, Donald Crowhurst and Bernard Moitessier, were battling it out on two fronts. Each was focusing on his own survival, pitted against the elements, and each was wary of the others' positions on the globe, determined to win a place in the history books.

2 : GIANT LEAP FOR MANKIND

The *Sunday Times* Golden Globe race began as little more than an opportunistic newspaper stunt, typical of the sharp-witted editor, Harold Evans. It was becoming increasingly obvious that someone was going to sail all the way round the world on their own: Francis Chichester had just done it, in 1966/7, with only one stop in Australia. Known sailors were now planning non-stop attempts and their sponsorship was already being bought up by newspapers. Harold Evans, editor of Britain's biggest selling Sunday broadsheet, was missing out, so he simply hijacked the whole concept.

In the early spring of 1968, he announced there would be a race. It was a brilliant Fleet Street wheeze. There would be almost no rules at all, beyond not being allowed to have outside assistance, having to finish where you started, and that everyone had to leave during a five-month window, from 1 June to 31 October 1968 (as this was the only sensible time in the year to go, in order to avoid the worst of the weather in the Southern Ocean, it wasn't much of a rule). The real coup was in ambushing every sailor. They were part of the race whether or not they wanted to be. There was no need to enter. There were no forms. By leaving, you were in the race, like it or not. Several did not.

The first to make it home would win the *Sunday Times* Golden Globe. Mindful of the need to spin the story out for as long as possible, the newspaper also announced that the fastest boat round the world would also win a prize of £5,000. Interest in the race would therefore be prolonged beyond that of the first competitor home.

It was, arguably, a reckless stunt as there was, of course, no guarantee that anyone would actually succeed or, for that matter, survive. In the words of Robin Knox-Johnston: 'It sounds silly now but in those days no one knew whether a boat or human could make it all the way round. Chichester stopped in Australia where his boat had a big refit. A non-stop attempt would mean perhaps ten months at sea. It was far from certain that a yacht could stay at sea for that long, totally self-sufficient and unassisted, and we just didn't know much about the possible effects of the loneliness. Psychiatrists said a human would go mad.'

It was Francis Chichester who started it all. His derring-do, nine-month-long voyage had gripped the public. He had sailed single-handed from Plymouth in south-west England and had stopped just once, in Australia. Before the official start, he had put on a showbiz leg from the Tower of London on the Thames, to Plymouth, with family and friends on board. He was tapping into a public mood; the people of England were two weeks into celebrating beating Germany in the football World Cup final of 1966 when Chichester pumped up the media hype still further by moving his specially built boat, *Gipsy Moth IV*, to Tower Pier, ready for the off. There was short-term euphoria but, in truth, the United Kingdom of Great Britain and Northern Ireland had little to shout about. The nation's place on the world stage had been steadily declining; the once-mighty Empire had been unravelling since the end of the Second World War twenty years earlier. The economy was struggling and industrial strikes were commonplace. The young were okay – it was the swinging sixties. Beatlemania was well under way and John Lennon was apologising to the Americans for saying the Beatles were more popular than Jesus. For older generations, it was all somewhat unnerving.

With hindsight, it is little wonder that the Establishment pounced on sixty-five-year-old Chichester as he sailed triumphantly into his home port in the summer of 1967. The BBC broadcast live as he bent down for the Queen to wave a ceremonial sword over his shoulders. Nothing was left to the imagination. The setting was the Grand Quadrangle of the 18th-century Royal Naval College at Greenwich and, in case the masses were not quite getting the point, the public relations people let it be known that the very same sword was apparently used to knight Francis Drake 400 years earlier. Britain might no longer be great but the people were, was the clear message: you could take away an empire but not the fact that it once existed. Countries like Britain and France were turning to modern-day adventurers either to remind their people of the glory days, or simply to distract. None of this was lost on the men who were now thinking of going one better than Chichester.

It was no coincidence that Francis Chichester's route round the world was itself a throwback to the days of Empire. What is a voyage round the world? Who says it should start from Western Europe? To most people, Chichester was simply trying to get round the world with his one stop in Australia. In fact, he was racing the average times set by the old Victorian trade clippers. It was they who set the route, using prevailing winds and currents in a pre-engine age to sail from the English Channel with cargoes of gold, wool and grain. Chichester, in planning his adventure, researched the experience of the clippers so thoroughly that, before leaving, he wrote a book about them, *Along the Clipper Way*. He knew he could not beat the pride of the fleet, the *Cutty Sark*, but he fancied his chances against the ordinary clippers' average times. He would follow their route to Australia and on round the world. It would take him down through the aptly named trade winds of the North and South Atlantics, round southern Africa's Cape of Good Hope and, crucially, into what are known as the Roaring Forties. These are the westerly winds blasting around the Southern Ocean along the latitude of 40 degrees south of the equator. It was these wild winds that created a nautical conveyor belt and made this route profitable but dangerous. Once away from Australia, Chichester, using these winds, would pass New Zealand and continue eastwards along the second half of the Southern Ocean to Cape Horn, the southern tip of America. Assuming a safe rounding of this most infamous of obstacles – made dangerous by the winds funnelling and seas breaking in what is a relative squeezing of landmasses – home was back up the two

Atlantics: in all, around 30,000 nautical miles, more than a third of which was in the unforgiving Southern Ocean (nautical miles are linked to latitude and are 15 per cent longer than statute).

The old clippers were fast, faster than Chichester as it turned out. Most of the route was sailed with the wind coming from behind – the optimum direction for the clippers' unsophisticated sails, which were at their most effective when they worked like baggy sheets.

By Chichester's period, there was no technical need for yachts to slavishly follow the old routes. The improved sails meant the wind direction was less important to them, as the sails worked more like aerofoils – like an airplane's wing providing lift – rather than simple sheets of cloth. Subtle alterations in the shape and position of these new sails meant that a yacht could now travel much closer to the wind. Even with it blowing from near the front of the boat, the sails' dynamics gave a new-found driving force that still made for good progress, whereas the old clippers' sails would have been left flapping and powerless.

So, there was a modern choice. The age-old limitations were gone and there was no need to be hamstrung by the old trade wind routes, born out of necessity. Sailing boats could now realistically travel in any direction they wanted to go.

However, no one thought of racing round the world any other way. The Golden Globe, like almost every race since, was to start in Western Europe and follow the old trade routes. It would echo the days of Empire for no particular reason other than it simply seemed the right thing to do. History, not progress, was dictating the challenge.

That was ironic because the race was soon being compared with one of the great technological advances of all time – man flying into space. Back then, any landing on the moon, whether by the Soviet Union or the United States, was still an ambition. However, it was getting closer to happening. The East–West space race was at its height just as the Golden Globe came into being. The two dreams competed for column inches in the newspapers, and took on a kind of symmetry. They were both part of a wider picture in which whole nations were looking for new challenges to interest them. It was an environment that elevated the 'single-handed' adventurers further still.

Together, the names in the two races were becoming familiar to the public. As the Golden Globe was taking shape, the astronaut Neil Armstrong was almost killed while training for the Apollo programme. He was on board a contraption called a lunar landing training vehicle, nicknamed a Flying Bedstead, when his controls started to fail. The whole machine, hovering 30 metres above the ground, began to bank. Armstrong ejected only a fraction of a second before it was too late. His near-death experience introduced him to the public just two weeks before the first Golden Globe 'entry' was confirmed on the front pages.

A little over a year later, as the Golden Globe and all of its maritime drama finished, Armstrong uttered the words 'giant leap for mankind' as he became the first man to step onto the moon. Technologically, it was an infinitely greater achievement than sailing round the world single-handed but in the newspaper game a hero is a hero, and the Golden Globe sailors basked in the same kind of adoration that Armstrong enjoyed. The two goals had shared something that was increasingly in short supply. They were journeys into the unknown. It had by no means been certain that either could or would be done.

The sharing of a place centre-stage was all very well but it was a little superficial. In contrast with the moon landing, the Golden Globe had a level of chaos and amateurism that was to become part of its charm.

Robin Knox-Johnston had started thinking of a non-stop voyage a year before the *Sunday Times* had thought up the idea of sponsoring a race. Whilst on a month's leave from his base in Bombay, India, and waiting to join a new ship as first officer, he was sitting in his parents' home in Kent, in London's southern commuter belt. A chance remark by his father was to change his life. It was March 1967 and Chichester was still at sea but on the homeward leg of his record-breaking one-stop voyage. It was obvious Chichester was heading for success and that he would, in effect, raise the bar for all other sailors. Robin's father wondered aloud who would now plan to beat the time Chichester was clearly going to set or whether anyone would even make a non-stop attempt. 'That's about all there's left to do now,' were the words left spinning in his son's head.

The young Robin was stirred further by his father's suggestion that the most likely candidate was a Frenchman. Robin was a great believer in Britain's place on the seas. The idea that a Frenchman would surpass Chichester's achievement, claiming superiority over this island nation's ruling of the waves, made his blood boil. 'We'd never hear the last of it,' he said. 'By rights a

Briton should do it first.' Robin, twenty-eight years old at the time, felt it could be him.

Robin had been married to his childhood sweetheart, Sue, while living in Bombay, but after only three years she flew back to Britain with their young daughter, Sara. Their marriage was over. Sue left over arguments about a particular dream of Robin's. In Bombay, he had been supervising the building, by hand, of a yacht made from local wood. He worked from mail-order plans sent by a company in Poole in Dorset. The boat was named after a Persian Gulf wind, *Suhaili*, and was launched, on completion, with the cracking of a coconut on her bow and scripture blessings chanted by the men who had built her. Robin had expected Sue, with baby Sara, to sail *Suhaili* 15,000 miles home with him, where he planned to sell the boat for a profit. She refused.

Although his marriage was over, the dream voyage went ahead with a brother and a friend as crew. They sailed up the Thames just in time for Robin to get back to work and join his next ship. However, she had been held up on her journey from East Africa, and Robin was told to take a month off and wait. Had it not been for that delay, the conversation in his father's sitting room might never have happened.

The decision was made. Robin was determined that he would be the first person to sail round the world single-handed without stopping. The question was how.

Robin Knox-Johnston's family background is usually described as wealthy and privileged, largely on the basis that he went to a private school, Berkhamsted, in Hertfordshire. It is an assumption that irritates him if only because of the sacrifices his parents made for his education. Born in Putney, London, and spending his early childhood in suburban Heswall, Wirral, he sees his upbringing as having been normal and middle class, without an exceptional amount of money. Certainly, there was not enough money to bankroll another adventure.

It was obvious to him that although his own boat *Suhaili* was strong and seaworthy, it would not be right for a record-breaking attempt. *Suhaili* was built from heavy teak from top to bottom. The cabin roof and walls, the deck, hull and even the keel were all solid wood. The two masts were cut from Kashmiri pine. The boat was so heavy it floated two inches lower in the water than it was designed to. At 32 feet long, it was small and, as speed is partly determined by the length of a boat's hull, slow. However, at least *Suhaili* was an asset that could be sold to help finance a professional project. The young Robin quickly persuaded a naval architect to draw up plans for an impressive but low-budget boat. The target was for the new boat to be 53 feet long, exactly the same length as Chichester's.

Robin had decided to keep the cost down to £5,000 by not bothering about the inside of his new boat: a bit of DIY would suffice. Even so, *Suhaili* was worth less than the projected new boat and, worse still, was half paid for with borrowed money. Like almost all the nine eventual starters, Robin needed a sponsor. His month's wait to start his new job was over and he had to go back to work, but rather than allowing that to get in the way he put it to good use. First Officer Knox-Johnston took advantage of his access to the passengers. They were captivated by this young man's ambition and they helped him to write more than 50 letters to blue-chip businesses. However, the coming months were to become increasingly frustrating. Not only was there a series of polite refusals but *Suhaili* was not selling. There was only one logical answer: to go with what he had. *Suhaili's* length would raise eyebrows among the sailing fraternity who would regard a length of 32 feet as ridiculously small for the hideous conditions of the Southern Ocean but Knox-Johnston knew the small size would be compensated for by the fact she was built like a tank. Having sailed her from India, he knew the boat inside out and he was confident he was a better judge of her abilities than the usual doubters and know-alls; of which there was no shortage.

Speaking forty years on, he says: 'A guy came up to me when I was working on the boat before I left. He said, "You can't do it in a boat like that." It was a stupid remark and I just laughed at him. I said, "I hope you're not a schoolteacher." He said "Why?" I said, "Because it would be bloody depressing for the kids."'

Robin made a quick but well-reasoned decision that *Suhaili* would survive the voyage. The real question was how long it would take. The slow speed meant a departure as soon as possible was imperative because it was inevitable that someone, French or not, would be competing to be the first round. There was still a problem. *Suhaili* was laid up on the mudflats of Benfleet Creek, on the northern bank of the Thames estuary. She needed an extensive refit and overhaul, including a new mast, before she could be sailed anywhere, let alone round the world.

It soon emerged, albeit vaguely, that there was indeed likely to be competition. Other sailors appeared to have plans. One was pretending to be preparing for a 1968 transatlantic race, precisely the same ploy Robin Knox-Johnston was in fact using. The shorter race was being used as cover to hide true intentions, for fear of alerting any opposition. The sailors were being secretive. They generally felt that an attempt at a round-the-world voyage did not need any complication. Each man wanted to be the first to achieve it. He did not want to alert others and create a 'race'.

All too soon, a surprise disturbed their peace and changed everything. It came at the London Boat Show in January of 1968. It was announced that a 57-year-old English submariner, Commander Bill King, who lived in a castle on Ireland's west coast, was to sail round the world that summer in a purpose-built, revolutionary yacht named after his local fox hunt, the *Galway Blazer II*. It was quite an announcement. It was a surprise even to Bill King. He was one of the men who, indeed, had been planning to sail, but not until the following year: he had not been sailing for almost two decades and needed time to remind himself how to do it. He had brought his plans forward because he got wind that someone else, whom he had not been able to identify, was planning a voyage. However, it had still been a secret that he was keeping, even from close friends. His sponsor, the *Daily Express* newspaper, had kept it quiet until unilaterally deciding to announce all while he and his family were on holiday skiing in Switzerland. The *Express* had sent a 300-word telegram to Bill's chalet explaining that they had had to act quickly because they were worried there could be rival announcements.

If the news did not exactly flush out would-be rivals, it certainly brought their intentions forward. Another military man, Captain John Ridgway of the SAS, had been thinking of an attempt for five years. He was now well into his planning and had intended to leave in a year's time. The moment he heard the *Daily Express* announcement he knew King would be regretting it, as a whole gang of people would now come forward and turn it into a race. Ridgway understood sponsorship. It would be available only if there was a chance of being first. The economics of publicity had been made starkly clear by a shrewd local businessman who spelt out to him, in blunt terms, how it all worked. He said: 'This publicity can be achieved in two ways: firstly, if you succeed; and secondly, if you fail gloriously.' So far, the advice was fairly routine and, indeed, reasonably familiar to the British. But the businessman was not finished. He pointed out there were degrees of glorious failure and, therefore, media exposure. 'It would be preferable if you died – slowly, and over the radio,' he said. Ridgway preferred the option of succeeding by being first, so he made an immediate decision to go in five months' time, hopefully before King.

Ridgway had an advantage when it came to finding a boat. He was already famous. He had rowed across the Atlantic 18 months earlier, in 1966, with a fellow paratrooper, Sergeant Chay Blyth. It had turned into an unofficial race with two men in a similar rowing boat. The rival pair had drowned; Ridgway and Blyth defied death. Now they were enjoying success with a bestselling book of the adventure. It was the sort of success that opened doors and Ridgway was able to persuade a British boat builder, Westerly, to provide a 30-foot yacht fresh from its production line – the *English Rose IV*. At the same London Boat Show at which Bill King's plans had been announced to all and sundry, Ridgway had quietly and secretly sought the opinion of experts on a yachting panel as to whether such a production-line boat could take on a round-the-world voyage. They said it could, theoretically, go anywhere. It was an interesting verdict. Not only was the boat even smaller than Knox-Johnston's 32-foot *Suhaili*; it was built for the family cruising market.

Knox-Johnston was still struggling to finance his venture and there was now a real urgency. King had gone public and would be ready by late summer 1968. Ridgway looked as if he would be ready earlier, by the beginning of June. Then, just when he needed it, Knox-Johnston had some real luck. Having a boat handmade in India and then sailing it home had been unusual enough for a literary agent to contact him when he tied up at the Tower of London at the end of the voyage. The new, extraordinary plan to sail round the world took over and the agent soon had a book deal, complete with advance payment. It paid for the refit of *Suhaili*. The *Sunday Mirror* came on board too, despite the embarrassment of Knox-Johnston falling off his chair during a lunchtime meeting with the paper's executives on a floating restaurant on the Thames. He had lost his balance when the wake of a passing tug rocked the restaurant boat. Not a word was spoken as everyone at the meeting looked out of portholes or at their menus, anywhere to avoid meeting eyes with this young man who was proposing to sail around the world but couldn't sit down on a boat in central London.

Weeks later, in late February 1968, the *Sunday Times*

got wind of what was going on. The paper's senior staff knew that, at the very least, the *Mirror* and *Express* were involved with their own sailors' freelance voyages. The paper came storming in with its plan for a race, thereby hijacking the whole adventure from under its rivals' noses. The *Sunday Times* Golden Globe race was born.

The *Sunday Times*, for all of the simplicity and vagueness of its 'race', got into a bit of a mess over the start. In order to ensnare even the reluctant free spirits, the paper announced that leaving from any port anywhere in the British Isles would do. But then the paper discovered that an established French sailor was planning a non-stop voyage of his own. He had been quietly preparing in Toulon, on France's Mediterranean coast. The *Sunday Times* had unwittingly stumbled upon a rivalry, between Britain and France, which was to play out during the race and even have a strong influence on the result.

Bernard Moitessier was not only one of the most advanced in his preparations, he was also the most obvious person to succeed. He was already a sailing celebrity in his home country, having written books about his exploits that included sailing round Cape Horn with his wife, Francoise, at a time when people did not sail round the Horn for fun. He had a huge following, in part, because he was something of an amateur philosopher, always writing about more than simply sailing. He was an eccentric, a man of strong and colourful opinions who loved to share them with anyone who would listen. For the *Sunday Times* newsdesk in London, it was obvious this Frenchman's freelance voyage would generate international headlines. The paper faced the prospect of Moitessier making their race look ridiculous. A senior reporter, Murray Sayle, was dispatched to the south of France with one purpose: to make sure Moitessier agreed to sail from Britain and, therefore, become part of the official event and be eligible for a prize.

Moitessier was in a harbour-side café near his boat, enjoying a morning coffee, when Sayle introduced himself and explained the situation. It was a tactful and reasonable approach but Moitessier was an unpredictable man. The concept of a race was new to him, and he reacted badly. In fact, he was incensed. He made it clear to this journalist from London that the proposal made him want to vomit. A challenge as great as sailing round the world was not something to turn into a media circus. He was angry enough to later fire off a letter to a French yachting magazine. Characteristically, he expanded on why he felt such distaste. He wrote: 'In a passage like this, a man must look into himself without facing a competitor. I disapprove of a race. It makes you lose sight of the essential: a voyage to your own outer limits, this search for a profound truth with, as sole witnesses, the sea, the wind, the boat, the infinitely big, the infinitely small.'

Sayle was getting a first-hand insight into the often unconventional world of people who sailed single-handed for long distances. In fact, the race concept was unpopular with most of the nine eventual starters. They felt there was enough of a challenge ahead without turning it into a spectacle. However, boats and time cost money; a practical consideration to be overcome no matter how great the search at sea for a profound truth.

All the men, despite a widely held desire for solitude, were looking for sponsors or publishing deals.

The *Sunday Times*, taking no risks, was in the process of altering the departure rules to include French ports when Murray Sayle returned to have another go at persuading Moitessier to embrace the event. There was no need for Sayle's second assignment or a rule change. Moitessier, who had thought of little else between the journalist's visits, had changed his mind. Performing a spectacular U-turn, he was to sail for Plymouth from where he would start his voyage. He justified this change of heart with a promise. He told Sayle that if he won, he would snatch the cheque and leave without a word to the *Sunday Times,* thereby demonstrating his contempt for the paper's race.

News of Moitessier, a formidable opponent with a proven ocean-going yacht, was soon circulating. He would be ready to start from Plymouth in September. Knox-Johnston calculated Moitessier would take nine months to get round the world, finishing in May 1969, whereas his smaller boat would take ten months. His chances of winning the £5,000 prize for the fastest voyage looked slim but he could still win the more historic prize, the Golden Globe trophy. He decided *Suhaili* had to be ready to go right at the beginning of the *Sunday Times* window, 1 June, or as close as he could get to it, to have the best chance of getting home before Moitessier or any other competitor.

Others were plotting too. The London Boat Show of 1968, at which Bill King's voyage had been announced, had been quite a farce without anyone realising it at the time. While Ridgway surreptitiously weighed up one production boat, none other than Sergeant Chay Blyth, his rowing partner, was doing precisely the same with another similar make in the same exhibition hall. Neither man knew what the other was doing nor, for that matter, what he himself was doing: they had become heroic adventurers together and it was obvious now to each of them what the next adventure should be, but they were both leaning heavily on others for discreet advice. Remarkably, both men were being offered nearly identical British-built, 30 feet long, mass-produced, family, weekend cruisers. It was surprising anyone was considering such a boat for a round-the-world voyage. But it was no coincidence: Blyth and Ridgway probably knew less about sailing boats than any of the other competitors. Both were looking to be convinced that their boats would be up to the task and both were utterly dependent on others to make the crucial decisions. It would be difficult to imagine Knox-Johnston or Moitessier relying on others, or allowing others, to make such assessments. So shrouded in secrecy were the plans of Ridgway and Blyth that these two men, who had survived three months of unspeakable highs and lows in the tiniest of rowing boats in the biggest of oceans, were now secret rivals. The public knew them as a double act. The reality was now very different. Ridgway did at least have some sailing experience. He had used the time since rowing the Atlantic to network, and had found a novel way to get on the water: bidding heavily at a charity auction for a handbag when he heard it came with a promise of ocean racing on one of the yachting scene's major boats.

Blyth, on the other hand, was breathtakingly ignorant

of what he was letting himself in for. He was, quite simply, the Golden Globe's comedy turn.

It was an unlikely role for a man who was already a household name. Blyth and Ridgway were to be the most famous men in the race. Along with the Frenchman Moitessier, they were the ones whom the public saw as cut out for this great challenge – the only true adventurers.

In later life, Blyth would indeed go on to become one of the giants of sailing, responsible for breaking records and for enabling hundreds of fare-paying amateurs to sail round the world on his fleet of Challenge Business yachts. However, at the time of the Golden Globe, he was making it up as he went along. Put bluntly, he had no idea how to sail. He had never done it before, but then he had never been to sea before he rowed across the Atlantic, so he did not see why being a complete novice should stop him now.

Speaking 40 years later, he says: 'You have got to remember that sailing then, and still pretty much now, is a pretty elitist sort of sport. It is surrounded and cocooned by some sort of aura. In the old days, it used to be the navigation because unless you were ninety with a long white beard there was no possibility of you being able to navigate by sextant. I think that's partly why, being a bit of a maverick, I just suddenly jumped in when I couldn't sail and I couldn't navigate. I didn't see it as a problem, you see. I wasn't bothered. As far as I was concerned, if Columbus could do it why the hell couldn't I?'

Blyth did at least realise some lessons might be a good idea, but he went about them in a preposterously casual manner. Because of his new-found celebrity status as an Atlantic rower, he was invited to join fare-paying pupils on a basic Day Skipper course on the sheltered waters of the Solent, on England's south coast. It was free of charge, so he had to settle for spending much of the time making coffee and just watching the others. He had a mere seven day trips in that summer of 1967. The sum total of his single-handed experience, outside Langstone Harbour near Portsmouth, was three miles out to Nab Tower, a wartime construction in the Solent's eastern approach, where he was becalmed.

'I didn't see it as a problem,' he says. 'I have never been a good sailor. All I was good at was raising the money. That's all I was good at. If you think about it, Robin already had his own boat because he saved up his pennies and he came from what I call a "quack quack" family, and he probably had money helping him, and a naval officer and all that crap, and Ridgway of course, well, his family was very rich, he already had a boat and so on, so I went along to sponsors and asked them if they would sponsor me.

'I well remember the interviews. I went down to Morgan Giles in Teignmouth. They said, "How much sailing experience have you got?" I said, "None." The guy said, "Well, can you navigate?" I said, "No." The interview almost terminated there and then. They were polite, of course, being yacht people.'

The fact that he did eventually get a boat – *Dytiscus III* – and was able to take part in a round-the-world race says a lot about the Golden Globe. The challenge was so groundbreaking that it was not fully understood. Blyth's entry epitomised both the amateurism of the entire event and its absolute charm and spontaneity. It was becoming obvious that the people involved were a special breed.

Blyth's conversation is peppered with references to social status and upbringing. From his days as a young man in the Scottish border town of Hawick, he has not tolerated being 'put in his place'. He was a roughly hewn, blunt, working-class lad when he left school at 15 to work at the local knitwear factory as a frame worker. Even speaking now, ever the competitive one, he cannot resist a boast: 'I was actually a very good worker. I was the youngest person to get a frame, having only been there for five months. You're usually there for about eight months before you get a frame.' But the proud teenager got the sack for hitting a foreman. 'He started poking me in the chest. I was a Teddy Boy, the bee's knees, and you don't allow that. That was on the Tuesday. On the Thursday I went to the drill hall to sign on to the army, to the Parachute Regiment. He [the foreman] came on the Friday with my pay packet and he said: "We've had a talk about you and we've decided we are going to let you stay." I said: "You're too bloody late, I've joined the army." On the Monday I was on the way to the army.'

Blyth has never been good at letting other people tell him he is wrong. It is a trait that has tended to get him into trouble throughout his life, and which has shown no sign of diminishing. When he launched his Challenge fleet in 1992, with the intention of racing amateurs the wrong way round the world, against the clipper routes' prevailing winds and currents, some in the yachting industry questioned whether this was wise. A broadsheet journalist, a few days before the start of the first race, suggested the participants did not realise how much danger they were exposing themselves to. 'I read the story and I was so angry,' says Blyth. 'The office phoned me up and said we were getting phone calls from grannies and aunties and cousins saying this journalist was saying we were all going to die.' Blyth's response when he heard that the journalist was in the fleet's marina was drastic. 'I said I'm going to whack this guy. So I went down there with every intention of filling him in, bearing in mind I'm an ex-paratrooper. I got there and he looked at me. Of course he's half my bloody size and I thought shit, if I hit this guy I'll bloody kill him. So I just grabbed him and threw him into the water.'

Telling this story nearly two decades on, Blyth becomes almost worryingly animated and excited. Certainly, there is no hint of regret. 'What was funny about it, the best thing about it, was he was fumbling with his glasses and got up to the edge to pull himself up onto the pontoon, and whack ... ' Blyth is now almost choking on his own laughter as he demonstrates how to dispense with any need for the Press Complaints Commission by placing a foot on the head of a journalist who is frightened of drowning. 'I got a three-line whip from the RORC [Royal Ocean Racing Club] saying if you don't write and apologise we'll ban you from racing. I'd stopped racing anyway so it didn't really matter. Anyway, I had to write this apology and the editor wrote back and said "If that's an apology ...". I had offered to pay for his dry cleaning.'

Blyth is proud of literally fighting for what he has

got. It seems strange that he should want to meet in, of all places, the grandiose headquarters of the Royal Ocean Racing Club, the organisation that had felt it necessary to broker a peace deal between the press and sailing's wayward ambassador. The RORC occupies a majestic Georgian town house in the heart of England's Establishment district, St James's, a pocket of central London between Piccadilly and The Mall. It is blue plaque country. Chopin departed from a house in the same street to perform for the last time. The corner shop is William Evans, gun and rifle maker: 'For the sporting gentleman since 1883'. Chichester, by delightful coincidence, lived a few doors down for almost thirty years. This area is defined by 'quack quack' money. Yet Blyth is at ease here, in his private club, helping the staff make the coffee. He moans about the fees but in fact the bedroom deals mean he probably saves the fees several times over every year whilst staying in London. Priding himself as a shrewd Scotsman, it is possibly why he is here.

Captain Ridgway and Sergeant Blyth were an odd couple on their rowing boat in 1966. Ridgway, educated at public school and brought up in a rambling Victorian house on the Thames riverbank near Windsor, had recruited the rougher Blyth to join him. He was very much the senior of the two. At the beginning of the trip, they were still calling each other by their surnames. To get over any embarrassment, they changed to numbers. Ridgway was Number One. Even when they finished and both went on lecture tours for the army, Ridgway did the public schools while Blyth did the state-run secondaries.

If there was any doubt about who was the more important of the two, the Establishment sealed it with a decision so bizarre it placed the pair back on the front pages. The workings of the British Honours system are a mystery to most, a throwback to another time, but it was fairly obvious that the two men had been bold and brave together in equal measure and should be rewarded accordingly. Yet Ridgway became a Member of the British Empire (MBE) while Blyth received the lesser British Empire Medal (BEM). 'The stupid thing about the army is that they made them military medals,' says Blyth. 'That's why they had to be separate. If they had made them civilian medals they could have done what the hell they liked but of course being the army they were a bit dim. The press were on about John getting the MBE because he had longer oars. He hadn't!'

Despite the inequality between the two men, they did operate publicly as a partnership. 'It was an extraordinary time. They always wanted the pair of us to go on talks and appearances. They always wanted the pair. It wasn't quite the same with one of you, somehow.'

But behind the scenes there was tension. Four decades on, Ridgway declines to talk about it. Blyth is not so shy. 'It was to do with money. The deal John and I had was not 50-50.' Blyth believes status played its part in the friction too. He traces the problems back to one particular public appearance in London. 'John used to do all the talking. I just sat there enjoying myself, and I only ever had to speak once at a presentation we were doing at a hotel in Kensington. He was the captain and all this sort of thing. The hotel was absolutely packed, you'd got generals and Christ knows what and the television chaps. John stood up, and he was desperate to come up with what I call an awe statement. He wanted to say something, rather like "One step for man, a giant leap for mankind". He wanted to do that. So deep and meaningful and fantastic that we would all sit back and go ooooooh! But he could never get it. He used to get up and just mumble away happily. So it came to my turn to speak. I thought, "Jesus!" So I stood up, and I'm an off-the-cuff sort of maverick sort of guy, so I stood up and I said, "Thank you very much, it's very kind of you,' – just echoed John's words. I said, "There's been a lot of controversy lately over the fact John got an MBE and I got a BEM. There's a very strong rumour that John didn't row and that I did all the rowing." There was a lot of titter titter, and I said, "That's not true. I'd like to lay this completely to rest. John did in fact row ... but only when I was cooking." The place fell apart. Absolutely fell apart. I couldn't have got the timing better. Absolutely fell apart. Of course, the outcome of that was any time we then went to be interviewed they wanted me to speak because making jokes was as easy as pie for me. I felt that John used to get pissed off about it. Because I was always taking the piss out of us, you see.'

Before long, the tension became too much. 'Something happened, and I said to John, that's me finished. I am not going to do any more jobs, with the pair of us, with the two of us. That's me finished. I'm going to go on my own from here on in. Of course John wasn't happy. It felt like he took to his officer mode, which was "Don't be so bloody stupid, you'll never make as much money like this in your life again, this is fantastic." He did a similar thing with the BEM and MBE. So I just said, "Right that's the end of the story, I'm not doing any more." We split up.'

It was the start of a spectacular falling out between the two men that has never been resolved. It goes some way in explaining the quite astonishing few months that were to come before the Golden Globe. The cloak-and-dagger secrecy of the London Boat Show in January 1968, when Blyth was looking for a boat without Ridgway finding out, would pale into insignificance. When Blyth had his boat delivered in early February, his one-time ally knew nothing of his plans. Yet Blyth knew exactly what Ridgway was up to because Ridgway had told him. Blyth was even going so far as to copy Ridgway's intended departure date, aiming for July. With breathtaking audacity, he set up camp right under Ridgway's nose at the top end of the picturesque River Hamble, a rural idyll seemingly far from the dockland commotion of nearby Southampton. Ridgway was based at the Hamble's Elephant Boatyard, a rambling site steeped in the history of traditional boatbuilding. It was later to become famous as the setting of a BBC television soap opera, *Howard's Way*, where it would play host to many a scurrilous plot. No scriptwriter could ever have matched the real-life drama being played out now. Blyth was at Swanwick marina on the opposite side of the river. To keep costs down, his boat was on mooring piles in the river itself, taking him closer still to his rival. The two men were working within a few hundred yards of each other. 'I was in the river. I could see him quite easily. I had line of sight,' says Blyth, laughing loudly.

It was pure pantomime. Blyth's sails were even delivered to the Elephant Boatyard, yet Ridgway still had no idea what was going on. There was no reason why he should. In March, just after the *Sunday Times* announced the creation of the Golden Globe race, Ridgway brought his departure date forward. He had heard about Robin Knox-Johnston and his aim of leaving at the beginning of June, so he set himself a new goal, to be the first to leave at the start of the *Sunday Times*'s window of 1 June. Blyth unashamedly copied Ridgway again, knowing he could not afford to give his former partner a head start. He also knew he had to break the news to Ridgway some time.

The two men still had enough of a relationship to meet with their wives for dinner at Blyth's house on 5 May. Ridgway later described how his host put his spoon down and announced he was going to join the race. He wrote in his autobiography: 'The eating stopped. Nobody said a word. Marie Christine and I just looked at each other, stunned. Maureen and Chay looked anxiously at us both.'

Ridgway described how he felt he had been hit with a hammer. The two men have barely spoken since. Blyth speaks about that dilemma now with a matter-of-fact air, dismissing its importance. He says: 'John felt the whole thing was disloyal. I could understand that. But it wasn't like he had copyright on the idea. Well, I mean, it was pretty obvious if you had come from rowing, it didn't take a lot of brains to work out sailing was going to be a bit easier than rowing, wasn't it?'

A suggestion that his behaviour had been deceitful does not go down well. Blyth becomes restless, his voice louder and higher pitched. 'Yes, but I came from the military. We're secret.' Bringing the departure date forward? 'Yes.' Doing so without sharing plans? 'No. Well, because why would I? But you have got to go back in time, you see.'

Blyth points out, rightly, that Ridgway's idea to row the Atlantic had been copied from the two other men who set off just before them, after their plans were published in a newspaper. Ridgway had even met one of the other pair. 'John did exactly the same to them. We had about two or three months to get this ready, get a rowing boat together to race them. So he did QED really. And, besides, why did I have to? I wasn't his keeper or he my keeper.'

On 19 May, two weeks after the dinner at Blyth's house, Ridgway formally and publicly announced he would be in the Golden Globe and that he would leave from the Aran Islands off Galway Bay on Ireland's west coast. It was where he and Blyth had landed in their rowing boat. Blyth was still playing games, admitting to the press that he was interested if he could find a boat. He did not mention the boat he had been working on since early February.

There was an irony in Ridgway deciding to start from Galway. He would be starting a mere thirty miles from Oranmore Castle, the home of Commander Bill King. King's boat, *Galway Blazer II*, meanwhile, was about to be launched in Cowes on the Isle of Wight, ready for its start in Plymouth. His sixteen-year-old daughter Leonie, who was discovering flower power while at boarding school in London, was to perform the launch ceremony. She went on to create a stir in Cowes with her partying friends.

Bill King was another of the great characters. At 57 years old, he was often compared to Chichester, who happened to be a good friend. He was the only commander of submarines to serve throughout the whole of the Second World War and live to tell the tale. He had married the author Anita Leslie, whom he met in Beirut during the war. Her Anglo-Irish family owned Castle Leslie, in Ireland's border country. Winston Churchill was a relative whom they regularly visited at Chartwell in Kent. Yet the family was also close to Irish republicans Eamon de Valera and Michael Collins. Bill King was not an easy man to pigeonhole.

Forty years on, at the age of 97, he is still in his castle, looked after by Leonie, now an artist, and her husband. There is a ramshackle eccentricity to the place. Oranmore Castle is a single tower perched on the edge of Galway Bay, with a slipway into the rocky water. Anita and Bill bought it after the war and added rooms to the side with bricks from the redundant Protestant church. A pair of Victorian stuffed golden eagles at the entrance door is an early warning that nothing is conventional here. Bill swears like the submariner he was, and revels in shocking visitors with his dirty jokes, which somehow feel all the more startling coming from a man close to one hundred years old. He is also charming and modest. He reveals that he decided to sail round the world to shake off the awful effects of war. 'War takes the mickey; certainly did out of me,' he says. 'The fire, energy, strength, health and all that sort of stuff. I discussed it with my wife and an old admiral friend who was one of the rudest men in Australia – you have to work very hard to be that – and we decided I should go round the world to loosen up. I was suffering from too many submarines and too much war. Too much bloody war. I commanded submarines right through the war from start to finish. Jesus. Bloody rough.'

Bill King shared Moitessier's dislike of the round-the-world voyage turning into a race. 'I had my own plan. I tell you, I was very little to do with it really. I was going to sail around the world on my own. I had that plan. The Golden Globe sort of caught up with me. I was nothing to do with it. I was to sail round on my own.' But King, just like Moitessier, discovered there was no escape. Even all these years later, it still gets to him. 'I never entered the Golden Globe. I didn't want anything to do with it. I was just sailing around the world. The Golden Globe was nothing to do with me, nothing.' But of course it was. King was soon drawn into the whole *Sunday Times* hype and razzmatazz. The launch of his boat, which used a radical design that looked remarkably like a submarine hull, drew a large crowd to Cowes. Leonie was an attractive teenager, heavily influenced by growing up in the smart parts of central London. She remembers it well. 'It was a great weekend. I was a bit of a wild child. There was indeed a circus. My friends and I were creating it! I remember launching the boat but the champagne bottle didn't break. I also remember it more for sailing round the world rather than specifically the Golden Globe. I thought it was cool, but my mother was bewildered.'

Commander King had been the first to announce his voyage and, in doing so, flushed out a string of rivals: Knox-Johnston, Ridgway and Blyth. Then the *Sunday*

Times announced it would be a race – their race – and the rest of the names started coming forward.

On 17 March 1968, Lieutenant Commander Nigel Tetley's wife, Eve, brought the Sunday papers on board *Victress*, their trimaran and home. They included the *Sunday Times* with its grand announcement. Nigel thought it would be a good idea to enter. Eve agreed, and that was that.

Speaking now, Eve says: 'When you think about it, it was quite a moment but it was as if this is what I have got to do. No question of well, that is something I would love to do if, but. No ifs. It was something I have got to do, to the extent of making sure he could get enough leave so he could do it before he actually retired. And, yes, it did make a difference that it was the family home.'

Tetley, like Knox-Johnston, was both an experienced professional seaman and yachtsman. He could improvise, as he proved when he hired a coffin maker to repair *Victress* after he bashed one of her hulls into a harbour wall in Cornwall just weeks after reading that edition of the *Sunday Times*. He was supposed to be taking Eve and his two sons on a sailing holiday to Ireland but the accident meant an early return to Plymouth. It gave him time to focus on his round-the-world plans. Like so many of the others, Tetley immediately set about finding sponsorship so he could have a new 50-foot boat built. Like so many of the others, he ended up settling for what he had, *Victress*, although he did stumble upon limited backing. His on-board music system had prompted a newspaper headline: '*Around the World in 80 Symphonies*'. The next day, the record company Music for Pleasure was on the phone offering sponsorship and a pack of music cassettes to take with him.

News broke of a second Frenchman entering the fray. Forty-two-year-old Loïck Fougeron from Brittany was another experienced sailor. He had been living in Casablanca, Morocco, for 20 years, where he was manager of a motorcycle engineering firm. He too had been planning the voyage before the Golden Globe race was announced. He had a secret weapon, the perfect answer, he thought, to the dilemma of the loneliness that lay in the months ahead. It was a wild Moroccan kitten, Roulis, named after the motion of a boat's roll from side to side. (Roulis would later prove a handful and find himself all over the newspapers.) Fougeron was an old friend of Moitessier and the two had been preparing their boats together. They sailed for Plymouth together – Fougeron on *Captain Browne*, Moitessier on *Joshua* – and they would eventually start the race on the same day in August. In a field dominated by the British, they were described always as the two Frenchmen. Fougeron, in truth, was in the shadow of his more famous friend.

Of all the nine starters, Donald Crowhurst was the most surprising. He was a Liberal Party borough councillor in Bridgwater in Somerset. In his mid 30s, he had four young children and a little blue day-boat, *Pot of Gold*, on which he used to take them sailing in the Bristol Channel. The other Golden Globe challengers were established sailors or adventurers. Donald Crowhurst was neither. He was unique for being ordinary. He was the armchair adventurer who instead of simply dreaming of being like Francis Chichester was now daring to believe that, indeed, he was. This owner of a small electronics business was putting himself alongside the likes of a wartime submariner and two thick-necked paratroopers who had rowed the Atlantic. He was portrayed as a weekend sailor, a derogatory term in ocean-going circles but not necessarily as amateur as it suggests. Crowhurst had years of sailing experience and most of it had been in difficult tidal waters. He was used to crossing the English Channel but, like most recreational sailors, he would rarely be at sea for more than 24 hours at a time and would never be far from a safe haven in bad weather. Sailing round the world without stopping would take nine to ten months. Whatever the weather, he would be in it. There would be nowhere to hide. When the gales came in the Roaring Forties, as they inevitably would, there would not be any help if he got into trouble. Firstly, no one would know. Secondly, even if they did they would not be able to get to him. Even now it is too far for modern helicopters and lifeboats to reach much of the vast wilderness that is the Southern Ocean.

It is no coincidence that the modern races which have grown out of the Golden Globe consist of large fleets which start together and go through the Southern Ocean broadly at the same time. It provides safety in numbers. British sailors like Pete Goss and Mike Golding have become famous rescuing fellow competitors because there has been no one else around to do it for them. Competitors nowadays are each others' lifeboats: Donald Crowhurst, who would in fact be departing well behind almost everyone else, would not have one.

It was not a foregone conclusion that Donald, the weekend sailor, would not be able to cope but it was certainly a distinct possibility. Most sailors graduate to long-distance passage-making by pushing the boundaries over time, not in one fell swoop in front of the world's media.

Crowhurst had read Chichester's books and followed the media coverage of his voyage, although he chose not to be at the heroic homecoming in Plymouth and instead listened to the radio commentary while out on his own boat. Aside from the lure of adventure in trying to beat Chichester's record, there was a commercial attraction. Crowhurst had designed and manufactured the Navicator, a hand-held device to help sailors pinpoint where they were. It detected radio signals from coastal stations. By holding it up like a gun, the sailor could point it at the signal and read a bearing on its compass. The Navicator had its following but Crowhurst's company, Electron Utilisation, was struggling. He had scaled down from factory premises and half a dozen staff to stables in the garden and one part-time worker.

Crowhurst was another round-the-world hopeful at the London Boat Show in January 1968, where the announcement of Bill King's plans caused such a stir. Crowhurst was selling his Navicators but he also took time out at the show to speak to the designer of King's boat. As a businessman with a small company, Crowhurst knew all about the difficulties of raising money and he knew getting a boat of his own would be, at best, a major challenge. He hit on an idea that was to divide the yachting scene, and he used the show to launch an audacious campaign. He wanted to use Chichester's boat, *Gipsy Moth IV*. Plans were well afoot for displaying the yacht on the Thames waterside at Greenwich, next to the famous *Cutty Sark*, which was already a tourist attraction: given that clippers were Chichester's inspiration, there was a certain resonance to the plan. However, *Gipsy Moth IV* was to be lowered into a concrete hole so that visitors could walk round and look down as if she was in a dry dock. That was controversial and unpopular with many in the yachting world who agreed with Crowhurst that such a boat should be on water rather than entombed in concrete.

One fundamental flaw in Crowhurst's campaign, though, was that the boat's suitability for another voyage was questionable. Despite Chichester's success, he hated the yacht and spent much of his book, *Gipsy Moth Circles the World*, saying so. It did not help that Chichester himself was suspicious of Crowhurst's sailing credentials when he struggled to find anyone who had heard of him. Crowhurst, after months of lobbying, was eventually turned down.

He had shown considerable vision, though. He was arguably proved right decades later when *Gipsy Moth IV* was closed to the public and abandoned to rot in her hole in the ground. It took a new public appeal, organised by the editor of Britain's *Yachting Monthly* magazine, Paul Gelder, to enable her to sail again. It was not quite what Crowhurst envisaged but, in 2007, *Gipsy Moth IV* completed a round-the-world voyage crewed by relay teams of disadvantaged children.

Not one to be undone, in March 1968, just days after the Golden Globe announcement, Crowhurst declared himself in the race. He still had no boat or sponsor. He was saying little to the press at this stage on the grounds that there was not much to say. He became known as the mystery man. It was not until late May, with Ridgway, Blyth and Knox-Johnston almost ready to set sail, that he won over a local caravan dealer, Stanley Best. It was testimony to Crowhurst's impressive skills of persuasion. Best was already a backer of Electron Utilisation but was growing understandably nervous and had been asking for his money back. Instead, for reasons that Best was later quoted as saying he did not fully understand, he agreed to pay for a new boat to be built. It perhaps helped that Crowhurst wanted a trimaran and he said they were to become the caravan of the sea. He also promised an array of technical devices that would make a trimaran safe and would therefore return the company to profit. Crowhurst was saying the voyage would be good for business but he was careful to add that the commercial considerations alone would not induce him to make the attempt.

He had written to Best on 20 May, the day after Ridgway's entry had been announced in the papers. Time was running out but Crowhurst did have on standby two boatyards that would share the work. The rest of the field would be long gone while he was still having a boat built and was working on the inventions that would make it radical. Undaunted, he drew up a table of estimated speeds for the whole fleet and, there-fore, finishing dates. He reckoned that his trimaran would be the fastest boat, faster even than Tetley's similar yacht because of his adaptations. Not only was Crowhurst aiming at the fastest time, and the £5,000 prize, but also his table showed he could be first home even though others would have a four-month head start. It was a wildly optimistic assessment although not entirely without logic.

There was one more entry, announced long after most of the field had set sail. It took everyone by surprise, and had the effect of making Crowhurst's hectic schedule appear more sensible than it was. Alex Carozzo, known as Italy's Francis Chichester, had secretly been having a boat built in Cowes on the Isle of Wight. At 66 feet, it would be the longest boat in the race and 13 feet longer than Chichester's *Gipsy Moth IV*. There were question marks as to whether one man could really handle such a big boat. The Italians, though, had confidence in their man.

Carozzo was only 36 years old and already a legend in his own country. The story was of him, a young merchant officer, building a 33-foot boat in the cargo hold of a ship en route to Japan, from where he sailed his makeshift craft to San Francisco. The boat he had built for the Golden Globe voyage was no less extraordinary. It was launched only seven weeks after work began, thanks to 15 men working in three shifts around the clock. Even the boatyard managing director said it was a 'bloody miracle' and he did not quite know how they had managed it. Carozzo had achieved what most of the other competitors had set out to do but had given up on; building a large, state-of-the-art boat specifically for the task. However, the price, in racing terms, was that he would be starting at the back of the field.

After a confusing few months, it was now clear that the prize for being the first person to sail round the world non-stop was being chased by nine men, and a strange collection they were.

There would in effect be three waves of boats leaving during the *Sunday Times*'s window of 1 June to 31 October 1968. First off would be the two paratroopers who once relied on each other for survival but had now fallen out, the officer John Ridgway and his pugnacious junior, Chay Blyth. Within days, the young seaman Robin Knox-Johnston, in his lumbering, Indian-teak boat, built from mail-order plans, would follow them. They were the three young guns in this race, eager to get off. They would have a considerable head start on the rest of the fleet as no one else would be ready for almost three months.

The second wave would consist of four older men who were planning to leave at the theoretically ideal time of late August or September, all from Plymouth. Leading this chase group, the two Frenchmen would fly their country's flag in what many were seeing as a battle of nations. Bernard Moitessier, the philosopher who said the idea of a race made him want to vomit, and Loïck Fougeron, the kitten-owning Breton in the shadow of his more famous countryman, would leave together. Close behind would be Commander Bill King, still trying to shake off his wartime ordeals. Completing the chase pack in the family home, Lieutenant Commander Nigel Tetley would be going round the world with his 80 symphonies.

The third and final wave would be very late to leave, the two skippers setting sail at the last possible moment, on 31 October itself, beating the *Sunday Times* deadline by a matter of hours. The town councillor, Donald

Crowhurst, keen to promote his direction-finding navigation device, and keener still to be taken seriously, would be watched by a sailing fraternity interested in his promises of computerised gadgetry. Italy's Chichester, Alex Carozzo, would add another international dimension with his super-yacht. He was young, single and resourceful and clearly in with a chance of the fastest time.

There were nine men. They each prepared in their own idiosyncratic ways, whether based in the Mediterranean or on England's south coast. Through inexperience or nostalgia, some would choose unlikely starting places, from the River Hamble far up the dreaded shipping lanes of the English Channel, to the sparsely populated islands on the west coast of Ireland. Wherever they started, wherever they were, there was one basic rule: finish in the same place without receiving any assistance along the way.

Few of these offbeat characters wanted this to be a race. They wanted to do it alone, in every sense of the word. Nine diverse characters with their own egos were brought together reluctantly, each driven by a desire for a place in history.

3 : RACE ON

On 1 June 1968, John Ridgway was the first to start. To the relief of everyone, the talking appeared to be over and the race was beginning. Ridgway, seeking an emotional tranquillity in the Aran Islands, told the press that he was in the remote west of Ireland because he would have hated the kind of fuss that would have surrounded a start from Portsmouth, where the boat was built. Ironically, this simply served to increase interest in his start by presenting the media with an even better story than they expected. Here he was again at Inishmore's Kilronan Pier, the very same tiny refuge into which two years earlier he and Chay Blyth were towed by the island lifeboat at the end of their epic row across the Atlantic.

On the morning of his departure, Ridgway received a telegram from Blyth. It said: 'Last one home's a cissy. Who cares who wins.' Twisting the motto of the SAS regiment, Blyth was perhaps trying to make peace. Ridgway did not send a reply. Now, on a harbour-wall berth just a couple of hundred yards from the plaque marking the earlier homecoming, he stood on a sailing yacht instead of a rowing boat. Unlike last time, the sun was out and the sea was calm. The same lifeboat crew prepared to tow him out to sea. The 29-year-old ex-paratrooper looked handsome and rugged in the Aran Islands sweater and knitted tam o'shanter cap that the parish priest had presented to him the night before. Ridgway had unwittingly put in place the ingredients for a wonderful, romantic and swashbuckling story. His naivety in believing he could escape attention had created a media circus that was getting out of control. Two of the world's biggest news broadcasters at the time, Britain's Independent Television News (ITN) and the BBC, had chartered their own boats and were determined to out do each other. In Ridgway's own words, they were at each other's throats. The two organisations had fallen out the previous week when they were filming a heart transplant patient in a London hospital. Subsequently, the daily tension between them was far deeper than normal and now it was surfacing during Ridgway's big moment. Even without that, he was anxious about the start, knowing a collision was possible if one of the many boats in the farewell flotilla got too close.

Within minutes of his gliding out of the harbour, and while he was still under a lifeboat's tow, it all started to go horribly wrong. ITN had scored a victory in the television war. They had chartered a 25-ton fishing trawler, a bigger boat than the BBC's motor launch, and crucially they had secured exclusive rights to the human element of the story by having on board Ridgway's wife, Marie Christine. Fighting back, the BBC squeezed their boat between ITN and Ridgway's yacht. When ITN shouted to them to get out of the way, the BBC slowed down to move around the stern of the yacht. They were too close. There was a glancing blow, only narrowly missing the vital self-steering apparatus. Although it was a minor bump and there was no damage, Ridgway was furious. He screamed abuse at the BBC. It was a surprising reaction from an SAS captain with a reputation for coping under extreme pressure. The occasion was getting to him, but no one seemed to notice. He calmed down, hoisted his sails, slipped the towrope from the lifeboat and posed on the yacht's bow for the cameras, letting the self-steering system guide his path through the water. Now ITN were too close on the starboard side. Ridgway sensed danger and shouted out as he dashed the length of his boat to get back to the tiller. He was too late. ITN's trawler banged into the side with what Ridgway described as a 'horrible crunch'. The wooden rubbing strip that ran along the joint between the hull and the deck was smashed where the two boats had collided.

It was a dreadful moment in which Ridgway's voyage could have been over before it had even started. He managed to put on an impressive show of nonchalance as he inspected the damage and decided it probably was not structural. Learning quickly from his earlier outburst with the BBC, he was precisely the unruffled superman everyone expected to see.

Privately though, he was bordering on meltdown. It was only months later that he admitted that he had felt an awful sickness, with his stomach tied in knots. Remarkably for a man not known for giving up, he said defeat filled his mind and he was overcome with bloody despair. The surrounding boats soon turned for home and Ridgway was alone. Less than an hour into his voyage, this action man was sitting in the cockpit of his small yacht, with, in his own words, tears of self-pity streaming down his cheeks and with his world crashing down around him.

The next day's *Sunday Times* newspaper reported the collision thus: 'Captain Ridgway remained calm, almost impassive ("an indication of how he will react to real emergencies," as someone said).'

The *Boy's Own* hero had got away with it but this was not how the Golden Globe was meant to start.

Chay Blyth planned to leave a week later. He was concentrating on how to hide his ignorance, at least from the public if not from his friends.

When he had first stepped onto his new yacht back in February, he was left alone for the morning to start the time-consuming process of preparing a boat for a long voyage. Any sailor would immediately have known there was an endless list of jobs, checking and adapting a myriad of items. Blyth was utterly clueless, bereft of any idea whatsoever. He stood there alone and bewildered. Forty years on, he accepts with good grace that his role was comical. 'Oh Christ, not half, of course it was. I got on board and looked around and I thought, "What the hell am I supposed to do?" I just looked around. I thought, "Well, I've got no idea. It all looks ok to me!" I had to do something, so I cleaned the cooker. That's what I did. I cleaned the cooker. I had nothing else to do!'

A sailing friend helped him sort the boat out but when it came to the departure in June, there was no getting round the fact that Blyth still barely knew how to sail. He had certainly never been out of sight of land on a yacht. His half-baked intention was to learn as he went along. That was a little like a learner-driver lining up on the grid of a Formula One race, hoping to work out the gears and steering as the race progressed. It was a barely credible plan but it might just about work out at sea where there was little to bump into. Leaving a home port, on the other hand, surrounded by media boats and well-wishers, was another issue altogether. To complicate matters, the strength of the story guaranteed there would be a huge crowd both on and off the water. This 27-year-old Scotsman was chasing Ridgway, his former partner in adventure. It would have been an even bigger story if the public had had any inkling of Blyth's inexperience.

It seemed odd to the sailing world that Blyth chose to leave from the River Hamble. Almost all the other sailors were planning to set sail from the West Country. They would quickly be out of the English Channel's shipping lanes and in the open sea, vital for a single-hander who had to sleep. Blyth would spend half a day negotiating Southampton Water and the Western Solent and, at best, in favourable conditions, would then have 24 hours before he got to the area from which the others would be starting. So he, unlike the others, would need to sleep while still in the proximity of shipping lanes. There was, however, a method included in Blyth's madness. The extraordinary plan of this young soldier who was taking on sailing's Everest, challenging the great seamen like Chichester and chasing the greatest maritime prize of all, was to follow a mate in another yacht. He would copy every move for the few hours it would take to pass the Needles lighthouse on the Isle of Wight. A second friend would sail behind to keep other boats at bay, as Blyth had little idea of the rules of the road. By starting from the Hamble, Blyth would be surrounded by friends who would cover for him. Even the issue of getting off a pontoon and hoisting the sails became part of the plan as Blyth did not know how to do either. Both tasks would be done for him. Friends would set up the boat, point it to the start with the self-steering lined up, and then they would jump onto other boats, leaving Blyth single-handed. It was agreed that the start gun would be fired not, as tradition dictates, at a certain time of day but at the moment Blyth's boat was about to cross the start line, whenever that would be. It was an unbelievable plan and, on 8 June, it worked a treat. Blyth was off.

Once past the Needles and out of the Solent, he had to start sailing for himself. He also had to watch out for shipping. 'I went straight to sleep,' he says, 40 years later, almost in disbelief at his own response to the challenge that was rapidly descending into a farce. 'I put on the self-steering and I went straight to sleep. I was so tired that I slept right through the night. I relied on other people seeing my little white masthead light. It's incredible. I look back on it now, the luck of the devil.' Blyth woke up the next morning to find that he was lost, which was hardly surprising as most of his experience of navigation was practising in his bedroom. Using a sextant to take sights of the sun and the stars was not proving to be his strong point. 'It was flat calm. I had no idea where I was. I took a sight and I couldn't make it work out, so I called up a friend. I then went across to France and again I couldn't get a sight to work out. I saw a buoy. Thank Christ it wasn't bad weather. So I sailed up to the buoy and looked it up in a book. I knew where I was then. I took a huge wide berth round the corner of France.

'Eventually the sights seemed to start working but of course I had to get verification so that I knew they were accurate. I decided to head for Madeira. I tell the story that my plan was always to head for there but, in fact, I made it up as I went along. My throwaway line is that if I couldn't find Madeira, I'd turn around and start looking for Britain!'

If Blyth was where he thought he was, he could expect to find Madeira, a Portuguese-run island 350 miles off the North African coast, two weeks after setting sail from the Hamble. Passing close to the island, as he now planned, and doing so at the time he predicted, would prove that his navigation could be relied on. If he missed Madeira, he knew he would be in serious trouble, unable to find his way round the world. He became strangely superstitious about looking out for what he so desperately wanted to see. He had a nervousness that stemmed from rowing across the Atlantic with Ridgway two years earlier; then, as Ireland's west coast seemed to be emerging on the distant and indistinct horizon, Blyth had told Ridgway that he would not turn round to look until there was no doubt that what Ridgway said he was seeing was indeed land. Now, alone on his yacht at dusk, and worried he would fail the test he had set himself, he once again refused to look. It is a moment in the voyage that Blyth still remembers with great clarity. 'I decided I had to make sure I could actually see the lighthouse on Madeira and there would not be illusions or convincing myself or anything like that. You can make situations where you believe what you want to believe. You can tell yourself: "That's it", so it is it. It's all part of the confidence business you hear about in lectures. So I said, "Right, it's getting dark and I should see the bloody light soon." So I purposely went down below and I stayed there and wouldn't come up until it was dark. Eventually, I said, "Well, now's the time." So I went up. I put my hands on the cockpit roof and I looked out. It was pitch black. I'm sitting there in the dark watching where the light should be, knowing that I must see it within a few seconds, otherwise it's not there. Suddenly the light flashed. I can tell you, the exultation, the excitement, knowing I had got to it. It was very Columbus in bloody America, I can tell you. It was just fantastic. I thought, bloody hell. Wow. It was just terrific.'

Blyth was on his way, chasing Ridgway who was still a week ahead. He was getting away with it. He was fooling everyone. He must have been because it was at this point that the *Sunday Times*, wary of criticism that the entire Golden Globe was a reckless and irresponsible venture, wrote: 'It must be emphasised that the *Sunday Times* has no desire to encourage undue risks. To have a hope of success, yachtsmen must have seamanship of the highest order. Only men with considerable long-distance ocean-yachting experience should consider competing.' The paper published potted biographies of the nine sailors. In Blyth's, they wrote that he would not specify what single-handed experience he had gained in preparation for the voyage.

Six days after Blyth's departure, on 14 June, Robin Knox-Johnston left Falmouth in Cornwall. Such was the sense of mystery surrounding the challenge ahead that his sponsor, the *Sunday Mirror* newspaper, had sent him to be analysed by a psychiatrist. The verdict was 'Distressingly normal' but the real test would be a comparison after ten months at sea alone. Knox-Johnston's laid-back approach to the voyage ahead was anything but normal. His barometer was borrowed from the wall of a pub. More seriously, his boat, *Suhaili*, had been leaking for days and he could not work out why. He decided to depart anyway and deal with the problem as he sailed. Likewise, the self-steering apparatus he had constructed was not performing properly. Either problem could end his challenge but he was anxious about the head start he was handing to both Ridgway and Blyth, so he set off. Barely six miles out of Falmouth, and with the obligatory farewell flotilla having turned back for port, he got out a chart of the world and planned his route.

On first appearances, Knox-Johnston looked as though he might surpass Blyth for recklessness if not incompetence. However, he had good reasons to be confident that he could overcome the compromises he was making in order to start his voyage quickly, and although Knox-Johnston was late in plotting a route, Blyth was still working out the basics of how to plot while also learning how to sail.

Knox-Johnston also had the upper hand over the other early starter, John Ridgway. Although Ridgway did at least know how to sail a boat, he was more comfortable as a paratrooper than a sailor.

So, of the three early starters, Knox-Johnston, the professional seaman, was the one who most knew what he was doing.

To the press, Knox-Johnston bordered on being dull, certainly in comparison to the two soldiers who had left before him. In Galway, Ridgway's last words as he was about to set sail had been inspirational. He talked about endurance and survival. Blyth had colourfully told the press that he was worried he might come back 'queer as a nine-bob note' but at least, he added, he would have done something with his life, unlike the journalists around him. There was an expectation that these men would come up with great or entertaining words to fit the occasion, like George Mallory's reason for climbing Mount Everest: 'Because it's there.' Ridgway and Blyth fell short of Mallory's succinct eloquence but at least they went some way towards meeting the demand for pithy quotations.

Knox-Johnston, on the other hand, as he prepared to sail round the world non-stop, had simply said: 'It hasn't been done before and I'd rather like to do it.'

No wonder the papers described him as 'pleasant', damning him with faint praise. Prominent in their reports was the fact that his father was a churchwarden and that he was taking a Bible with him. Indeed, accompanied by the Falmouth port chaplain, he had bought the Bible on the morning of his departure. Somehow he did not seem, to the press at least, to be quite the all-action, all-conquering hero who was likely to win. The media was underestimating this young man.

Knox-Johnston spent much of the first two weeks sorting the self-steering (an automatic system that uses a wind vane to keep the rudder on a certain course, freeing the single-hander to work on running the boat and to sleep). It was the emergence of self-steering systems in the early 60s, just before the Golden Globe, that was making single-handed sailing a more practical proposition. However, *Suhaili*, a twin-masted ketch, was an awkward design for these new devices. The vane had to be high enough to be in the airflow and was normally on the stern of the boat where it could easily be linked to the rudder. The problem for *Suhaili* with two masts and, therefore, two large sails, was that the boom on the second mast stretched out beyond the stern and so would have demolished any vane. So Knox-Johnston had come up with a bizarre solution. From an initial design that he had chalked out on his parents' garage floor, he had built a network of scaffolding and ropes which now extended three feet out of each side of the boat and four feet up above the height of the deck. Each side held a plywood wind vane, clear of the aft boom and sail, and linked to the rudder by a web of lines and pulley blocks. It was a contraption that would not have looked out of place in a Heath Robinson drawing. It was so complicated that getting it to work efficiently took days of experimentation.

Three weeks into the voyage, now 400 miles off the coast of Senegal and close to the Cape Verde Islands, Knox-Johnston felt uneasy at the increasing amount of water leaking into the boat's bilges – the area between the hull and the floorboards – as he was pumping it out at least twice a day. *Suhaili*'s Indian-teak planks appeared to be leaking somewhere near the join with the keel but it was impossible to be sure from inside, because the fresh-water tanks blocked any inspection. The only way to find out was to dive overboard and swim under the boat: no mean feat alone in the North Atlantic. When the weather was calm two days later, over the side he went. Immediately visible, there was a horrendous gap running for about seven feet between two planks and, on the other side of the keel, the same again. To make matters worse, as the boat rolled gently in the swell, Knox-Johnston could see the gaps opening and closing. He climbed back on board. It had been an awful sight. Most sailors would have been filled with horror, and even the laid-back Knox-Johnston was alarmed. He feared that this could be the start of all the planks working loose. If so, he knew it would be suicidal to continue but he convinced himself that *Suhaili* was still strong or, if the boat did break up, she would do so slowly, allowing him to reach a port. But even if these seven-foot-long leaks were an isolated problem, they still needed plugging. The question was how. They could not be reached from inside the boat. The obvious solution would normally have been to turn around and go back to the Cape Verde Islands, which he had passed two days earlier, but assistance was forbidden. He would be disqualified. Knox-Johnston's race was in danger of being over already.

He decided that the answer was an improvised version of the traditional boat-building technique called caulking. He would dive again, hold his breath for as long as he could, and try to fill the gaps by hammering in long strands of cotton fibre. Underwater, it was a highly ambitious plan, fraught with complication and risk. One issue was weighing on his mind more than others: sharks. It was obvious he would need to make repeated dives, and there was no one to keep watch.

This particular moment in the crisis would have been when most people would have given up, but Knox-Johnston was nothing if not resourceful. He decided to dress in blue shirt and jeans to hide the whiteness of his body, which would attract the sharks. If that failed, he hoped he would notice them while they were still circling, giving him enough time to climb out of the water. Finally, in case it all went horribly wrong, he strapped a knife to his leg.

He jumped over the side. Right from the start, he struggled in vain to get the cotton strands to stay in the gaps. Always glancing nervously over his shoulder, he would tap in a few inches of the strands and then come back up to the surface to breathe. When he went back under, he would find the cotton had fallen out. It was hopeless. After half an hour, he climbed back on board to rethink.

He decided he would have to construct a way to keep the strands in place. He set about sewing them down the middle of two long strips of canvas that he then strengthened and waterproofed by coating in tar. He pushed copper tacks through the canvas, ready to bang into the hull. The canvas strips, with their cotton strands, would cover the leaking gaps. To give the canvas a better chance of staying in place, he would then nail pieces of copper over the top.

Halfway through the job, Knox-Johnston was having a break out of the water on the boat, when he suddenly noticed '... a lean grey shape moving sinuously past the boat'. It was what he had feared. A shark had arrived and was circling *Suhaili*. It was a lucky escape, but immediately his thoughts were on what to do then. He had a rifle but he knew that shooting the shark could spell danger. The blood and the death convulsions could lead to others moving in, and he had a job to finish. He watched the shark for ten minutes. It kept circling, showing no signs of leaving. Knox-Johnston got his rifle. He dropped sheets of toilet paper into the water and waited for the shark to come and investigate. It moved in, staying several feet under the surface. It came again, this time slowly rising. Through the rifle's sights, Knox-Johnston tracked its moves, finger on the trigger. The shark's head broke the surface and Knox-Johnston fired. There was an explosion in the water as the shark thrashed around briefly before its lifeless body started to sink slowly.

It might have been prudent to abandon the DIY for a time, but Knox-Johnston was determined to finish at least one of the two leaks. He watched carefully for half an hour to see if other sharks would appear. They did not, so he jumped overboard again. For an hour and a half, he dived and dived, constantly glancing around, expecting to see an approaching shark. By the time he had finished, he had spent a total of four hours in the water. Two days later, when the weather was calm again, he went back over the side and did the same to the other leak, never knowing for sure whether sharks were around.

The entire intrepid episode was extraordinary. It was the sort of eccentric pragmatism that pioneering ventures such as the Golden Globe were all about, exploits that the armchair adventurer could read about in a state of disbelief. Yet, when Knox-Johnston wrote a book about his voyage, this part of the story occupied little more than one page. His account was understated and matter of fact. It was a measure of the man: modesty personified and hugely capable.

Throughout the first few weeks at sea, Ridgway, Blyth and Knox-Johnston were keen to know how they were progressing in comparison with each other. Details were hard to come by but they were all receiving some information in radio calls to England. Knox-Johnston was confident he could catch the two soldiers by the time they reached the Southern Ocean, a third of the way into their ten-month-long voyages. Just as important, though, was how the second wave of boats would fare when they set off in August. The public was already questioning how seriously the three early starters should be taken. Ridicule was beginning to creep into the press coverage. Francis Chichester, now chairman of the Golden Globe panel of judges, said: 'Some of these chaps don't know what they are letting themselves in for. If any of them succeed in getting round it will be remarkable.' Even the *Sunday Times* joined the backlash, going so far as to say the three sailors had left England ill advisedly. Apparently forgetting its own race timetable, the paper said most seasoned yachtsmen agreed that a June start was almost bound to spell ugly weather in the Southern Ocean. The paper stressed that the three who had already left were all young men in small yachts and that one, Robin Knox-Johnston, had left Falmouth in an '... untidy boat as casually as if sailing her to a painting yard'. The clear implication was that the three were being reckless. The 'canniest sailors' in the race would all leave later in the summer, said the paper. 'It seems that the younger, rasher men have started first.'

Of course, there was some truth to this but the three knew that if they had started at the same time as the bigger, faster boats they would have had little chance of finishing first.

The serious contenders – the second wave – were starting to gather in Plymouth. They were the favourites, the ones to watch. Nigel Tetley was still living chaotically on his trimaran with Eve and the boys, berthed alongside a bleak dockside wall in the heart of the city. Plymouth, then, was a huge sprawl of commercial and naval docks, less sanitised and equipped for yachts than it is now. By coincidence, the Frenchmen Bernard Moitessier and Loïck Fougeron motored in to the same part of the complex as the Tetleys and berthed alongside walls nearby. During the following weeks of preparations, the three sailors and Eve became good friends, regularly eating and drinking together and even swapping ideas for the race. Bill King, the wartime submariner, now 58 years old, arrived at the Royal Naval Dockyards a mile away, still trying to imagine he was on his own voyage and not part of a media circus. The others, armed with two bottles of champagne, soon introduced themselves and the Plymouth party was complete.

The press was fascinated by the fact these rivals were enjoying each other's company. London-based journalists were in search of eccentricity and oddness, as they began to build up a picture of the individual characters, and they did not need to look far.

Bernard Moitessier was waxing lyrically on life and philosophy. He wanted to borrow a cine camera in order to film his voyage, but he quickly stressed that this was not to make money. 'Screw the money,' he said. 'I just want to record my emotions. Money is all right as long as you have enough for a cup of tea. I don't care for it any more than that.' The press and public loved this 43-year-old's pearls of wisdom and oddball ways. His boat's cabin was full of mementoes from his wanderings: a goatskin, a mandolin made from a turtle shell, an albatross feather. He talked of living on rice and mushrooms, yet he had a penchant for English powdered potato. Here in Plymouth, his initial ghastly encounter with the *Sunday Times* back in Toulon was a thing of the past. Indeed, he liked the paper's staff. They, in turn, were beginning to understand the need to tread carefully with this man of unconventional ways. They were desperate to ensure a regular supply of stories during Moitessier's race but he had no radio. In an age before satellite communications and without global positioning systems, bulky and expensive radios were the only hope of getting information. Moitessier could not afford one but, as with most things in life, the issue was more complicated for this free-spirited Frenchman. The *Sunday Times* offered a set along with a generator to power it. In return, all they asked for was two messages a week. Moitessier took one look at the radio. He described it as a big cumbersome contraption. He turned the offer down, saying it was not welcome. His peace of mind without distraction was more important. Instead, he would communicate the way he had always done, with a catapult. He would fire aluminium film cans, containing film and notes, onto the decks of passing ships. However, aside from the risk of valuable material missing its target and falling into the sea, there was the issue that, for most of the voyage, there would be no passing ships. Yet all Moitessier would say was that a good slingshot was worth all the transmitters in the world. On the eve of this historic voyage, Britain's biggest Sunday newspaper was reduced to helping Moitessier find a supply of good-quality rubber bands to aid the propulsion. To the journalists' credit, Moitessier later wrote that they did understand the 'how and why'.

For a man who liked a simple life, Moitessier's planning in Plymouth was complicated. He was forever phoning home, in the south of France, with lists of things he needed. Francoise would have to drop everything and abandon her three children. She would jump into her old yellow car and drive for twelve hours to catch a ferry to England. Devoted to her husband's dream, she made the return journey to Plymouth an exhausting nine times, clocking up no less than 15,000 miles – halfway round the world.

Loïck Fougeron, who was a year younger than his fellow Frenchman, was known as the most superstitious of all the sailors. The papers quoted him on old maritime tales like never speaking of rabbits at sea for fear of provoking a storm. He was ruthless in his preparations, discarding as much as possible to reduce weight and therefore make his boat faster. His kitchen crockery came down to one plate and one cup. Any visitors who were offered an aperitif were confined to gin, which they had to drink from the bottle. Yet there was room for Roulis the cat, for now.

Of the four boats preparing in Plymouth, the Tetleys' trimaran was the most disordered. The job of transforming the yacht while living on it was formidable. Domestic trappings such as a coal-burning stove and copper chimney had to be offloaded. Mattresses, bedding, clothes, a fridge, record player, sewing machine, iron and ironing board, pots and pans and so on all had to come off the boat to be stored in a rented flat into which Eve and the boys were moving. Whilst Nigel dealt with boat jobs, everything was ferried backwards and forwards by Eve in her little MG, the only working vehicle the family owned. Many a head would turn on the industrial dockside as this tall, glamorous young woman struggled to keep everything from falling out of her open-top sports car.

Eve was determined that the man she had fallen in love with was going to live comfortably on his voyage. She bought a pile of cheap pillowcases so he would always have a clean one. She hunted for men's disposable underpants. When she couldn't find any, she bought a supply from a women's range instead, and was delighted to see that they fitted. Meal planning became a major issue. Eve was not prepared to see her husband eat with the tedious monotony so many of the single-handed sailors tolerated: Moitessier and Fougeron were basing their meals around rice; Ridgway had 400 identical ration parcels from Horlicks; Knox-Johnston had 216 tins of corned beef and 144 tins of stewing steak; Blyth had several hundred 24-hour army ration packs that, unknown to the public until now, 40 years later, were stolen from the army with the help of a friend. Variety was not a priority for these men in a hurry but it was going to be very different indeed for Nigel Tetley.

Eve spent evening after evening studying any book she could find on diet and nutrition. Her final shopping list was a table with the headings: vitamin A, vitamin B, vitamin C, vitamin D and protein. Much to the media's amusement, the eventual supplies included: roast duck, octopus, oyster, venison in wine, jugged hare, smoked turkey, smoked eel, Chinese chicken and beef, mussels, prawns, Hungarian paprika-stuffed pork, lobster, roast goose, Polish sausage, stuffed carp and a pheasant for Christmas. Somehow, Eve had found that most of the meat was available in tins. Nigel Tetley would certainly be the best-fed sailor, thanks to his dedicated wife.

Out at sea, the three young early-starters were conscious of the need to make the most of their head start on the Plymouth four. Ridgway was having an abysmal time. He had not recovered psychologically from the stressful chaos of his departure in Galway. The collision with the ITN trawler was constantly nagging away at him, to the point that he felt unnerved in a manner he had not experienced before. As early as two weeks into his voyage, still close enough to home to listen to BBC Radio 4's *Woman's Hour*, he felt mentally bruised and unable to relax. The condition of the boat did not enhance his mood. There were hairline cracks in the deck's surface coating around one of the shrouds that held the mast up. The bottom of the mast itself looked like it might have shifted slightly. Ominous creaking noises emanated from around the collision area. Ridgway's boat was damaged. Alone at sea, without answers, he felt extremely nervous. He pressed on, wondering how Chay Blyth and Robin Knox-Johnston were doing, one and two weeks behind.

Manhood personified, Ridgway should have been at ease now that the adventure was well under way. Yet in the weeks sailing down towards the equator he felt terrible, wrestling with what he described as an emotional loneliness. A gale caught the boat and he had a fierce struggle to control the sails. Sudden gales happen on long voyages. Ridgway should have taken this one in his stride. Instead, after he had won his battle with the flailing sails, he crept down below, as if to hide. Then the paratrooper whom the media saw as being as tough as nails simply burst into tears.

The officer who, only two years earlier, had risked his life by spending three months crossing the Atlantic in a tiny rowing boat realised this venture was different. It did not mean as much to him. He was not hungry for success. Still inside the boat, hiding from the gale and trying to pull himself together, he realised he had cried at some point on each of the last 27 days.

Ridgway's troubled voyage continued south. His mind frequently wandered to dreams of the adventure school he planned to build in a remote Highlands wood called Ardmore, on the north-west corner of Scotland. His heart was not in this sailing race, but Ridgway was a stranger to the concept of giving up.

Six hundred miles south of the equator, the deck began to bulge around one of the shrouds supporting the mast. Either the boat, a family cruiser, was not strong enough for the task, or the collision in Galway had sent a shock wave through the rigging, causing structural damage away from the actual point of collision. Whatever the cause, the mast was unlikely to stay up for long unless something was changed. Ridgway strengthened the deck with plywood and spare bolts. Still it bulged. There was no solution. To take the boat into the windswept Southern Ocean would have been insane. Ridgway made the decision to quit. His race was over six weeks after it began. He turned the boat round so that the wind was coming from behind. That way, there would be less strain on the rigging as he limped to safety. He was pointing to the north west, to the coast of Brazil, and defeat. Seven hours later, he changed his mind, altered course and was back in the race. He simply could not give up. For another four hours, the bulging deck tormented him until he could stand it no longer. Once again, he altered course and headed for Brazil. This time, his race really was over.

Despite Ridgway's public profile, the emotional calamity that he suffered on the Golden Globe could have remained a private matter. The very isolation that contributed to his crisis meant no one knew it had even happened. Yet, to Ridgway's credit, he bared all three years later in an autobiography he called *Journey to Ardmore*. The Golden Globe was pointedly just one chapter. On the effect of the decision to drop out, he wrote: 'For two days I lapsed into a dangerous state of mind, while we ran 260 miles downwind. Listless and dejected, I lay on my bunk, my mind crowded with all the thoughts of misery and self-pity which from time to time engulf every human being. I failed to make any entries in the log, I did no cooking. The great dream had folded before my eyes. I thought of all the work and hope so many kind people had put into this grand design. Now I had let them down. In an awful fatalistic sort of way, I looked forward to my return home; I would feel more suited to the inevitable denigration and contempt than I had with all the embarrassing praise after the rowing.

'I wrote in my log: "I don't think I have ever given up in my life before. Now I feel debased and worthless. The future looks empty and, and, and, I won't write any more, there must be something to fill this vacuum."'

That vacuum was undoubtedly filled by the reality of the adventure school, which opened two years later in 1969. Forty years on, John Ridgway and Marie Christine are still based in their stone croft house above the loch at Ardmore, a hundred miles from the nearest town. The adventure school is still a thriving business, now run by Rebecca, the daughter who was born only months before the Golden Globe, and her husband. John and Marie Christine have sailed around the world three times.

Of all the key players in the Golden Globe story who were approached for this book, Ridgway was the only one who declined to be interviewed. In a polite but short response, he added only: 'Into the mist …'

So, the Golden Globe had claimed its first victim even before most of the competitors had set sail. Chay Blyth did not hear about his one-time soulmate dropping out of the race until three weeks later. His radio was out of action because seawater had contaminated his supply of petrol which powered the generator which, in turn, recharged the batteries. Blyth was worried by this problem. The prospect of at least another eight months without batteries to power the radio or navigational lights filled him with horror.

There was an additional problem – coping with sailing.

Blyth was caught in his first gale, the same one that reduced Ridgway to tears. In keeping with his voyage so far, he did not know what to do, other than lowering the sails and turning to prayer. He was frightened and realised his belief in God might not be enough, so he started reading a sailing manual on how to cope with storms. Once again, Chay Blyth was making it up as he went along. As his small boat pitched and rolled in heavy seas, he was looking through a book to find out what to do. It was, he said, like 'being in hell with instructions'.

After the wind dropped, Blyth decided his experience had been character forming. He felt humbled. He read Francis Chichester's book, *Gipsy Moth Circles the World*. The disparity in boats and equipment left him feeling depressed but he pushed on south, still believing he was chasing Ridgway and that Knox-Johnston was not far behind.

The closer Blyth got to the Roaring Forties, the more he thought about the problem of not having petrol for the generator. The rules of the race were clear. He could not pull into a port or seek outside assistance, but Blyth was not interested in what he saw as bureaucracy. He would make his own rules. He decided he would try to get petrol at the South Atlantic volcanic island of Tristan da Cunha, inhabited by more than 200 British citizens.

Tristan, known as the most isolated settlement in the world, was not the most likely filling station but Blyth was staggeringly lucky. When he arrived on 15 August, a South African fuel ship was anchored off the island, waiting to pump ashore one of the three deliveries of petrol it made every year. Blyth tied up next to it, with the intention of receiving petrol and then sailing off in the knowledge that he could say honestly he had not been ashore. He was not expecting the captain to be a fellow Scot with an offer of a dram of whisky should he wish to climb aboard. It was too much for Blyth. As he saw it, he was bending the rules already so there could be no harm in bending them just a little bit more. He climbed onto the ship. It was while enjoying the hospitality that the captain mentioned the news of Ridgway's retirement from the race. Blyth was stunned. The cocky self-belief that had helped get him this far was shaken. He thought the rowing success had made both of them 'unsinkable'. Now he realised that he was just as vulnerable as the other competitors.

Technically, Blyth was now out of the race but that was not how he saw it. He sent several telegrams home saying he had received petrol, but stressing he had not been ashore. He set sail for the Roaring Forties with the intention of continuing around the world.

Robin Knox-Johnston's heroic patching up of *Suhaili* was holding out. His biggest problem as he crossed the equator was no longer his boat's bottom, but his own. He had probably the most bizarre accident in the entire Golden Globe when he was cooking a large stew in a pressure cooker, whilst naked. He put the hot pan aside on the cabin steps, turned to put the kettle on and then sat back on the pan. He let out a yelp of pain. His bottom was burned and he was unable to sit comfortably for three days.

Boredom became a problem for Knox-Johnston. He read Tolstoy's voluminous *War and Peace*, one of 105 books on board, and listened to a Gilbert and Sullivan cassette. British heroes such as Drake and Nelson dominated his daydreams. He felt proud that his voyage was, in a small way, continuing in the same vein and he noticed how it was mostly Britons who had risen to this new round-the-world challenge. Knox-Johnston was again enjoying his British heritage.

Communication with shore-based radio stations was very limited because of range and the need to conserve battery power. Knox-Johnston was increasingly experiencing the frustration that all the competitors would eventually endure: a lack of information on their rivals' positions. Even when radio contact was established, the information was often out of date and unreliable. A week after the defeated Ridgway had arrived in Brazil, a Cape Town radio operator told Knox-Johnston that Ridgway was still believed to be in the lead. It took another week for the truth to get out.

On 22 August, Cape Town made contact with Knox-Johnston again. This time their information was up to date. Bernard Moitessier and Loïck Fougeron had that day sailed out of Plymouth to start their race.

It was a Thursday. Fougeron saw to that. Superstitious sailors do not leave on a Friday. The final farewells on shore had not gone well for the Moitessiers. Francoise was upset and in tears. Bernard was more concerned about himself and the effect his wife was having on his big day. 'Don't give me the blues at a time like this,' he said. Right from the off, Bernard Moitessier was wrapped up in his own self-discovery. He later wrote: 'I felt such a need to rediscover the wind of the high sea, nothing else counted at that moment, neither earth nor man.' The conventions of a parting moment were clearly too much for a man who was never happy living to other people's rules. 'You do not ask a tame seagull why it needs to disappear from time to time towards the open sea,' he wrote. Forty years later, Francoise laughs and looks to the ceiling as she recalls Bernard's words. 'We had been married for eight years, so I knew him well,' she says. 'Bernard was always having his own way and doing what he wanted whenever he wanted. He would be away on the other side of France and would ring me to say he was coming home. After two days of waiting, I would go to the harbour for a walk and find Bernard there on his boat. I was used to it. We really were very happily married.'

Two days after Moitessier and Fougeron, Bill King set sail. His days as a wartime submariner should have put him in good stead but he felt choked with fear, worried that he would not be able to deal with a crisis. He soon recovered and set about chasing the two Frenchmen. The fourth member of the Plymouth group, Nigel Tetley, would be leaving three weeks later.

The race was taking shape, and Knox-Johnston recognised the change. Until the Cape Town radio call, he had been focusing on catching Chay Blyth. Now he saw that he would be the hunted one and that his two-month head start might not be enough. He calculated that he was just short of the average speed he needed if he was to have any chance of staying ahead and beating the bigger and faster boats behind.

Knox-Johnston and Chay Blyth were about to enter the Southern Ocean: the occasional gale they had experienced to date would pale into insignificance.

4 : BOTTOM OF AFRICA

Robin Knox-Johnston crossed the latitude of 40 degrees south on 3 September, three days ahead of Chay Blyth. Both men were soon in the worst weather so far: the Roaring Forties were living up to their name, and the two boats and their skippers were thrown into a test that was going to make or break their voyages.

Knox-Johnston was several hundred miles ahead when the wind suddenly changed direction and increased to a force-eight gale. He battled in a hailstorm to reef the sails, and was relieved to get back down below where he turned to his brandy bottle. The change in wind direction was confusing the sea, with waves now coming in two directions. It was uncomfortable and dangerous. As night fell, Knox-Johnston lay on his bunk but stayed in his oilskins, ready to jump up if anything went wrong. He fell asleep.

Just before 3 am, his world turned upside down. Boxes, tins, books, clothes, food, medical supplies and tools came crashing down onto his bunk. *Suhaili* was on her side. The light of the cabin lantern was knocked out. Knox-Johnston lay for a moment in the pitch darkness trying to sense what had happened. He struggled to climb out of his bunk just as *Suhaili* lurched upright, throwing him, and all that had landed on him, over to the other side of the cabin. It was bedlam, but the urgent, shocking concern was that damage was bound to have occurred outside. The voyage might be over. Still in darkness, he climbed over the cabin debris and onto the deck, expecting to discover that the two masts had been swept away. They were still there. He was so convinced that they would be gone that he had to look twice. Surely he could not have escaped so lightly. Then he saw that there was damage to the self-steering system; it was working, at least for now. He carefully scrambled around the boat, inspecting everything. Another huge wave rolled in, crashing and boiling over Knox-Johnston as he hung on for his life. He altered course slightly to change the waves' angle of approach, and then went down below to light the lantern. The place was an indescribable mess, with most supplies tossed out of their cupboards and now sloshing around in water, yet Knox-Johnston was feeling he had come off lightly. Then, to his absolute horror, he realised where the water had come from. Every time a wave swept over, water poured in around the joint between the cabin top and the deck. There were cracks all around it. The force of the knockdown had almost ripped the cabin top off like the lid of a sardine can. He felt sick: this was major damage. He had missed it during his inspection because it was so improbable. Now there was a real risk that the weakened structure would be swept away by another crashing wave. That would leave a hole 12 feet long and six feet wide. The boat would be opened up, changing in an instant from a capsule to a bathtub. It would have no chance here in the Southern Ocean, 700 miles south west of the bottom of Africa. It would simply swamp and sink. Knox-Johnston stood, all this dreadful imagery flashing through his mind. Another wave hit the boat and the whole cabin top seemed to wince, but it did not shift. Nothing could be done in the dark while a gale howled outside. Knox-Johnston took a slug, this time from a whisky bottle, and decided he might as well sleep for three hours until daybreak.

The sea seemed less angry when he woke up. The cabin top needed strengthening urgently, irrespective of whether the voyage could continue beyond Africa's Cape of Good Hope. He set about the task with the same matter-of-fact resourcefulness he had demonstrated when patching the leaking hull back in the Atlantic's shark-infested waters. Using the longest bolts and heaviest screws he could find in his spares box, he spent the entire day reinforcing the brackets that joined the cabin top to the deck. He felt a lot safer when the job was finished.

The entry into the Roaring Forties had been dramatic, and there was no let up. In the ten days from the knockdown, there were five gales. They were exceptional conditions, even at this latitude, and Knox-Johnston was appalled. Physically and mentally, he was suffering. He felt constant pain from the torn skin and ripped fingernails on his hands. His body was bruised all over. He could not remember the last chance he had to wash, and now his skin itched from the chafing of constantly wet clothes. Always conscious of Blyth and the Plymouth four, he felt he could not ease off. Lowering the sails to ride out each gale was not a realistic option. It meant progress was too slow. Yet not all his thoughts were on a competitive level. He knew Blyth was in the same area and he wondered how his rival was coping and, in particular, how he had fared in the knockdown gale.

Chay Blyth was frightened, cold, depressed and, in his words, cursing the point of the whole miserable exercise. Right from the beginning of the trip, he had been praying each evening. Now he was praying in the mornings too. Caught in the same weather system that hit Knox-Johnston, he described the waves as mountainsides of liquid hell. His earlier, albeit belated, study of storm tactics told him to run away from the wind. His storm sails should be enough to provide power for steerage and control without being overwhelmed. However, the reason why eyebrows had been raised back at the London Boat Show in January had become apparent. A 30-foot family cruiser with two shallow keels was always likely to struggle to stay in a straight line in these conditions. The short keels would not bite into the water as much as a larger, deeper, single one. Blyth had never fully understood the theory. Now he was experiencing a startling demonstration of the practical implications, as he attempted to stay in control. He described the outcome as keeling, crabbing, toppling and slithering, with as much say in his destiny as a matchstick in a waterfall. Perilously, he broached an incredible three times in one hour. Blyth did not know what broaching was until he read Chichester's book, and discovered it happened when a boat had too much sail up while running. The outcome was like a car making a handbrake turn, only more dramatic and dangerous because of the sheer energy involved.

Speaking 40 years later, Blyth knows he was lucky to get away with it: 'Chichester wrote a whole chapter on broaching once. Not only did I broach three times in one hour; but on one day – and I counted each time it happened – I broached eleven times.' Laughing, as if unable to believe even his own story, he says: 'I thought this was normal sailing! I didn't know what to do. Even today, I still don't know whether the boat could have run or not. It could very well have been me. I wouldn't like to criticise the boat. It could easily have been my lack of skill.'

Not surprisingly, there was a price to pay. The broaching had broken a vital piece of the self-steering gear. Blyth decided to sail to the South African port of East London, 400 miles and almost a week away to the north, to pick up spare parts. Once again, he was planning to break the rules of the race, but he felt he would still be making a non-stop voyage if he did not go ashore and touch land.

Tied to a jetty, and refusing to get off his boat while waiting for the parts, Blyth spent a bizarre three days playing host to an old friend who now lived in South Africa. Chick Gough had been a fellow member of the Parachute Regiment before leaving to play football for Charlton Athletic. Together, the two men sat on Blyth's boat and got thoroughly drunk.

On 16 September, the final day of Blyth's drinking session, Nigel Tetley was at last ready to leave Plymouth. The involvement of his sponsors, Music for Pleasure, meant that the gimmicky slogan, 'Around the

World in 80 Symphonies' had firmly caught on. The music, combined with the glorious food supplies organised by Eve, saw his voyage portrayed as a cheerful affair. There was an added excitement in the harbour as he set sail because Nigel was the local boy in the race, married to a local teacher. Yet Tetley felt subdued. His mood was not helped by the news of Knox-Johnston's knockdown in the Roaring Forties. The race leader was quoted as saying he had never seen such seas in all his years as a professional seaman. Tetley also knew that John Ridgway was both out of the race and feeling distraught, and that Chay Blyth was having a miserable time. As he sailed out of Plymouth harbour, he tried to lift his mood by playing, on the cockpit speakers, the sponsor's recording of a brass band. He tapped his fingers to the beat and saw Eve doing the same on a nearby motor launch. Far from lifting his spirits, it reduced him to sobs of tears. He scolded himself, recognising that this was his adventure and that it was he who was condemning his wife to months of uncertain loneliness. He should not feel sorry for himself. Eve stood tall and proud on the bow of the launch, in her carefree way, waving and shouting her goodbyes, determined that she would enjoy this exciting moment. She told him to come back soon. He shouted back that he would.

Nigel Tetley was leaving three weeks behind Bernard Moitessier, Loïck Fougeron and Bill King, but that was a minor issue in a nine- or ten-month-long adventure. In theory at least, his trimaran was the fastest yacht. The four Plymouth boats were in effect one chasing pack. Their target was the leading pair, Robin Knox-Johnston and Chay Blyth, now at the bottom of Africa. The hunt was under way.

There were now only six weeks left to October 31, the final departure date in the *Sunday Times* race rules. Donald Crowhurst, the town councillor from Bridgwater, was still a mystery man because so little was known about his challenge. Now, as his boat was still being built, he was beginning to talk up his prospects. He predicted he would catch the others because his trimaran would be the fastest boat. It would be faster even than Tetley's because his design modifications meant it would be three-quarters of the weight, yet eight times as strong.

Trimarans – the type of boat that Crowhurst had told his sponsor would become the caravan of the sea – were new in recreational boating. They had, and still have to this day, two major advantages over the more common monohull yacht. They can offer more accommodation space, hence the caravan epithet, and they are typically faster. They benefit from the way they form a platform on the sea, dispensing with the need for a heavy keel under the boat. However, the very same platform that enables a multihull to stay upright becomes a liability if, for some reason, the boat capsizes and continues to turn all the way upside down. The boat becomes stable the wrong way up, and is impossible to right. The mono-hull, on the other hand, has a natural tendency to get back to where it was because the heavy keel acts as a counter-balance, swinging the boat upright. At the time of the Golden Globe, there was a fierce debate as to whether multihulls were safe for ocean sailing. Tetley and Crowhurst were sailing the same basic design as each other – the *Victress* class – and they had few doubts about its seaworthiness. However, their cause was not helped by the disappearance at sea of the class designer, shortly before the Golden Globe began.

Crowhurst was keen to tell the world he had answers. He had what he called a computer: 'a box of tricks you can pick up in your hands'. It was a captivating claim in an age when computers were little understood and certainly were not in people's homes. He said it was programmed to set off an alarm if the boat was in danger of tipping over, and it would automatically slacken the sails to spill the wind and remove the threat. If that failed, electrodes would send a signal to the computer which in turn would fire off a carbon dioxide cylinder that was connected by hosepipe to a buoyancy bag at the top of the mast. The inflated bag would stop the mast from sinking, keeping the boat lying on its side at ninety degrees and preventing it from turning turtle. A pumping system would then kick in to move water around the hulls, using it as ballast, so that the entire boat would be righted by wave motion.

The *Sunday Times* proudly declared that their race would have the first known computerised yachtsman. The yachting press spoke well of the apparent inventions. However, Crowhurst's desire to be taken seriously had led him to exaggerate. In reality, the box of tricks was a box of bits, awaiting assembly.

The computer story was a microcosm of Crowhurst's entire project. He was full of interesting ideas, including intelligent and ultimately successful design changes to his boat, but there was a spectacular scramble, bordering on pandemonium, to get everything ready on time. The boat was under construction at a yard near Norwich in Norfolk, on England's east coast. It was supposed to be launched at the end of August. Corners now had to be cut if Crowhurst was to be in the race at all, let alone in a position to beat the opposition. He was, however, soon to have one less opponent.

Down in South Africa, on 17 September, Blyth received the delivery of parts he had been waiting for on his jetty in East London. He sailed off immediately, adamant that he was still on a non-stop voyage. Two days later, he was battling in a storm force 10, gusting force 11. A hurricane is force 12. Blyth was running out of words to describe what he was seeing. Colossal seas were throwing his boat around in what he said was a terrifying pantomime in which he was always on the brink of catastrophe. The boat broached repeatedly, simply unable to cope with conditions in which it was not designed to sail. Three times it was knocked right over, before the weight of the sloop's twin keels slowly brought it back upright. The self-steering system broke again. Blyth thought about the fact that he had been in the Roaring Forties for two weeks, and had been having the frights of his life; there were still about four months of this to go until Cape Horn. In the early hours of 20 September, after the third knockdown, he decided to quit and head back to a South African port. There was no ambiguity now. Blyth was out of the Golden Globe race and his round-the-world voyage was over.

Forty years later, he describes, in stark terms, how quitting was more difficult than carrying on, despite the obvious risk. 'It would have been easier to die because [if you don't] you are coming back to face people,' he says. 'What am I going to say to them? "Terribly sorry."

'To understand what it was like then, you have to forget modern racing and instead think of *Boy's Own* and *Biggles*, and all that. It wasn't like nowadays where if they have a boat that is damaged they pull out of the race because, "What's the point of continuing?" They're not going to win, so why waste all that time? If they're not in the game, get out, come back, and get prepared and ready for the next one.

'But then, it was sail off, over the top and fanfare – so it really would have been easier to die.'

Blyth says he might have continued if he had not been married with a newborn child. At the time, as his boat tossed around like flotsam, he looked at the photograph of Maureen and baby Samantha that was hanging in the galley. He decided he had no right to die just because he was afraid of being accused of failure.

Speaking now, he says the mental approach to making the crucial decision was the same as that which he has employed throughout his life. 'Even to this day, you look at all the factors, you see what the aim of the exercise is, you segment the factors out and then go through each one and you come to a conclusion.

'The situation needed a decision. I made it probably within about an hour. The boat could not go on, so the decision was to call it a day. Once you've made that decision you shed everything else; finished. You don't sit down and cry about it: "I wish I'd done this, I wish I'd done that." You have to call it a day, get on with the next thing. Shed that. See what's next.

'I sent a message that actually stood me in enormous

stead later on. I said: "Boat will not track downwind. Common sense must prevail. Turning into Port Elizabeth." The decision was there. It was a big occasion.'

Three years later, Blyth famously did succeed in sailing round the world, and he went one better than the Golden Globe. He sailed the 'wrong way', against the prevailing currents and winds. British Steel, whose directors were impressed by his earlier 'common sense' message, sponsored him in the belief that he had proved he would not embarrass the company by being reckless.

They might have been less confident if they had known that the idea for the new challenge had stemmed from a delightful ignorance, based on the Golden Globe experience of the boat failing to run with the wind without broaching. 'It was my wife, my ex-wife I should add, who suggested in her quite obvious logical way that if the boat couldn't go one way, why didn't I go the other way,' says Blyth, thumping the table with delight.

'I was so naive, I didn't see the difference. We were on a high. Yet, to go one way with the prevailing winds and currents is fairly daunting, but to go the other way you are talking about a quantum leap. The public never really has got the difference.

'These were adventure days. That's the distinction you have to make.' Even now, Blyth, who was knighted in 1997, simply cannot resist being provocative. 'Nowadays, it's all about records. Records in sailing are a load of bollocks. If you want to go faster, you buy a bigger boat. It's all about money. Just buy a bigger boat.'

So, did Blyth go the wrong way around the world because he had something to prove after the Golden

Globe? 'No, it was for adventure. I didn't even think about it. I had done that. It didn't work. Shed it. Forget it. And that holds good to this day.'

Blyth's philosophical approach has needed to hold good. Challenge Business, the high-profile company he had run for almost twenty years, collapsed and went into administration in 2006. He suffered financially on a personal level and had to sell his home in Gloucestershire: a country house sitting in 12 acres with stables, three cottages and a duck pond. Blyth was reduced to making a deal with the new owner, allowing him to live for a year in one of the cottages while he wrote his autobiography and renovated a house back in his home town in the Scottish Borders.

In 2008, at the age of 67, Sir Chay Blyth and his second wife, Felicity, moved back to Hawick. He says: 'It doesn't make any difference. Shut it down. End of story. Let's move on. I've just done a talk about work–life balance. What the hell do I know about work–life balance? I made it up!' The remarkably robust Blyth has changed little, it seems, since the days when he tried to sail round the world while reading instructions.

Back in 1968, Ridgway and Blyth were now officially out of the Golden Globe. Donald Crowhurst was getting closer to being in it. At last, on 23 September, his boat was sufficiently near completion to be launched, although there was still a mountain of work ahead. She was named *Teignmouth Electron*, an amalgamation of the name of the South Devon town from which Crowhurst would set sail and the name of his electronics business. Donald's wife, Clare, made a short speech and swung the customary bottle of champagne onto the hull. It failed to break at first, but at least the boat was now in the water. There was another week of construction work before Crowhurst was able to make his maiden voyage of 300 nautical miles down the English Channel to Teignmouth. The trip should have taken three days. It actually took two weeks. Bad weather was partly to blame, but so too was *Teignmouth Electron's* inability to sail close to the wind. By the time Crowhurst arrived in Teignmouth, it was mid October. He would have to start his round-the-world voyage in two weeks' time whether or not he was ready. There was so much to do that even workmen from the Norfolk boatyard were back on the boat. Crowhurst was increasingly tense. Workers said he was in a daze. An old friend said he was peculiarly quiet, as if his mind was paralysed. The task was threatening to overwhelm him, but any suggestion that he should give up was dismissed. Crowhurst felt there was no turning back, even if he had to finish the boat while sailing.

He may have been influenced by Alex Carozzo, the man known as Italy's Chichester. Coincidentally, the two men met in Cowes when Crowhurst stopped on his maiden voyage, and where Carozzo's boat was being built. They were bedfellows, in the sense that they were the only two competitors yet to start and both were running the risk of disqualification for not leaving before the October 31 deadline. Both boats had been built in a race against time. The two men chatted while Crowhurst spent a day in the harbour, reportedly impressed by the Italian and his new 66-foot yacht. Once in Teignmouth, Crowhurst at least knew he was not alone in his state of chaos.

The chances of either man being the first to sail round the world single-handed were rapidly diminishing but each thought he could still be the fastest.

The rest of the fleet was stretching out, although information at the time was sketchy to say the least. There were long periods in which little seemed to happen. After the drama of Knox-Johnston's knock-down and Ridgway and Blyth's retirements, the biggest news had been about Fougeron's cat, Roulis. Fougeron, who had declined the *Sunday Times* offer of a radio transmitter, had managed to throw a package of notes and film onto a fishing trawler. It was a rare, photo-graphic account of life in the race, even if it was not quite the adventure story the papers had been hoping for. Roulis, the wild kitten from Morocco, was causing trouble. She had chewed through the wires of the domestic radio, and made a tremendous mess by chewing open bags of powdered egg and spreading them around the cabin while Fougeron was up on deck. She also had fleas and, most worrying of all, appeared to be pregnant. The Frenchman had brought Roulis along for company but the idea of a whole litter of cats was too much. He said he considered building a raft and setting her out to sea but decided he was too fond of her to take such a risk. Roulis instead became an undignified part of the press package handed over to the trawler. Film, notes and mischievous cat were soon in the hands of the British consul in the Cape Verde Islands. The consul sent the film and notes to London, and kept the cat; until, that is, he discovered her powers of destruction. He sent a cable to London asking to be relieved of Roulis as soon as possible, and arrangements were made to ship her to Belgium to a friend of Fougeron.

Stories for the newspaper-buying public were more frequent from the competitors who did have a radio transmitter on board, but even that did not guarantee exciting copy throughout. Nigel Tetley, who was too old-fashioned, honest and charming to take naturally to hyperbole, had been listening to what he described as a 'very interesting' record by the Mousehole Male Voice Choir. Apparently, it took him back to his youth in Cornwall, Mousehole being a tiny fishing village near Land's End. With a delightful desire to please, and honour his commitments, he peppered his logbook with references to his sponsor's music. He had discovered a mystery tape among the hundred or so Music for Pleasure had given him. 'I found an unmarked tape and put it on ... Acker Bilk! ... most reassuring music to hear with the yacht banging about,' he wrote. Hardly a day passed by without a less than subtle plug: 'Played "Music Hall Hits" – several splendid old tunes'; 'To match the mood, I put on a record of Stanley Holloway'; 'Listening to Beethoven over the wheelhouse speaker'. When not playing cassettes, Tetley was coming up with novel ways to tell how fast the boat was going. He had lost the use of both speed logs, so was reduced to guessing, until he realised the answer lay in the toilet. The forward motion of the boat had a siphoning effect on the water in the bowl. Tetley realised it was happening in direct proportion to speed. A half-full bowl happened at four knots; an empty bowl at eight knots. One month in, and closing on the equator, it would be fair to describe Tetley's voyage so far as relatively uneventful.

If the race felt like it had become dull for a while, it was only because of the lack of reporting from the boats that were in the thick of it. Knox-Johnston was in fact having a particularly cruel time. He had spent almost two weeks recovering from the knockdown off Africa. The reinforcements to the cabin top appeared to be working and repairs to the self-steering system were looking promising, but it had taken three days to rebuild a self-steering rudder. He made a new one from a teak bunk board, and reinforced the metalwork with home made rivets, cut from a six-inch nail and heated on the primus stove. He bound the finished article in fibreglass to make it stronger. Once again, Knox-Johnston proved to be as much a resourceful handyman as sailor.

However, a disastrous effect of the knockdown had been lurking undiscovered. So far, Knox-Johnston had been drinking water from plastic containers to preserve the supply in the boat's tanks. Now he connected a feed pipe from the forward tank to the pump and began to suck up the water. It was pale brown and smelt unpleasant. Knox-Johnston was alarmed. He quickly got to the tank's inspection cover and took it off. There was a putrid smell of bilge water. The other tank was the same. The water had been contaminated in the knockdown and was undrinkable. Knox-Johnston lit a cigarette and sat down. He could turn back to Africa, only four or five days away. Or he still had ten gallons of water in plastic containers and reckoned he could stretch that out for 40 days. He had another six months of sailing ahead of him so he would obviously have to catch rainwater. He wondered if he really should continue, knowing his life depended on the rain. Australia was just under two months away. If it did not rain, he had 300 tins of fruit juice. Perhaps he could survive the last couple of weeks to Australia by boiling seawater and condensing the steam. The answer was to continue and see how things went. His non-stop voyage might not get any further than Chichester's, but he did not have to make the decision now.

A medical crisis almost made the decision for him. While testing the batteries, in yet more bad weather, *Suhaili* broached and he fell over. Battery acid flicked across his face and into his left eye. He was still close enough to turn for Africa. He thought about Bernard Moitessier and Bill King, the two most serious challengers in the race, and where they were positioned. Knox-Johnston was in the lead and knew he had at least a slight chance of winning. He felt that would be worth giving an eye for.

Again, Knox-Johnston refused to give up. He was now firmly in the Southern Ocean, committing himself to the longest and most treacherous part of the voyage despite doubts about the structural strength of his boat, his self-steering, his water supply and his left eye. Initially, the eye hurt so badly that he felt he had been through ten rounds with a boxer like Cassius Clay. After a week, it stopped throbbing and was back to normal. However, the list of doubts and worries was soon to get longer.

The winch handle for reefing the mainsail was lost overboard. Knox-Johnston turned blacksmith to manufacture a new one from half a rigging bottlescrew, heating the tube of metal over the stove until it was red-hot and could be hammered into shape.

The engine, useful for charging the batteries, had seized up. Hours of frustrating work with levers and screwdrivers led to a slip. His forefinger was gashed right down to the bone.

The gooseneck metal joint between the mast and boom sheared off. Knox-Johnston had been worried about it since shortly after crossing the equator two months earlier. He had even wondered whether its weakness meant it would be unwise to continue. Now he was lashing the mast and boom together, a temporary affair while he worked on a solution. For two days he reshaped the metal with a file and, somehow, precision-drilled new holes while clinging on to the mast as *Suhaili* lurched in awkward seas. He had to stop when the wind rose to storm force ten but started work again when it dropped to force seven. Eventually, he created a new joint to hold the two spars together with a long bolt. Knox-Johnston was getting into the habit of solving problems that would each have been enough to force lesser men out of the race.

Another crisis was in the making, though, and, yet again, it was caused by the knockdown off Africa. Since then, the radio transmitter had not been working properly because, like everything else in the boat, it had been soaked in water. Knox-Johnston now spent two days with it stripped down, cleaning out the encrusted salt and looking for faults. For once, he was baffled and beaten. His radio was unable to transmit. No one would know where he was or even if he was still alive.

On 13 October, Knox-Johnston thought his voyage

was over when he encountered the worst conditions so far. Again, the wind was storm force ten but, this time, huge waves started to hit the boat from the side, shaking it with such stunning force that shudders and cracking noises left him terrified. Water poured through the cabin roof gaps that had been created by the knock-down. The reinforcements Knox-Johnston had done were tested to the limit, and he did not see how any boat could stand up to this punishment, let alone one he had patched up. He thought of getting the life raft ready and hoped the wind and currents would push him the 2,000 miles to Australia. He would have to try to row north while drifting, so as not to miss land, and risk carrying on round the Southern Ocean. Knox-Johnston snapped out of his thoughts, unimpressed by his own defeatism. He set to work, improving the motion of the boat in order to survive this latest drama and stay in the race.

At the end of October, Knox-Johnston reached Australia and was only 60 miles off the coast. He was halfway round the world and he had sailed this far against the odds. However, the constant crisis management had taken its toll. He felt fed up and exhausted and, more seriously, was scared about the state of his boat, wondering what would break next. He thought about giving up in Melbourne.

It was the worst possible time for a major crisis, but that is precisely what happened. The self-steering rudder broke again and this time part of it was lost to the sea, so there was no chance of repairing it. Halfway round the world, Knox-Johnston had a dozen reasons to admit defeat. He thought of Chichester, and was proud that

Suhaili was the smallest boat to make it this far non-stop. It would be a pity, he thought, to waste all the work so far and not get all the way round.

Knox-Johnston gave himself a history lesson in which the central character was an American called Captain Joshua Slocum. In 1898, Slocum became the first person to sail around the world single-handed. He was, in some respects, the 'grandfather' of the Golden Globe generation. The crucial difference was that Slocum's voyage, remarkable though it was, included frequent stops and took three years. His story, still a bestseller more than a hundred years on, was one about people as well as the sea. Nevertheless, Knox-Johnston turned to him, in his dark moment off Australia, for one reason – the lack of a self-steering system on Slocum's 37-foot yacht, *Spray*. Slocum had kept *Spray* on course by tying the tiller and balancing the power of the sails. A fixed position for a tiller, or wheel, is not normally enough to keep a yacht on a straight line because the force of wind in the sails overwhelms the rudder unless it is adjusted constantly. Many yachts, however, can be balanced to hold their course at least for short periods. Slocum proved it could be done for longer voyages. Now, Knox-Johnston wondered if he could do it for five months, for halfway round the world, and while racing. It was a formidable challenge. Unless he tried, he was out of the Golden Globe.

The end of October 1968 proved to be significant in the overall race. Knox-Johnston was halfway round the world, with a convincing lead but in a seemingly impossible situation. Moitessier had moved down the Atlantic faster than the rest of the Plymouth four and was now leading the chasing pack by a considerable distance. His boat, *Joshua*, named after Slocum, was proving to be the fastest. He was now round the Cape of Good Hope. Superficially, with approximately 6,000 nautical miles (6,905 statute) between Africa and Australia, it looked as if Knox-Johnston had an unassailable lead over Moitessier. However, this race was on a slow burner. Moitessier started nine weeks after Knox-Johnston. He was now six weeks behind, so it was clear that Moitessier was slowly reeling in the young Briton. That was to be expected, given the difference in the size of the boats, *Joshua* being 42 feet long and *Suhaili* 32 feet long.

Off Africa, Moitessier felt so invigorated that he wondered if he was in a hypnotic trance, born out of contact with the great sea and its many forces. Moitessier loved to talk and write about much more than simply the mechanics of sailing. Here, he imagined an escort made up of the ghosts of the sailing ships that had sunk around the Cape. 'I am full of life, like the sea I contemplate so intensely. I feel it watching me,' he wrote.

On 30 October, he sailed through his first gale of the Southern Ocean. The next day, the wind dropped to a gentle breeze, and Moitessier was struck by the contrast in the weather hour by hour. Late afternoon, the entire sea began to make a sound, reminding him of the angry termite colonies he would come across in Indochina as a young man. It was if he could hear the soldier termites, escorting the workers, clicking jaws in their thousands. Despite there being little wind, the surface of the sea shivered, each crest covered with foam. He had never seen anything like it. Moitessier wondered where the others were.

Bill King, the wartime submariner who, back in late August, had left Plymouth only two days after Moitessier, was a thousand miles from reaching the Cape of Good Hope, two weeks behind the Frenchman. He was bitterly disappointed when he heard over the radio that Moitessier was well ahead. Their boats were exactly the same size but King thought his would be faster, given that it was custom built for the purpose. Now his relative slowness, and the question of whether it was caused by seamanship or boat design, nagged away at his mind. It was strange that King should be so disturbed. He and Moitessier were the two who most resented their voyages turning into a race. He had always intended to sail around the world in his own time. Yet now, unable to cope with losing a race of which he was a reluctant part, he struggled with depression. He was, though, ahead of the other Frenchman, Loïck Fougeron, who had started his race at the same time as Moitessier.

Fougeron was only 400 miles, a few days, behind King. The two were close enough to be in the same weather system as they approached the Roaring Forties, still a long way ahead of Nigel Tetley who had started three weeks after them. King and Fougeron were about to experience the worst conditions either man had ever seen. On the last two days of October, they were hit by hurricane-force winds. At the same time that Moitessier was transfixed by a calm yet strange, termite-sounding sea more than a thousand miles away, King and Fougeron were thrown into what one described as the ultimate storm. Each man thought he would die. So powerful was the sea that Fougeron said he feared being crushed like a nut under an elephant's foot.

'Impossible to sleep,' he said. 'I curl up in the cramped bunk and wait for the unbridled sea to win its victory over me.

'What to do? The boat lunges sideways, driven by a frightful force. I am flattened violently against the side, and then in the middle of the bubbling waters everything goes black. A cascade of kitchen materials, books, bottles, tins of jam, everything that isn't secured, and in the midst of this bewildering song and dance, I am projected helter-skelter across the boat.

'At this moment I believe it is the end, that the sea will crush me and prevent me from ever coming to the surface again. I will join the legions of sailors who have perished along this ancient route.

'In a flashing instant, I think of my family, wife, all those whom I love and will never see again. I feel the boat making a desperate effort to right itself.

'My eyes burn, my teeth chatter – more from the diabolical sight of the enraged sea than from the unenviable situation in which I find myself. The waves rise up like cliffs. I am surrounded by buildings which collapse in order to stand up and fall down again.

'I loathe this sea, the sea that I love. I want to cry at the sight of the shambles.'

In the early hours of 31 October, with the force 12 still raging round his small 30ft boat, Fougeron knew he would be dropping out of the race and sailing to the nearest port the moment the wind dropped. He did not have to make a decision. He simply knew it was what he would do.

Bill King, 400 miles to the south east, was no less horrified. He felt he was in a witch's cauldron, a smashing tempest. Hurricane-force winds should not be happening here, or at this time of year. Why was it happening? For his whole life, he had been dealt lucky cards, surviving six years of commanding submarines throughout World War Two, dodging enemy bombs, depth charges, shells and bullets. He wondered why his luck was changing now.

The sea became more than violent. Now it was confused, with waves coming from two directions. *Galway Blazer II* was thrown suddenly onto her side at the top of a mountainous, breaking wave. The boat accelerated down, as if a surfboard, still at 90 degrees. King braced himself in the cabin. He had time to think. He waited for the weight of the keel to swing the boat upright but, in the trough, a cross-sea wave powered into the vulnerable *Galway Blazer II* with the impact of a train. To King's horror, the boat was 'turning turtle'. He found himself upside down on his shoulders, his head pointing to the bottom of the sea.

'Curiously, I felt no fear at that moment,' he wrote later. 'There was nothing I could do, except cling on to my wedged-in position. I stared, perhaps stupidly, at the in-rushing columns of water, and then looked away.'

The boat was full of water. Inexplicably, the sight of the oven hanging upside down transfixed him. He waited, knowing that another wave should knock the hull over to the side, hopefully far enough for the two tons of keel to act again as a counter weight. It worked. *Galway Blazer II* came back up.

King pumped furiously to bail out the water. Then he

climbed up onto the deck to survey the inevitable damage, knowing that *Galway Blazer II*'s two unsupported masts were potentially more vulnerable than the more common design of one mast held up by wire stays and side shrouds. He looked around. In a flash, he knew his race was over. The foremast had snapped in half. The main mast was still standing but bent over and fractured. King spent three days clearing up the mess and setting up a makeshift jury rig. It took him three weeks to reach Cape Town, his dreams and ambition shattered.

Both Loïck Fougeron and Bill King knew they had been lucky to survive. The outcome for both could have been very different.

They have been enjoying long lives since their brush with death. Fougeron decided not to return to the business world. He became a professional skipper, first for the wealthy owner of a 75 feet long schooner and then for yacht delivery customers.

He eventually retired home to his native France, where he lives now with his second wife, Anne, 60, and another cat, on a tree-lined road in a village on the southern outskirts of Perpignan, near the Pyrenees.

At the age of 82, he enjoys telling the story of his second, colourful attempt to sail round the world four years after the race. He was then almost 50-years-old. With a mischievous giggle, he says he decided at the last moment to take a tall and beautiful 35-year-old Belgian air hostess as crew, even though she had never sailed. They set off from Lorient in Brittany but the voyage ended in failure when they were beaten back by force 9 winds only five days from Cape Horn.

Fougeron did eventually sail round Cape Horn, on the third attempt, but this time he used the Panama Canal to minimise time in the Roaring Forties. He had had enough of danger, never allowing himself to forget how vulnerable he had been on the day when he was knocked out of the Golden Globe.

Bill King, who at 58 was the oldest man in the race, was more used to near-death experiences from his days in wartime submarines. Speaking in his Galway castle 40 years later, King has to take his time recalling past events in his extraordinary life. He frequently pauses, like a slow computer trying to find its place on the hard drive. On occasions, he has to give up, frustrated that at the age of 97 his memory is not quite as alert as it used to be. The force 12, however, is imprinted firmly on his mind. 'I was very lucky,' he says, sitting forward and pressing his hearing aid in anticipation of a response. He speaks in short, determined bursts as each detail of the memory comes to the surface. 'Really bad seas – Jesus – but I really was very lucky – happened to be inside the boat – coiling a rope – my shoulders braced against the top – if I had been lying in my bunk I'd have been knocked about – couldn't have been in a better position – completely fixed.'

King could have blamed the radical design of his boat for not surviving the hurricane-force winds, but he says the fault was in his own strategy, which was to abandon actively sailing the boat and, instead, leave it to its own devices; the hull drifting in the waves without involvement of the sailor. Sitting at the huge wooden kitchen table in Oranmore Castle, yards from a screeching parrot called Otis, his mind whirrs into action as he tries to recall the sequence of events. 'I remember doing something stupid. What was it? Yes, I started to sail downwind but I stopped doing that. I should have continued like that. Instead, I lay a-hull and rested. That was f****** stupid. That did for me. If I had gone downwind, the storm would probably have passed me.

'We make mistakes. You can make one mistake too many, you know. I don't remember the disappointment. I just remember having so much to do, to battle.'

In truth, King considers the Golden Globe as something of a footnote in his remarkable life. He talks more about the war, and that he did eventually sail round the world in *Galway Blazer II*, on the third attempt, in 1973. He enjoys, often mischievously, passing on the benefit of his own experiences. 'Best advice I can give about Cape Horn is, don't go there. The wind blows like shit.'

His one regret is that sailing round the world placed too much of a burden on his wife, Anita, who died in 1985. 'I shouldn't have done it,' he says. 'It was too much strain for her. She was delicate.'

King cannot stay serious for long. As he pours his third glass of white wine, he says: 'I am a small drinker. A small man who drinks.' He is distracted by Otis. 'The parrot is an awful bloody nuisance. Don't put your finger in the cage. It loves my son-in-law and loathes everyone else.'

He is proud of his fitness and longevity. 'I feel in very good shape considering my advanced age. I went walkabout the other day. I don't know about my marbles, that's another matter. I'm getting old and stupid. Not as bright as I used to be. My memory is pretty good considering.

'I enjoy old age. I can still climb a mountain and do a

hard day's work in the garden. It's good. If I live to be a century, we'll have a "PU". A piss up, or a run ashore.'

31 October 1968, the day Bill King and Loïck Fougeron were knocked out of the race as they arrived at the Roaring Forties, was the final day of the *Sunday Times*'s start window. Back on the south coast of England, Donald Crowhurst and Alex Carozzo had to leave on this day or be disqualified, their race over before it had even begun. Neither man was ready. Carozzo had asked the *Sunday Times* race panel for permission to delay his start, but the request was refused. He conjured up a solution that technically avoided a breach of the rules. He would sail out of Cowes harbour and immediately tie up to a mooring buoy in the sheltered waters of the Solent for a week while he finished preparing his new boat: Carozzo had found a loophole in rules that were as thrown together by the race's founders as the race was.

Down the coast in Devon, Crowhurst, who had made so many promises of radical designs and computers, knew he would be humiliated if he did not start on time. While the hurricane-force winds off Africa were knocking out two competitors, he was in a whirlwind of his own. The eve of his departure was to be a defining moment in the most extraordinary of all the Golden Globe stories.

5 : LATE STARTERS

The last time Teignmouth had seen anything like it was when the Beatles had stopped by in 1967 to promote their *Magical Mystery Tour* film. The Fab Four stayed, inevitably, in the Master Suite of the very grand Royal Hotel, which was built in 1825 and dominated the archetypal English seaside resort. Now, a year later, on 30 October 1968, the occupants of the Master Suite were Donald and Clare Crowhurst and their four young children: James, 11; Simon, eight; Roger, seven; and Rachel, five. Whilst the Golden Globe was not quite on a par with Beatlemania, it was important enough for the Crowhurst family to be honoured guests of the town. Certainly, it was expected that they would enjoy the hospitality in return, simply, for helping to maintain this south Devon resort's profile.

There was no time to enjoy or savour anything. *Teignmouth Electron* was in a state of chaos. In 24 hours' time, a crowd of well-wishers and media would be gathering to see Donald Crowhurst off. A regional BBC television team that had been documenting the build-up now sensed that all was not well. They stopped filming in the spirit of the optimism they had shown so far, and instead focused on the real possibility of failure.

Much has since been written about the final evening, not least in the *Sunday Times* book, *The Strange Voyage of Donald Crowhurst*, published soon after the race, in 1970 (later editions were called *The Strange Last Voyage of Donald Crowhurst*). There was a small dinner party in the Royal Hotel. The owner sent a bottle of champagne to the table to help the celebrations. However, the mood was subdued. Donald and Clare went to their room, and it was here that all the weeks and months of tension bubbled to the surface. This could be their last night together if the voyage went disastrously wrong. Lying in bed, Donald reportedly said he was very disappointed in the boat and that the project was in a hopeless state. He questioned whether he should go ahead with it. Clare, in turn, asked if he would be unhappy for the rest of his life if he gave up now. Donald began to cry.

There is no doubt that Crowhurst was under immense pressure. The short cuts in the building of the boat had left him apprehensive about its structural integrity. His 'computer' was not built and, therefore, the entire anti-capsize system that he had boasted would make his trimaran safe did not exist. With his electronics business struggling, he had staked everything on a successful voyage. He was in debt to Stanley Best, the caravan dealer, who had provided a loan against the value of the family house. Stanley Best still had money in Electron Utilisation and, such was his control over Crowhurst's financial affairs, he also technically owned the boat.

Crowhurst faced financial ruin if he did not set sail the next day. Even if he did set off, failure in the voyage would probably result in him having no home, business or boat. It was an intolerable position to be in.

In the decades since the Golden Globe, Clare Crowhurst has spoken out rarely but has never made a secret of the fact she deeply regrets, that final night in the Royal Hotel, not trying to stop Donald from going ahead with his voyage. She is still weighed down by an overwhelming guilt that has barely eased with the passage of time, resulting in a critical self-analysis of her role as wife of a Golden Globe competitor.

She feels she missed a subtle warning sign earlier that day. It was a minor moment, but one that a wife could, perhaps, have picked up on. 'A pot plant shed an insect into Donald's tea,' she says. 'Before he took the cup back to get another cup of tea, he very carefully rescued the insect and put it through the window. Stanley Best thought it was extraordinary. He said, "Why don't you swot it?" and Donald just looked at him as though he was a bit odd. Afterwards I thought he must have had some sort of fellow feeling, this insect floating on a cup of tea. He very carefully rescued it and put it out of the window. It was odd.'

An account of Chay Blyth dropping out of the race was another missed opportunity, in Clare Crowhurst's agonised retrospection. 'Stanley Best had a cutting from a newspaper, I think it was the *Sunday Mirror*, in which Chay Blyth was weeping and saying he'd had to come out of the race. He was totally broken down about it all, and Stanley Best asked if Donald had thought about this. I said, "We both have, actually," but it came as a shock to me that somebody would get so upset about having to say he couldn't do it. I said to Donald, "Isn't that extraordinary that he just could not face the business of coming back to people," and he said, "I can understand that." That should have been a terrible warning shot across my bows. I should have realised that it is very, very difficult to break off something like that, and come back and say, look, I failed.

'I have never, never understood how difficult it is to back off from something like that, in spite of reading the Chay Blyth article. I think that is horrendous, because I don't go in for competition, I'm just not at all competitive, and it is apparently incredibly difficult to come out once you have started in something like that.'

At the age of 75, Clare Crowhurst is as fiercely protective of her husband as ever. Her regret at not trying to stop him is based on her own shortcomings, not his. She says Donald's misgivings during the final 24 hours before departure were exaggerated at the time and since. 'The BBC reporter says he was definitely filming for a potential disaster. I certainly didn't get that impression,' she says. 'Certainly, when we got back to the hotel that evening there was a private party with our friend Ron Winspear, my sister and one or two others. Donald was fine and very relaxed and chatty.'

However, Clare does accept that there was a great deal of anxiety. 'He had a boil on his forehead which worried me, because often that is a sign of tension. He said, "No, it's just that I'm not paying enough attention to hygiene." He was very dismissive of that.'

Looking back, she slowly and thoughtfully tries to recreate in her mind the scene in their suite after dinner.

'He was very, very upset, suddenly. It is a very emotional thing separating from your wife and your children – they were all in bed by then – and he was certainly very upset indeed.'

Even now, as she pauses to recollect and build a picture in her mind, she jumps between differing interpretations of Donald's behaviour.

'We were in bed. He was saying that things were too chaotic on the boat. He certainly didn't say to me it was definitely a mistake or a disaster. No, definitely not. He just felt things weren't quite as he would have liked them to be. He said things aren't right.

'I said, "Can't you sort out an awful lot while you are actually on it?" I think I completely underestimated the whole trip, actually. The idea that you could go out on that and start sorting the groceries on board, you know, because once you are on a trip like that presumably your whole drive is to get on with it. He was left with piles of stuff on deck. It was a bit chaotic.'

It is obvious from the way Clare speaks that she was happy to let her husband get on with his project, while she kept a healthy distance and got on with running the family and the house. Such an approach, though, meant she was under-qualified to judge the enormity of the challenge.

'I probably wasn't picking up enough on what he was saying to me. He was very upset. He was crying. He was really crying. That was pretty frightening actually. It was for at least an hour. I don't remember why he started crying, what started it. Probably just a slight upset to begin with and then you become more aware that somebody is actually weeping. It was beginning to be very cumulative, the whole business.'

With the children asleep in the next-door rooms, the tears and talk carried on quietly through the night. This was their secret. The press and public would know nothing of it.

'We did both go to sleep very late in the night. We slept for a very short time. It wasn't a very nice experience.

'He was very pale in the morning. I did notice that,' she says, once again drawing attention to her own perceived failings of not noticing the bigger picture.

The day of departure, 31 October, the last possible day within the rules, was a strange one, but not as bizarre as it could have been if Crowhurst's publicist had been able to have his way. Rodney Hallworth was an ex-Fleet Street, tabloid journalist who now owned the Devon News Agency and doubled up as public relations officer for Teignmouth Town Council. He had met Crowhurst when the *Sunday Times* commissioned his agency to take a photograph. Hallworth, a huge, heavy-drinking man, was the archetypal hack. Like any local freelance journalist who wanted to make money, he was always brimming with ideas of contrived stories and photo opportunities. Now, not content with the imagery of a lone man sailing into the unknown, he wanted to spice things up. Miss Teignmouth 1968 was to be on board with the heroic sailor as they left the harbour. Shortly before the start line, she was to give him a kiss and jump off the boat. It did not happen.

Donald Crowhurst was at long last about to leave, almost five months after Robin Knox-Johnston set sail. It was a cold, wet and grey day, typical of an English autumn, itself a reminder of how late in the race his departure was. A band of 40 or 50 supporters gathered in front of the buildings that were just a few yards from the water's edge as the Crowhurst family boarded a small motor boat to be taken the short distance to *Teignmouth Electron*'s river mooring. Every step, every tense word and gesture was filmed at close quarters by the BBC as Donald struggled to contain the inevitable stress of such an occasion. The family made a strange, peculiarly English, sight, as if off to church in their Sunday best. The three boys, James, Simon and Roger, all wore ties as they waved to the cameras during an adventure that they were too young to understand. Bizarrely, for a man about to sail off around the world, Donald, too, wore a shirt and tie. Clare was unruffled in her smart, beige mac and patterned headscarf, as she sought, without disturbing Donald, to involve the children in this once-in-a-lifetime experience.

At 3 pm, *Teignmouth Electron*, with only Donald on board, was towed the short distance from the town moorings to the narrow river entrance and across the natural underwater sandbar to the open sea. Immediately, things went embarrassingly wrong. In front of the farewell flotilla, which included the ever-present BBC film crew, Crowhurst realised he could not hoist either of the two headsails. The halyards were underneath the lashings for the revolutionary buoyancy bag at the top of the mast, which had been hurriedly installed by helpers only the day before. Crowhurst, still wearing his shirt and tie but now underneath an all-in-one yellow jumpsuit, called for a tow back into the sheltered waters of the river. The mess at the top of the mast was sorted, and Crowhurst started his voyage again, two hours later, at 5 pm, seven hours before the *Sunday Times*'s deadline. After all the secret tears of the night before, Crowhurst was off. He was in the Golden Globe race, but it was an inauspicious start.

Alex Carozzo, meanwhile, was moving onto his mooring off Cowes to avoid disqualification. A week passed before he set sail, chasing after Crowhurst, the fellow competitor he had met a few weeks earlier. Carozzo was delighted with the huge yacht, *Gancia Americano*, that had been built in a record-breaking seven weeks. She stood up to the gale that he sailed straight into in the English Channel and the Bay of Biscay and, when the conditions settled, flew along at a satisfyingly fast speed. However, the stress of the build-up had taken its toll. Of the weeks before the race, he said: 'I was on edge. I was not in the right frame of mind.' Now, only a week after setting sail, he was suffering from a stomach ulcer. He was vomiting blood, and struggling to cope.

'When you are alone at sea in a big yacht and the weather is poor, then it is bad enough, but when you are ill it is terrible,' he said. 'When the seas were rough in the Bay of Biscay all I wanted to do was sleep and be sick. I was vomiting blood and felt terrible. I was very weak but I had to keep control of the yacht. No one can understand what it was like for me. To make things worse, the thought kept pounding through my head that I would have to retire. All the preparations that I and so many other people had made would be wasted.

'Out at sea, I had no one to help me, no one to talk with me. I am a bloody fool to try to sail round the world alone but I am not a complete idiot. I was beginning to feel a little better but, I thought, it is bad enough to be ill near land – what happens when you are in the middle of the ocean?'

Carozzo knew he could not go on. He radioed London and said he would make for Porto in northern Portugal. Long-distance sailors generally have a spirit of independence and are reluctant to seek outside help. They usually prefer to solve their problems on their own. Carozzo maintained the tradition. Despite his desperate state, he said he did not want to be rescued. He would make for port unaided.

The authorities, however, decided differently. The Portuguese sent a search-and-rescue plane out to sea. Its crew found him just 15 miles from Porto, making frustratingly slow progress in the now light winds. Carozzo signalled that he would now accept help, and a pilot boat was sent out to tow the Italian into port.

Wounded in more ways than one, he spent the first night in Porto on board his boat, reluctant to see a doctor. He was merely delaying the inevitable. The next day, from a hospital bed, he agreed to talk to the *Sunday Times* but there was no hiding his embarrassment at dropping out so early in the race. 'Now there is so much fuss over me,' he said. 'I did not want all this fuss. It is turning into a comedy.'

Waiting for his operation, as with so many of the men who were attracted to the Golden Globe challenge, he could not help but plan for the future and another attempt at sailing round the world. He had read about

Bill King's retirement and that King had said he wanted to try again. Carozzo was keenly aware of the possibility that no one would finish the race. He hoped the *Sunday Times* would organise another attempt the following year, and he would be in it.

That was to prove a forlorn hope. Carozzo went home to recuperate. It was six months before he could recover his boat and take it back to Italy.

He launched himself into a busy career of boat building and, for 30 years, has lived in a two-storey villa 100 metres from the southern shore of Lake Garda, Italy's biggest lake.

At the age of 77, he says of the Golden Globe: 'For me, it was a very bad time. The race was very important to me. I had a good boat for it but I had to abandon it all because I had been working like hell and that made me sick. It was a shame.

'But I would like to meet Robin Knox-Johnston again because he is "everything". I liked him, and I remember Donald Crowhurst from when we met in Cowes. I still have the Navicator which he gave to me as a present.'

The closest Carozzo ever got to a circumnavigation was to translate Chichester's *Gipsy Moth Circles the World* into Italian, but he remains a favourite among the sailing community in his home country.

In November 1968, there certainly was, as Carozzo had thought from his hospital bed, a real chance of the entire race being a failure. Five of the nine starters had now dropped out, none of them getting further than one third of the total distance. Of the four who were still standing, two, Knox-Johnston and Moitessier, were in the Roaring Forties, and Tetley was approaching this key stage of the route. Crowhurst, only a fortnight into his voyage and still off the coast of Portugal, was beginning to respond very oddly to the challenge.

It had taken him two weeks to sail to where he thought he would be in well under one week. There had been a series of new problems aside from the existing headaches such as his 'computer' being little more than a tangle of unconnected wires. He was struggling to keep the self-steering system in one piece, and he was paying for some of the short cuts in the building of the boat. Leaking hatches meant a vast quantity of water was getting into the hulls and, worse, into the generator compartment. Crowhurst was already wondering if he could, or should, continue.

Throughout his time at sea, Crowhurst made a series of recordings on equipment lent to him by the BBC. He often used them to present a public image of a heroic sailor in the mould of Chichester, sharing his thoughts on life at sea and life generally. Talking into a microphone is a type of public performance even when alone on a boat, and Crowhurst rose to this particular challenge with some relish and panache. Now, a fortnight into the voyage, he took to the stage for his first recording. For a man facing humiliating defeat, he spoke with remarkable optimism, even detailing the route he would take in the months ahead. He was 'a little worried' about arriving late at Cape Horn. In reality, the bottom of South America, which was a scheduled six months away, was the least of Crowhurst's problems. Shortly after making the recording, on 15 November, he set down his dilemma on paper. On nine pages of his logbook, he wrote a detailed account of the pros and cons of continuing, beginning by writing: 'What a bloody awful decision – to chuck it in at this stage – what a bloody awful decision!' He wrote about his fears for the Roaring Forties with the boat, and its self-steering system, behaving as it was. He feared repeated broaching while running in the big seas. Without his anti-capsize system, he calculated he would have, at best, a 50 per cent chance of survival. Crowhurst wrote that the odds were unacceptable. His whole race was falling apart.

He wondered if he could turn failure into a marketing success, writing: 'So: some form of salvage is necessary.' If he sailed to Cape Town in South Africa he would have got further, or as far as, Ridgway, Fougeron, King and Blyth, and there would be no disgrace. However, he wrote, there was no market there for Navicators, his hand-held direction-finding device.

Writing on through the night, Crowhurst agonised at length about the financial implications of giving up. He wrote that he would lose the boat, would be bankrupt, the company finished, his house sold and ten years of work and worry down the drain. Uppermost in his mind was Stanley Best, the sponsor. Perhaps he would maintain interest in the project and would finance another attempt next year.

Crowhurst decided to put off making a decision. He would keep sailing south and would try to get the flooded generator to work so that he could get the radio back in action. He would then be able to speak to Best and get his views.

He finished his hypothesis with an intellectual comment about failure, as if to dilute the impact of the terribly bleak decision he had reached but was not yet committed to. 'Superficial assessments of success or failure are worthless,' he wrote. 'What Nazi party member would have thought Hitler a failure in '41? What Pharisee would have considered the carpenter a success as he hung dying between the two thieves? Success lies in the satisfaction of having done one's utmost, I think, more than anything else. Having honestly tried to see the best course and then pursuing it.

'Philosophising is irrelevant, however, and must stop. I have things to do! It is also wasting the torch battery.'

On that night of 15 November, it seems that Crowhurst was tantalisingly close to making the sensible decision to stop and accept failure, however it be defined. The next day, the generator was back in action and he was able to radio home.

Whenever a competitor managed to get through to shore-based supporters, the one piece of information that mattered most was location. The latitude and longitude readings from a chart are the nautical equivalent of a map's grid reference. During the Golden Globe, these were the little nuggets with which supporters could tell how their man was progressing and with which the *Sunday Times* was able to build, slowly, a bigger picture of the race overall. Yet Crowhurst was starting to become vague, possibly, at this stage, to hide the embarrassment of poor progress and to hide his general predicament. He had a partial excuse in that he was having difficulty with his chronometer (a clock that keeps accurate time in varying temperatures and hostile marine environments – accurate time is essential for determining longitude), so a precise longitude reading, showing how far he was from Portugal's coast, was unavailable. However, he could have been more helpful than saying simply he was 'going on towards Madeira'. The Portuguese island, off Morocco, was in fact still hundreds of miles away but the newspapers, using Rodney Hallworth's embellished copy, reported Crowhurst not as going to Madeira but being near to Madeira. It was not a major crime, not even, arguably, a lie, but it was the start of a slippery slope. As the weeks went on, Crowhurst became increasingly vague. Hallworth perfected the black art of spinning what little imprecise news he was receiving into glorious success stories. His man may have been late into the race but he was on course. The combined effect of vagueness and spin resulted in a preposterous exaggeration of Crowhurst's progress, to the extent that some were soon predicting he could win.

The reality was awfully different. The secret predicament of a 50-50 chance of survival had not gone away. In fact, it had got worse. A new table of forecast progress, based on lower speed expectations, showed Crowhurst that he could not get to Cape Horn and out of the Southern Ocean before the local winter set in. Now he speculated there was a 60 per cent chance of capsizing, and there was still a major issue of the boat leaking severely. He actually went so far as to write down that he 'could conceivably get to Australia but certainly no further'. The voyage was doomed to failure yet, again, in more radio calls to Clare and Stanley Best there was no mention, whatsoever, of his utterly hopeless situation.

Crowhurst's intentions during the end of November are unclear. There is a lack of hard evidence to determine, conclusively, that he was intending to deceive. However, there are signs. The *Sunday Times*'s *The Strange Voyage of Donald Crowhurst* was written by two of the paper's senior journalists, Nick Tomalin and Ron Hall. With the full weight of the paper's resources behind them, they set to work scrutinising and collating evidence soon after the race finished. They uncovered two significant moments that they believed to be the first signs that Crowhurst had made a decision to fake his progress. On 21 November, Crowhurst had a seven- or eight-minute radio conversation with Stanley Best in which there was no mention of even possibly having to retire. The clue that Crowhurst might already have been setting the stage for his future actions came at the end of the call. He said there might be radio silence because of water getting to the generator. At a stroke, there was the excuse for no position reports at all, let alone vague ones. It is, however, possible that Crowhurst was simply telling the truth.

Clue two was found in Crowhurst's logbooks. Tomalin and Hall hired Captain Craig Rich to search through all the navigational records. Rich was an energetic 29-year-old master mariner and navigation instructor who was first recruited to help the *Sunday Times* during the race itself. Now he was back in the offices after taking an urgent phone call from Harold Evans, the editor. The team combed through everything Crowhurst had written. They found what they regarded as a peculiar logbook entry on 26 November. It said, simply: 'I am obviously going to run out of logbook space.'

Superficially, it was innocuous enough but why write it down? Crowhurst knew, of course, that his logbooks and charts would be scrutinised by the race judges. He needed to justify the subsequent tiny writing, which from here on was small enough to put two lines in each space. There is to this day uncertainty as to whether Crowhurst took three or four blank logbooks to sea. Clare Crowhurst says she bought them, and there were only three. Tomalin and Hall, pointing to a pre-voyage shopping list, said there were four. Therefore, they say, Crowhurst was not going to run out of space. They concluded that he wanted to use one of his spare logbooks for secret notes and calculations that he could hide from any end-of-race examination.

The *Sunday Times* found the clues convincing but they were looking for hard, indisputable evidence.

At the age of 70, Craig Rich, now a grandfather, has a boyish enthusiasm for a story that people still ask him about. He is a familiar face to many in the West Country where, for 25 years before retirement, he was a weather forecaster on the regional BBC television news programme. Sitting in his study, overlooking the River Tamar in Plymouth, he proudly places battered old boxes of Golden Globe paperwork onto his desk. Some documents are original, others are photocopies. Dominating the piles are the hardback notebooks on which he set out his own meticulously detailed calculations; each mathematical jotting an exciting journey of discovery to him, tortuously long to anyone else.

Rich has the sea and navigation in his blood. On the wall next to him is an early Hydrographic Office chart of the English Channel, the area he loves to sail in his own yacht, of which there is a photograph on his desk. When his grandson visits, he teaches him to dinghy sail on the waters below the modern apartment where he lives with his wife, Pat.

In 1968, Rich was running a Yachtmaster course at a sailing school near London when the *Sunday Times* phoned the school to ask for help. It was already October, and the paper's delightfully amateur attempts at following their own race for the previous five months were becoming comical. 'I was called up to the offices in Gray's Inn Road and met Ron Hall,' says Rich, chuckling over what happened next. 'He pointed to the *Sunday Times* map of the world and said, "Look, we've been all right when the boats are running roughly up and down; then we've been able to work out what they have done. But when they're going diagonally, we're buggered."

'They'd been using the wrong scales and everything. It was a mess. They wanted me to calculate, once a week, how far up or down everyone was on Chichester's progress. If I got latitude and longitude I could work it out. When I got no information I had to estimate.

'I started on the 23rd of October, just before Crowhurst set off from Teignmouth. I'd get the likes of the Rodney Hallworth press releases.'

He produces the original copy paper from a box, like a satisfied magician pulling a rabbit from a hat. Rich's job, working out where everyone was, became the core of the *Sunday Times*'s weekly reports. Tetley's position, as he headed towards the Roaring Forties, was being reported by radio reasonably frequently but information on the others was still scant. Knox-Johnston's radio had been out of action and Moitessier's catapult was of little use in the lonely ocean at the bottom of the world. As for Crowhurst, the diagonal problem that had 'buggered' the *Sunday Times* was even more complicated than they had realised. The number of miles travelled through the water was not necessarily the same as the number ticked off along the route. In the first couple of weeks, Crowhurst had difficult, head-on winds that meant he had to zigzag in the same laborious manner as his earlier delivery trip down the English Channel. He was managing to sail only an average of 80 miles a day (all miles here are nautical) and, as that was often in the wrong direction, he was moving towards the equator at only 50 miles a day. That was less than half the progress of his competitors and a spectacular disappointment when compared to his original target of 220 a day – a target that was always going to be wildly optimistic. In comparison, a typical family yacht, in ideal conditions, cruises at approximately six knots – 144 miles in a 24-hour day. On long passages, in which the conditions inevitably vary, the average would be expected to come down to four to five knots – 96 to 120 miles a day. (A knot is a nautical mile per hour and, therefore, 15 per cent more than a statute mile per hour).

Suddenly, out of the blue, Crowhurst sent a radio message saying he had broken the world record for the number of miles sailed single-handedly in 24 hours. He said he had sailed 243 miles in perfect trade winds on Sunday 8 December. Rodney Hallworth went into overdrive. Rather than the contrast in the record and the first few weeks' poor progress being cause for alarm, it was reason to regard the achievement as all the more remarkable. The papers had a new hero and a new, true competitor to spice up the race.

Crowhurst was exaggerating, although not as outrageously as it might first appear. With more favourable winds, he had in fact improved his speed to up to 170 miles in 24 hours. However, the claim of 243 miles was simply made up. It was designed to generate exciting headlines and hide the miserable reality that his voyage could not succeed. He even created another mini-table, this time with his actual and claimed mileages alongside each other in two columns.

It may seem incredible that Crowhurst was able to pull off such a stunt without more scepticism being expressed in the sailing world, but the fact is that almost everyone was fooled. Publicly, there was an occasional hint of it being a 'forthright claim', but little more. Privately, within race circles, there were only two people who had not been completely taken in. They were suspicious enough to, at least behind the scenes, ask questions. One was Francis Chichester, who said Crowhurst's claims needed careful examination. The other was Craig Rich, who had, indeed, been examining Crowhurst's progress as closely as was possible without modern communications.

Such scepticism, however, risked getting in the way of a good story. Speaking from his study in Plymouth, Rich says: 'I said to them, look, this just doesn't add up. I just didn't think it added up. You knew there were porkies going on but no one could say "This is ridiculous." You know the laws of libel. We didn't have any evidence. It just seemed very unlikely.

'After that I never really trusted anything. It just wasn't right. So I didn't trust him.'

Editor Harold Evans says no one told him that they thought Crowhurst was cheating. Rich believes there was a failure in the chain of command. 'I kept telling the *Sunday Times* all the time, this and that was unlikely. But don't forget I was telling just the reporter, and sometimes different reporters. They didn't really take much notice of it. Remember, they didn't really know me, so I'm sure they probably felt they couldn't use it.

'When Crowhurst claimed the 243-miles-in-a-day record, it was a nagging suspicion I had at that stage. His speeds had been all over the place whilst everyone else's had been consistent, as you would expect them to be. Then, suddenly he claims a record. I wondered, "Just what is going on here?"'

For Rich, examining the logbooks and paperwork after the race, the mini-table of the actual and claimed miles was enlightening but not the breakthrough he was looking for. All it proved was that Crowhurst had exaggerated a few days' sailing in order to be a hero back home. The suspicion, after the race, was that petty cheating had in fact been fraud on a grand scale.

The real revelation was, however, linked to that same week's sailing. Rich vividly recalls the moment he found the hard evidence, the conclusive proof that Crowhurst had, indeed, not simply been exaggerating his speed but that he had begun to fake his actual route, an altogether more serious affair.

'We couldn't crack it,' he says, re-enacting an intense and fevered search of everything on the desk before him. 'I suddenly asked if they had brought anything other than the logbooks off the boat. Nick dug out a roll of plotting charts. On one, down the side, very neatly written, for December 5, 6, 7, 8, 9, and 10 were calculations which *started* with the latitude and longitude and then worked backwards to the altitude of the sun and the time, and then was turned upside down and written into his logbook. Somewhere, he had to work backwards, and here it was. I said we've got him. That was the proof. He was putting fraudulent positions in his logbook.'

To appreciate what Crowhurst was doing, it is helpful to know a little broad-brush history. Navigation during the Golden Globe, indeed right up until the Americans fully introduced their global positioning System in 1995, had changed remarkably little since the previous breakthrough in the 1770s, when Captain Cook tested new ideas during his voyages in the Pacific. Sailors had always been able to determine their approximate position relative to the equator, their latitude, whether by simply noting the length of the day or by actually measuring the angle from the sun, at its highest point in the sky, to the horizon. However, determining longitude – how far east or west they were from a given point – was more complicated and was not possible until Cook's time. (Latitude is the horizontal hoops round earth. To picture longitude, imagine a chocolate orange and its slices). The inability to calculate longitude was why Columbus, in 1492, sailed straight out into the Atlantic until he discovered land, America. He was 'sailing the parallel' (parallel to the equator), keeping to the same degrees of latitude, so at least he had some idea of where he was on the planet. Knowing one geographical co-ordinate but not the other was, of course, hazardous.

The solution proved elusive for centuries. King Charles II, in 1675, ordered the building of a Royal Observatory, to be perched on a small hill overlooking the Thames at Greenwich in London, specifically to solve the problem of finding longitude at sea. Paris and Berlin did the same. Empires were at stake.

Yet some of the theory was well understood and was remarkably simple. The earth revolved once, in other words 360 degrees, every 24 hours. It did not take a genius to work out that the extent of the earth's movement each single hour could, therefore, be established by dividing 360 degrees by 24, and that the answer was 15 degrees. All you needed to know, for a rough idea, was the difference in time between where you were and where you started. If there was one hour difference, you had travelled 15 degrees east or west, two hours meant 30 degrees and so on. An alternative was to know the difference in time between where you were and a fixed reference point such as the Royal Observatory in Greenwich.

The problem, surprising though it may seem now, was that there was no way of keeping track of the time other than at your current location. Locally, noon was when the sun was at its height. However, the time back home soon became little more than a wild guess because the pendulum clocks that existed then were useless at sea. The quest for establishing longitude was as simple as manufacturing a timepiece, a chronometer, which could be accurate on a rolling ship and in varying climates. Thanks to an obsessive, Yorkshire-born clockmaker called John Harrison, such a chronometer was eventually achieved in time for Cook to prove it worked, in the early 1770s.

The broad principles of navigation were almost child-like but precision location finding was also possible, by taking the process a step further and combining time zones with a nautical almanac of lunar tables, compiled at the Greenwich observatory. The world of navigation had changed. Greenwich became the world's fixed point, zero degrees of longitude, the Prime Meridian and the vertical equivalent of the horizontal equator.

For the modern sailor, like Crowhurst, the process had changed little since Cook used Harrison's chronometer. Celestial readings still had to be translated for use on paper charts. It was a wonder of nature and science, but it was also a time-consuming process involving mathematical data. That is why most sailors, post GPS, don't bother with the stars and sun. Crowhurst, during those six days in early December 1968, was doing it all back to front: he worked it all out on plotting sheets and then copied the calculations, the correct way round, into the official logbook. His pencilled sums were meaningless to the few, select *Sunday Times* journalists poring through the logbooks and charts after the race, but to Craig Rich, however, they revealed the level of calculation, literally, to which Crowhurst was prepared to go. Rich says: 'One of the reasons why Crowhurst's fiddle was so plainly obvious to me, as a lecturer, was we didn't have computers in those days, and when we set examination questions on celestial navigation we would have to work backwards from latitude and longitude in order to set the questions. We were used to doing it all the time, so it was immediately apparent to me. That was the kernel of the story. It was the crucial finding.'

The level of fraud in Crowhurst's voyage became

increasingly intense, yet those six days in December were the only ones in which he bothered to do the back-to-front calculations, itself a sign of how much work was involved. 'It takes a long time to work out one of these fictitious calculations backwards, especially making sure you don't have any mistakes,' says Rich. 'It is difficult for laymen to imagine the scene, although anyone who sails could. You're in a boat in the Atlantic. You have to do your own real navigation as well, he's terrified of being spotted by a ship, the boat isn't all that good and, on top of that, he has to do these long complicated fiddles. And then you can copy things out wrong. There were errors because of his copying, which if they had happened for real would have put him in the wrong position. He knew it wasn't on.'

Tomalin and Hall, working with Craig Rich, discovered that Crowhurst then gave up using the fake logbook for a time. He took one of the spares and began to use it to track his true progress, presumably for his own benefit and not the end-of-race judges. He still had to juggle his real route with the fake one. Tomalin and Hall point to considerable evidence that Crowhurst, mid December, was still unsure what the level of his own fraud was and what it was turning into. He had started a plan of his false progress on an Admiralty Routing Chart, taking him right down to Tristan da Cunha in the Roaring Forties.

On 17 December, his radio communication with Rodney Hallworth was, for the first time, not just ambiguous but deliberately misleading. He sent a short telegram saying three things: he was over the equator, through the Doldrums and sailing fast. In fact, he was almost 200 miles north of the equator and was making slow progress.

Yet, right up until shortly before Christmas, it appeared that Crowhurst still intended to sail round the world or at least into the Roaring Forties and, therefore, presumably Australia. He had drawn up a list of tasks that would make the voyage possible, including constructing a mechanism for the anti-capsize buoyancy bag at the top of the mast.

However, Tomalin and Hall believed everything changed on 21 December when Crowhurst recorded that he had found a split in the skin of the starboard hull. It was another weakness in the boat, and a further sign that *Teignmouth Electron* might not survive the wilds of the Southern Ocean. The evidence, including drawing a map of the port at Rio de Janeiro in Brazil, pointed to Crowhurst seriously thinking of giving up. Yet three days later, he sent another telegram boasting of great progress. He gave the impression, arguably, of a position up to 900 miles ahead of where he was. He was making increasingly reckless claims, but that paled into insignificance compared to the ludicrous interpretation back home, and the subsequent press reports. Crowhurst, using his by now familiar ambiguity, had said he was heading to the Brazilian island of Trindade. Lost in transmission, it was written as Trinidad. Rodney Hallworth knew he could not have meant the West Indies, and concluded, somehow, his man must have meant the island of Tristan da Cunha down in the Roaring Forties. The resulting press reports put Crowhurst a flabbergasting 2,700 miles ahead of where he was. The reporting of

Crowhurst's voyage was descending to the level of a *Carry On* farce. Even the *Sunday Times*'s own Tomalin and Hall accepted that at this point the press coverage became absurd, crediting only the *Observer*'s yachting correspondent as being cautious enough to say Crowhurst was presumed to be somewhere in the Southern Atlantic.

Incredibly, it got worse. On Christmas Eve, Crowhurst blundered badly. During a radio call to Clare, he was again refusing to give a precise latitude and longitude position, saying he had not had time to take the relevant sights of the sun with his sextant. Under pressure, he inexplicably said he was 'somewhere off Cape Town'. Suddenly, with one careless stroke, he had lost any resemblance whatsoever between his actual and faked progress. His actual position was close to Brazil, still only two or three days' normal sailing below the equator. He had yet to sail the entire length and width of the South Atlantic to get to where he had just claimed to be. Quite simply, he was now in a different part of the world to where he said he was. The appalling predicament he had just put himself in was that he could not, now, give up without disgracing himself. If a sailor is 'somewhere off Cape Town', he does not limp into Brazil. And as if that was not bad enough, he would not be able to retire in Cape Town either. It was more than 4,000 miles away. He had claimed to be somewhere off it, yet would probably take more than a month to get there. Crowhurst faced total humiliation, and financial ruin. He had talked himself into a corner. He had built himself a monstrous trap.

6 : DEEP SOUTH

Market reports from the Albany wool sales in South West Australia may seem an unlikely navigational tool, but they were useful to Robin Knox-Johnston. Out of sight of land, he was tracking his progress off the south of Australia by following the local radio stations from Perth in the west to Sydney in the east. Their signals were reassuring as he had not seen land since he passed the Cape Verde Islands in the North Atlantic four months earlier, and he had little trust in his sextant since it had taken a bashing in the big knockdown off South Africa. The radio transmitter was still not working, which was a great worry to people back home as it meant nothing had been heard of Knox-Johnston and *Suhaili* for two months.

His attempts at copying Joshua Slocum by balancing the sails after losing the use of the self-steering system were proving comical at times. Much of the sailing was running downwind, so the mainsheet was loosened to allow the boom and mainsail to swing out almost 90 degrees to the side of the boat to catch as much wind as possible, emulating the old clippers with their big downwind and billowing sails. The problem in not having an automatic steering system was that there was now no constant adjustment to avoid the boat turning slightly and accidentally allowing the wind to get onto the back of the sail. If that happened, the sail and boom would be blown right across from one extreme side of the boat to the other – a crash gybe. Such uncontrolled violence can cause catastrophic damage to booms, masts and man. A gybe was all the more likely to happen because the fixed tiller, lashed into position, meant *Suhaili*'s hitherto graceful dance with the wind had turned into a robotic and rigid performance that took little heed of the ever-changing elements. To stop the boom crashing, Knox-Johnston rigged a gybe preventer; a long line from the front of the boat tied to the end of the boom, holding it back. The problem with a preventer, however, is that it only stops the symptom, the crashing outcome; it does not stop the wind getting to the wrong side of the sail in the first place, and that puts a tremendous strain on the sail and rigging. This needs to be dealt with quickly when it happens, which is a problem if the sailor is fast asleep down below. Knox-Johnston needed an alarm system. He came up with something that was startlingly primitive.

He altered his bed. When the wind pressed against the back of the sail, straining against the gybe preventer rope, the force would heel the boat over to its side. Knox-Johnston figured that he would then be thrown out of his bunk: alarm raised. It was a little rudimentary and drastic but enchantingly effective, for now.

Forced to experiment, Knox-Johnston learned as much about *Suhaili*'s sailing ability in two days as he had since having her built in Bombay. Not to have self-steering was a huge disadvantage but he was confident he could continue beyond New Zealand, a decision that would commit him to the second half of the Southern Ocean and, therefore, South America, although he had to get past Australia first.

Of course, the other problems had not gone away: the leaks and structural concerns, seized engine, reliance on rain water, failed radio transmitter and general equipment failures that required constant engineering ingenuity. However, Knox-Johnston felt this was no time to give up. He had equalled Chichester and now had a chance, of sorts, to go one better. He would never forgive himself if he did not press on.

The proximity to Australia's coastline did present an opportunity for Knox-Johnston: there was a reasonable chance of coming across another vessel. Then at least his position might be reported and people would know he was still alive and still in the race. In case he got lucky, he prepared a waterproof box of letters, articles, films and charts showing his route, and headed for Bass Strait, the stretch of water between Melbourne and Tasmania, to increase the chances of contact. The plan worked. Off Melbourne, he attracted the attention of a pilot boat and managed to pass over the box. The next day, while allowing every inch of his body to enjoy the rare sunshine, he was buzzed by two planes and a helicopter, creating comic-book moments as he dashed for his trousers. Word had clearly got out. It was a huge relief. Now his mother and father would know he was well.

Knox-Johnston headed south east to clear the bottom

of New Zealand. Now, history truly was being made. For the first time, a sailor had single-handedly passed Australia without stopping. Whatever happened now, this young Briton had broken a record. Knox-Johnston felt proud of the fact he had got further than Chichester but not proud enough to be satisfied. The clear goal now was to get all the way round. In a few days' time, he would turn left a bit and would be back on course heading east round the bottom of planet earth with just one more turning mark, Cape Horn.

There was a rude interruption. Seconds after hearing a worrying weather report on the still-functioning receiver, a radio message was broadcast for 'Master *Suhaili*'. The radio operator was not expecting a reply but was clearly hoping the call would be heard. It was a message from an Australian journalist called Bruce Maxwell. He was working for Knox-Johnston's sponsor, the *Sunday Mirror* newspaper, and had helped sail *Suhaili* from London to Falmouth in preparation for the race. Now he wanted a rendezvous outside New Zealand's Bluff Harbour. Knox-Johnston was delighted. It would be great to see a familiar face and catch up with news back home. However, over the next couple of days that radio call came very close to destroying Knox-Johnston's entire voyage.

Bluff, with a huge industrial port, is New Zealand's oldest European settlement, proud of its position at 46 degrees south, making it one of the world's most southern towns. It lies on the tip of South Island and is the gateway to Stewart Island, now a national park just an hour's ferry ride further south.

The stretch of water between the two land masses,

Foveaux Strait, is about 80 miles long and in places only 15 miles wide. For a man who had seen little land in months, it presented a new challenge. Ordinarily it would not be an issue, but the earlier worrying weather forecast was now turning into something quite frightening. A weather front was expected to bring force-ten winds just as Knox-Johnston would be in the Strait. He was now too close to be able to sail south of Stewart Island without a considerable risk of being blown onto land. To make matters worse, Knox-Johnston's meagre set of 24 charts did not include an adequate one for where he now was, and the strait was dotted with obstacles, all of which could end his race and even his life. In the wrong conditions, its geography makes Foveaux Strait a treacherous stretch of water that even today regularly kills people. Knox-Johnston was now deeply regretting getting so close to land. Just like the old clipper ships without their engines, *Suhaili* was in grave danger of being overwhelmed by the wind and waves and being swept onto rocks. Considering the months of open sea both before and after this moment, it was a ridiculous situation.

It had to be dealt with. It was night-time. An attempt to wait outside the strait for daylight failed because the wind was now gale force and was pushing Knox-Johnston where he did not want to go. He decided it would be better to sail a definite course rather than simply drift, even though that would take him into the danger area more quickly. He identified a lighthouse on an island, so he knew exactly where he was, for now. It was a lucky break, because for the next few hours driving rain brought visibility down to almost zero.

Knox-Johnston could just about see the front of his boat. He was worried he was getting closer to the island. He knew the tide would be strong but had no idea how much it would be pushing him backwards or forwards, so it was impossible to know how far he was travelling. If he turned away from the island too soon, he risked hitting other rocks; too late, he would run aground. The rain eased off momentarily. Knox-Johnston still could not see the lighthouse. He was seriously worried. That one light was the only way he could tell where he was relative to the island and relative to the many other unlit rocks in the straits. Despite rolling seas, a howling gale and the return of driving rain, he climbed high up on the old scaffolding that had once housed the self-steering system, holding on with one hand, swapping it for the other every few minutes to fight the cold, straining into the darkness in the hope of seeing a light somewhere, anywhere.

Daylight arrived, but still visibility was no more than a mile. Knox-Johnston thought he was in the centre of the strait but he was not sure. There was little chance of seeing Bluff and now he wondered if he had even passed the town. It was a frightening thought, not because it would mean missing the rendezvous but because it would mean he was heading straight for rocks that lay across much of the far end of the strait. Knox-Johnston's heart was sinking. He was in a force-ten storm, surrounded by invisible land, and he simply did not know where he was and he could not see where he was going.

He started to imagine shapes ahead of him. At 7.30 am, he saw one for real. Through the mist, he could see a blurred outline. He was heading straight towards it. It was downwind of the boat so he had to turn and fight into the wind if he was to get clear. That meant he had to raise the mainsail to give *Suhaili* extra punch and drive. She would not manage under storm jib alone, but Knox-Johnston feared the strain would be too great. If the mast did not break, the sail would be ripped to shreds. He had no choice. He was being swept towards the land. In no time at all, it was much closer and he could see the spray from waves hitting the shore. *Suhaili* struggled against a confused sea but started to draw clear. Through the rain and mist, Knox-Johnston could now see the end of the headland. He would clear it, but only by a whisker. He had survived this awful scare.

Knox-Johnston had been closer to the southern side of the strait than he realised. He headed north and, at last, found Bluff but the wind was still a force ten and *Suhaili* was blown straight past the harbour. The poor visibility, strong wind, close brushes with land and general confusion continued for another 24 hours as Knox-Johnston sailed round the south-east corner of New Zealand's South Island, hoping to get a message to Bruce Maxwell. He tried to sail up to a rural harbour and, struggling to beat an ebb tide, ran aground on a sandy seabed. He would have to wait until the tide came back in to lift him off. After the sightings off Australia, the passing of *Suhaili* was expected and looked-forward to in New Zealand. Before long, day boats were gathering round to talk to Knox-Johnston. Running aground was a little embarrassing but he loved the human contact and conversation, albeit from a safe distance so as not to break the rule of no assistance.

Word got out to Bruce Maxwell, who had spent the day driving up and down the coastline, and he soon arrived on another boat. He broke the news that he could not hand over any mail from home because the rules had changed. Knox-Johnston was furious at what he saw as childish and silly bureaucracy. However, he was happy to be told everyone was well at home, and he heard news of the other competitors. Some, like Tetley and Crowhurst, he had never even heard of. Others, like King, he did not realise had dropped out. Moitessier, he was told, was 4,000 miles behind. Based on the speeds averaged so far, a neck-and-neck finish in five months' time was being predicted. It was enough to galvanise the young Briton into action.

Foveaux Strait and New Zealand had delivered the most frightening and harrowing experience of Knox-Johnston's voyage. The next few weeks, through December, were to prove the most frustrating. Anxious to avoid the risk of icebergs, he sailed a little to the north and then along the 44th parallel towards Cape Horn. It was a mistake. His cautious route choice had taken him out of the best of the Roaring Forties' westerlies and into head-on easterly winds. In the first 15 days, the winds were against him on all but one day. Instead of being blown along in the direction he wanted to go, he was forever bashing against the wind and sea, and in a longer zigzag direction. With Bruce Maxwell's news on the competition, he knew Moitessier was averaging 130 miles a day, so he would have to do better than 100 miles a day in order to finish first. Some of the sailing back up the Atlantic would be against the wind, so he was hoping to clock up higher mileages while down in the Southern Ocean. He was falling well short, making less than half the expected progress. In three weeks, he wasted ten days' sailing, a loss of at least 1,000 miles. He thought the elements were being 'diabolically unfair'.

It is often said that the Golden Globe was not a true race, and that the competitors really only cruised round the world. Knox-Johnston's reaction to these frustrating weeks goes a long way to contradicting those modern, airy dismissals. Exasperation exploded onto the pages of the young Briton's logbook. He wrote that he felt a hopelessness eating at his insides as he saw the race slipping away and a Frenchman closing rapidly. 'If the Frogs are meant to win – OK, but there is no need to torture me as well as allowing me to lose.'

The cross-Channel rivalry was back with a vengeance, as was his sense of national pride. 'Poor old Britain,' he wrote. 'She has a poor enough champion in this race as it is, but even our best could not do much better in these conditions. Drake and Nelson must be weeping.'

Knox-Johnston's self-deprecation belied a hunger for victory. Whilst still in a state of despair and tormented by thoughts of Moitessier closing in behind, he worked to improve his situation. He decided on a drastic response to all the time wasted. He would head south, where he would find the westerly winds, even if he risked hitting an iceberg. He would keep going down to below even the 45-degrees parallel which the Admiralty Pilot book said was the ice limit. His chart of the Southern Ocean was more up to date than the pilot book and it showed the ice limit as further south. Most unusually for a master mariner, Knox-Johnston decided to throw caution to the wind. Against every instinct, he placed all his faith in one source and discounted the other. He knew that was unwise, flying in the face of years of the best maritime training in the world, but he wanted to be first home and he was haunted by the invisible presence of Moitessier somewhere behind, probably flying along in the Roaring Forties.

The loss of the self-steering system was taking its toll. The bruises on his body were proof of success of the unorthodox method of alarm, but being tossed out of the bunk was less than ideal. However, Knox-Johnston was more concerned with the strain on *Suhaili*. Ropes, shackles and sails were all suffering. The boat lost speed every time he had to lower a sail to repair split seams, and that was happening frequently. He started to reduce sail at night to keep *Suhaili* under control and under less pressure. That way, there was less chance of gybing while he was asleep but that too meant speed was lost.

One ongoing irritation was the radio transmitter. Knox-Johnston's handyman-ingenuity did not extend to electronics, something he had demonstrated off Africa when he spent two days stripping the radio down to no avail. Now he got out the instruction manual and had another go. He found a wire that had corroded and short-circuited. All he had to do was solder it back on, without any solder. He was back in his element; able to fall back on his good old-fashioned resourcefulness. He broke three navigation light bulbs and melted down the little scraps of solder on the terminals, scrambling around the cabin floor on all fours whenever he dropped so much as a pinhead's worth. It almost worked. A radio operator on Chatham Island, 500 miles east of New Zealand, heard him call out but not clearly enough to identify the caller or have a conversation.

The race leader remained out of touch. However, there had been enough information from his sightings off Australia and New Zealand for the *Sunday Times* to establish that the race for first place was an exciting affair. The forecast of a dead heat may have been a little premature given that it was made when the race was only half completed but it was not an unreasonable prediction when based on the progress so far. Once Chichester's record had been broken, the headlines in the *Sunday Times* centred on a 'duel of stamina' between Knox-Johnston and Moitessier. The Frenchman was indeed slowly closing in on Knox-Johnston. His bigger and faster boat was making steady progress.

Bernard Moitessier's story in the Golden Globe is harder to relate than Knox-Johnston's, or any of the other competitors. In many respects, he had opted out of modern life. The rejection of a radio back in Plymouth was not merely pretentious posturing. He truly was a different kind of spirit. He had proved so, if proof was needed, during his 25 years of adulthood and nomadic drifting.

In his time teaching people to sail on the south coast of France, he refused to allow his pupils to use a compass, pointing out that the Gulf of Siam junks he knew well as a young man did not even possess one. On sailing-school cruises from France to Corsica, instead of steering to a course of 110 degrees, the pupils had to feel the mistral swell and keep it to the left-hand side of the back of the boat. At night, they had to use the Pole Star. Quite what this unconventional Frenchman would have made of GPS and its associated modern chart plotters is barely worth thinking about.

Moitessier's own account of his Golden Globe voyage, in his book *The Long Way,* is not a diary, or a logbook in the tradition of those gone before him or of those racing against him now. In his writings, there are ups and downs but his woes are rarely of a mechanical nature, his highs seldom only about speed and great progress. Instead, he talks about himself, the sea and the nature around him, as if on a mission to explain the inexplicable. 'The days go by, never monotonous,' he says. 'Even when they appear exactly alike they are never quite the same. That is what gives life at sea its special dimension, made up of contemplation and very simple contrasts. Sea, winds, calms, sun, clouds, porpoises. Peace, and the joy of being alive in harmony.'

Yet Moitessier's voyage was not solely about the blissful wanderings and wonderings of a hippy. He often struggled. A quarter of the way from Africa to Australia, he complained of a week in which he felt tired. He was losing weight and taking vitamin B tablets to fight his fatigue. The pre-race boasts of a simple diet dominated by rice, in deliberate monk-like contrast to Nigel Tetley's bloated gourmet menu, were not looking so clever now. He knew it was not right to rely on supplements, and that he needed to take more interest in cooking. There were moments, he said, when he felt a great emptiness inside and when he was no longer sure where to go. He looked longingly at Mauritius on his chart, to the north, and realised that if he did not get on top of things he would not 'reach the end of the long ribbon of foam that leads to Plymouth'.

Whereas Knox-Johnston wrote in the traditional, clipped style of adventurer battling against the elements, Moitessier filled pages with the vivid accounts of life around him. He marvelled at a flock of shearwaters gliding over the waves as he tossed a bag of rotten onions over the side. Why, he asked himself, did they fly over the bag ten times before one spotted it and the rest joined him? What the devil were they looking for? What were they so focused on that they missed the bag of onions? 'And how about you, old man,' he wrote. 'What are you looking for?' Moitessier was always asking questions; more often than not, centred on the meaning of life.

The race mattered, though. He longed for information on the others, especially those he had spent time with in Plymouth. He wondered on their tactics. Would they have gone a little north after Africa, into the Indian Ocean, to take what he called the half-quiet route, or would they have torn along below the 40-degrees parallel? Moitessier had opted for the half-quiet route, and told himself he did not regret it despite the slow speeds; Knox-Johnston need not have been so concerned at the price he was paying for doing the same further along the route.

In his writings, Moitessier could not discuss the race for long. He would always veer back to the world around him. On the approach to Australia, he was becalmed for a number of days. It is not clear how many days because Moitessier immersed himself in the antics of another flock of shearwaters, becoming so engrossed that he lost all sense of time. Day after day, he threw them bits of cheese and, when that was running out, lumps of butter that Francoise had mixed with salt to preserve in a large plastic jar. Each dawn, he came up to the deck to find a growing number of shearwaters close to the boat. He developed a rallying call, 'Kew-Kew!' and said he was offering them cheese and friendship. One in particular he singled out as his own. It was the only one to come and eat from his hand, and he could always tell him apart from the other hundred by his little mannerisms, such as cocking his head slightly to the left before taking the cheese or butter.

Sailors do not like being becalmed. Or if they do, they certainly do not like it to last days on end. Moitessier wrote: 'It's marvellous to have wind.' So far, so like every other sailor, but Moitessier was not like every other sailor: 'It's also marvellous to have a calm that seems always to have been. I have the feeling of having known my birds forever, of being here forever without time passing. It is like a book of images that one can leaf through endlessly.

'The wind will never come back. Yet I feel lighter with each dawn, happy to be alive, happy to feel all that life around the boat. The weather is fine, the sun is out, the birds are there.'

It is not uncommon for lone sailors in small boats, in large oceans, to bond with the surrounding wildlife, but Moitessier took this experience to new heights. Six whole pages of his book are packed with nothing but the behaviour of this flock of shearwaters, and his reaction to them. He finishes the story with an extraordinary account of just how far the relationship had blossomed, describing how he got up in the middle of the night and saw three of them sleeping on the still water a few yards from the boat. 'I went to the stern and spoke to them, very softly, just like that. And they came right alongside. I kept on talking the same way. They raised their heads toward me, cocking them to one side, right and left, from time to time giving a barely audible little cry in answer, as if they were trying to say that they liked me too.

'They may have added they liked cheese, but I could feel in an almost physical way that there was something more than food to that whispered conversation, something very moving: the friendship they were returning to me.

'I wanted to caress them, at least to try. But I did not dare; maybe it was too soon. With a clumsy and premature gesture I risked breaking something very fragile. Wait a while longer, don't rush things, don't force things. Wait until the waves of friendship, made of invisible vibrations, reach their full maturity. You can spoil everything, trying to go faster than nature.'

Moitessier never did get to caress his new friends. The wind returned and he was off again, heading for the bottom of Tasmania. After four months at sea, he was keen to use his catapult and make contact with a ship or fishing boat. The only contact on the voyage so far was as he approached southern Africa and he fired a message onto a freighter. The ship had got too close and the two collided. The damage was minor but, from then on, Moitessier was reluctant to take any risks when trying to deliver a package.

One week before Christmas, he was off Tasmania. He

thought of finding a bay and leaving messages and film in a plastic container anchored to a weight on the seabed, but decided it might never be found. He was nervous of being so close to land and coastal activity and, after a tense night of confusion as to where he was in relation to rocks, he vowed never again to take such risks in order to reassure his family.

He came across a fishing boat and threw the container to the three men on board. It was a rare opportunity to get information. One of the men had heard something about an Englishman passing New Zealand, without stopping, perhaps last month. Moitessier, who often listened on his radio receiver for news of the race but was always disappointed at the lack of mentions, knew so little that he was not certain who the Englishman was. He did not know Bill King was out of the race but anyway thought it was unlikely to be him. Of the three early starters, only Knox-Johnston had what Moitessier regarded as a real boat. The other two, Ridgway and Blyth, were in what he saw as little, fragile, plastic things. He decided to listen more carefully to Australian news broadcasts for a few days as they would soon have the fishermen's report of *Joshua* being in the area.

Considering Moitessier's rejection of all things to do with a race, he became peculiarly upset at the lack of news broadcasts on his radio. If he had been a little less pompous in Plymouth when he declared that a good slingshot was worth all the transmitters in the world, he would have been able to call for information. Yet here he was, Tasmania now in his wake, getting cross with the media for not appearing to be interested in him. He listened, religiously, to Australian radio and the BBC World Service, figuring that the BBC would have been told of his package as a matter of top priority. 'Yet nothing, not a word, not a mention,' he wrote. He became deeply unimpressed with the BBC for not letting the four friends, whom they had been filming together in Plymouth, know about each other's progress. He even went so far as to feel bitterness towards the media, saying he did not need anything other than just a little news from time to time.

Moitessier was unaware that Bill King and his friend Loïck Fougeron had both been knocked out of the race in the same storm off Africa. Nigel Tetley was, of course, still in the race, sailing in his new-fangled trimaran. Moitessier wondered how Nigel's boat would be faring. Recognising it would be fast at times, he thought, morbidly, of the five multihulls that were lost in Australian waters in the previous year. Fifteen men had died. Where was his new friend Nigel? It would really affect him if he was to learn that Nigel was not coming back.

Tetley was only doing moderately well. He had failed to make up any of the three weeks he had gifted Moitessier by starting late and he had actually fallen back another three weeks while sailing down the Atlantic. The theoretical speeds of the multihull meant Tetley would have been expected to close the gap across the Southern Ocean but it did not work out like that.

On the approach to the Roaring Forties back at the end of October, when King and Fougeron hit their hurricane-force winds ahead of him, Tetley had concentrated his mind on the very risks Moitessier had been ruminating over. The five Australian disasters had not escaped him. Arguably a little late in the day, he began to study the evidence of multihull capsizes in a journal written by the Amateur Yacht Research Society. His confidence cannot have been helped by the cover, on which there was a picture of the scenario so dreaded by multihull sailors – pitchpoling. One of the hulls of a trimaran was digging into a wave, leading to the front of the boat 'tripping' on itself and the stern lifting up out of the water. From that snapshot moment, the boat could have settled back or it could have continued the motion into an almighty, crashing somersault: a full-blown pitchpole, from which there is little chance of a trimaran recovering.

Tetley decided he would watch his speed. If necessary, he would reef the sails to slow down and lessen the chances of one of the bows tripping up. It would slow him down in the race but at least he had a better chance of getting home alive. He also decided to move a lot of his stores into the back of the boat to help keep the stern down.

Life had become considerably more interesting for Tetley since the days of judging speed by the toilet bowl. The deck covering had begun to lift on the starboard side and had to be nailed down. Leaks in the forepeaks, the front sections of the hulls, were getting unnervingly worse. He had to pump out 30 gallons of seawater in just two days. Still, he was able to take his mind off things by listening to Boccherini and Delius.

Mercifully, as Tetley headed more or less into the Roaring Forties in mid November, the noble but contrived plugging of his sponsor's music began to ease off. There was, though, one final flurry in his logbook, which was published after the race: 'I played the last recording to complete the full cycle of my Music for Pleasure repertoire. A few I have marked with a cross and will not play again, but I can say here with all honesty that the majority have given me great pleasure and contributed in no small way to my peace of mind.'

His mood may have been helped by the fact that *Victress* was now moving through the water with a kinder motion, thanks to the shifting of stores back to the stern. Tetley felt he would now be able to safely pick up his speed to more than 120 miles a day, a little slower than Moitessier but faster than Knox-Johnston.

At the end of November, he reached the position at which Knox-Johnston had been knocked down, south west of the Cape of Good Hope, back in early September. This was the story of 'worst seas in a life-time' that had been hanging over Tetley as he sailed out of Plymouth just days after it made the newspapers. Now, at the same location after two months at sea, he was conscious of the contrast as he plodded through in a near calm. Almost embarrassed, he spoke to the *Sunday Times* over the radio with an admission that there was little to report. If he was feeling anti-climactic, he could have done without the paper's journalist sounding disappointed over the lack of exciting news. Had he not fallen over the side or something – anything? No, was the honest reply.

In fact Tetley could easily have spun his story into quite a maritime drama. Here he was, at the spot of the leader's now famous near-disaster, close to where King and Fougeron were flattened and where the tough-nut

Blyth was beaten. He was taking on startling amounts of water and he was about to pass the point of no return and enter one of the most notorious parts of the seas. A modern adventurer would have had the media eating out of the hands of his or her public relations people. It just did not work like that then. It was all so much less sophisticated and so wonderfully amateur. Tetley simply was not interested. It is true that he had shown the value of sponsorship, and the need to give something in return with his clumsy logbook references to the music, but he did not see the need to go any further. His voyage, as with Knox-Johnston and Moitessier ahead of him, was about meeting a challenge, not selling a story. It was an indication of how 'adventure' was then in a different age. Today, the great challenges have been ticked off and any new exploit has, by necessity, become relatively contrived.

In the run up to Christmas Day, Tetley had his first taste of a Roaring Forties storm. All the sailors who made it this far spoke of their nervous anticipation for what became a sort of initiation process. For most, including Tetley, it was the first time their boats had been fully tested. The Plymouth four had discussed storm tactics in the belief that kindred spirits should share their knowledge rather than hide their secrets. Moitessier, who even then was concerned for his friend in a multihull, had advised Tetley to keep sailing and run away from the wind with just a scrap of sail to help maintain driving force and steerage. Now, in a severe force-nine gale, Tetley followed the Frenchman's advice. He was not happy. *Victress* did not feel under control. Tetley decided what was right for one boat was not necessarily right for another. He decided to 'heave-to' and ride out the storm. So he turned into the wind and stalled the sails by over-tightening them. That way, he hoped he would slow right down but would have a more stable boat than if he dropped the sails altogether. *Victress* stopped sailing, as planned, and rode out the waves with ease. Tetley was alarmed at the prospect of the inevitable bigger storms to come but was comforted by his apparently successful method of response. It did mean, though, he would lose time and progress.

Now that the race fleet was down to four, it was rare for any of the men to share the same experiences at sea. Each was in his own world, far from the others. It was unlikely that there would be a repeat of one weather system simultaneously affecting more than one competitor, as with King and Fougeron. However, Christmas Day 1968 was something they did share, in that all four had to get through it. It proved difficult for each of them. If Christmas can amplify loneliness at the best of times, then it can play havoc when sitting all alone in a very strange world of seemingly limitless water; a humbling world in which your place on earth can feel uncertain.

Robin Knox-Johnston, in the lead, was more than halfway between Australia and Cape Horn. On 24 December, practical problems such as the lack of self-steering and a radio transmitter paled into insignificance. He felt ruffled at the thought of Christmas alone. Now, for almost the first time since leaving Falmouth he was questioning the point of spending a year alone on a boat. He had a mental picture of home; a quintessentially English scene, with his father and brothers fetching logs from the garden, the family gathered round a roaring fire in the drawing room as they prepared to go to a midnight service at the village church. He turned to his whisky bottle and was soon perched on *Suhaili*'s cabin top bellowing out Christmas carols in his own impromptu, hour-long, surreal service. A little bit of England was in the Southern Ocean, more than one thousand miles from the nearest land.

Knox-Johnston's pride in his home country was ever-present. His biggest regret on Christmas Day was not being awake for the Queen's Speech, at 6 am local time. So, at 3 pm, he drank what he described as a Loyal Toast, and thought of all the people around the world who would have been listening to the Queen's words. It made the world feel smaller; if only, he thought.

The comparison of the Golden Globe challenge with man trying to reach the moon came to the fore that Christmas Day, and it horrified Knox-Johnston. He picked up a radio report of the Americans' successful mission to fly men around the moon for the first time, in Apollo 8. He marvelled at the three men risking their lives to expand frontiers. Suddenly, he was appalled at their magnificent effort in stark contrast to his own, which would add nothing to humans' scientific knowledge. He had been determined that a Briton would be the first person to sail round the world without stopping, but now he was seeing it as an act of selfishness rather than heroism. He remembered his mother being asked what she thought of his planned voyage. Her answer was to denounce her son's dream as 'totally irresponsible'. Now he thought she might have been right.

Bernard Moitessier was in sight of a distant New Zealand on Christmas Day, and got thoroughly drunk. The BBC was still saying nothing about the race. He was missing friends and family, and felt blue. He switched the radio receiver off because the stories of infant Jesus were getting on his nerves. Someway down a bottle of champagne, he had an alcohol-fuelled rant against religion, saying people used God as a shield, pretending they were facing up to themselves but all the while they were quietly going about their 'sleazy huckstering'. He philosophised about the meaning of life and the Bible, and how Christmas was the big truce with the whole world when he would invite not only the neighbourhood cats and dogs for dinner but the rats too. In addition to the champagne, he drank two mugs of wine. He went to bed, unable to tell what time it was because the hands of his watch were 'all mixed up'.

One of the most poignant photographs to make it in the sailors' rare packages home was of Nigel Tetley on Christmas Day. It was on one of many films in a parcel that included tape recordings, notes and a letter to Eve. It was February before he saw a boat and was able to hand the package over, at Otago harbour in New Zealand, the same harbour Knox-Johnston had run aground outside. When the photograph was taken, Tetley was still a long way from land, halfway between Africa and Australia. It was spread across the entire width of a broadsheet page in the *Sunday Times*, headlined: *'The day a sailor feels at his loneliest: Nigel Tetley drinks a champagne toast to his camera somewhere in the Indian Ocean.'*

It is a fascinating picture, in noteworthy contrast to

the more common self-portrait of a dishevelled sailor in a scene designed to reinforce images of basic living. Tetley is sitting in *Victress*'s cabin. It is obvious he has made the table setting as attractive as possible. The last of his oranges is propped up for display in a little bowl, like an egg on an egg cup. The last of his supply of nuts and raisins is on show too. Taking pride of place in the centre, next to the bottle of champagne, is a cooked pheasant that the *Sunday Times* mistook for a chicken. Tetley himself is unshaven but clean and groomed, with a hint of a slightly self-conscious smile as he looks into the camera and lifts his right hand for the toast. Sitting on his cushion, he has the unruffled appearance of someone waiting patiently for his Christmas meal. The viewer would barely know that he has just rushed to his seat from setting the camera's self-timer. On first glance, the only odd thing in this picture of domestic bliss is that he is on his own. Yet it is obvious that Tetley meant to impress. The galley sink is in view, with the washing-up already completed. Pencils on the chart table are neatly lined up together. Everything is in place, tidy and clean.

For whom was the effort made? Were we seeing Tetley the Royal Naval officer, unable to break the disciplined habits of a lifetime, or was he sending a message? There are clues that it was meant as reassurance for Eve. Tetley took more than one photograph of the same scene. The only slight differences are the positions, always prominent, of the huge and rather out of place pewter tankard he is holding up for the toast to camera. It is as if he is experimenting, searching for the pose that puts the tankard in the best light. That tankard was a

above: Eve Tetley, Clare Crowhurst and Francoise Moitessier together for the first and only time, at the mid-race photo shoot on *Discovery* in London

below: Francoise, Eve and Clare in one of a succession of poses for the *Sunday Times*

above: John Ridgway in new Aran Islands sweater and tam o'shanter departs 1 June 1968

above: Chay Blyth tries to look confident as he departs Hamble on 8 June 1968

above: Knox-Johnston on *Suhaili*, departing Falmouth on 14 June 1968. The self-steering scaffolding is already at work

above: Eve Tetley on shore in Plymouth as, left to right,
Nigel Tetley, Bill King, Bernard Moitessier and Loïck Fougeron
discuss King's new boat

below: Bill King, proud of the boat with similarities to a submarine

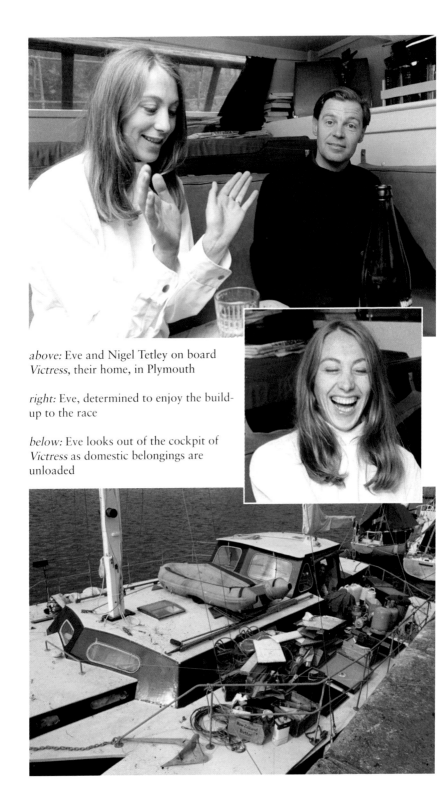

above: Eve and Nigel Tetley on board *Victress*, their home, in Plymouth

right: Eve, determined to enjoy the build-up to the race

below: Eve looks out of the cockpit of *Victress* as domestic belongings are unloaded

above: Bernard Moitessier demonstrates why he says there will be no need for a radio

below: Moitessier poses on his bunk during the weeks preparing in Plymouth

above: Joshua can be seen through the group but Francoise Moitessier looks away

above: Moitessier on *Joshua* sets sail from Plymouth on 22 August 1968

right: Bill King's radical *Galway Blazer II* leaving Plymouth on 24 August 1968

left: Lieutenant
Commander Nigel Tetley
on *Victress* in Plymouth

above: Tetley and *Victress*, a
trimaran, leave Plymouth on
16 September 1968

left: Alex Carozzo approaches
Gancia Americano on a mooring
off Cowes

above: Clare and Donald Crowhurst celebrate the launch of *Teignmouth Electron*

right & below: Crowhurst on board as helpers rush to get everything ready just three days before the deadline to start

right: Donald Crowhurst is taken to the boat for departure, accompanied for the last time by Clare with daughter Rachel in her arms, James and Roger, and Simon in the bow

below: Teignmouth Electron is towed to the open sea off Teignmouth ready to start, on 31 October 1968

above: Nigel Tetley self portrait as he seeks shade
from the sun and listens to his tape player

below: One of a series of Tetley's Christmas
dinner self-portraits

above: Bernard Moitessier's *Joshua* in heavy seas

below: Moitessier at one with sea and boat

opposite: Robin Knox-Johnston and his battered *Suhaili* on the triumphant approach to Falmouth

this page: The moment a lean Knox-Johnston steps ashore after ten months at sea

left: Falmouth lays on an open-top car parade

above: The first press conference. Sir Francis Chichester is nearest camera at the top table

right: In Falmouth with Chichester, Knox-Johnston signs a declaration that he kept to the rules

above: Eve Tetley creates a stir in Trinidad as she spots Nigel on his rescue ship

below: On the rooftop of a London hotel, Tetley is flanked by Knox-Johnston and Chichester

Donald Crowhurst's *Teignmouth Electron* drifts, complete with mizzen sail, like the *Mary Celeste*. A boarding party from a passing ship approaches. They are about to find that no one is on board

Christmas present from Eve, which he had opened that morning. Tetley started the day listening to Christmas carols from Guildford Cathedral and feeling festive. He finished it feeling very lonely.

Donald Crowhurst, the last of the four, was, as far as the public knew, chasing Tetley. It had been on Christmas Eve that he inadvertently set a trap for himself by telling Clare that he was somewhere off Cape Town. On Christmas Day, he was a mere 20 miles from Brazil, in sight of land if the visibility was good. After speaking to Clare, he had in fact turned the boat towards land before later turning away again. He made tape recordings and wrote about how he felt, trying to convince the eventual reader or listener that he was not under any great stress and was not depressed, even though he talked of loneliness and feeling melancholy. Tomalin and Hall, studying everything that he wrote and recorded, believed Christmas was full of introspection and self-doubt for Crowhurst. It is the time they believe he probably began to read his copy of Einstein's *Relativity*, a publication that was to feature heavily in the final days of Crowhurst's voyage.

On Boxing Day, Crowhurst's doubts about the structural integrity of *Teignmouth Electron* were justified when he investigated the split skin on the starboard hull that he first saw in the week before Christmas. Lifting the inspection hatch to look inside, he found that the plywood skin had come apart from its supporting wooden frame. It was as if the ribs in a ribcage were no longer doing their job. If he had been planning to stay in the race and sail on into the Roaring Forties, this might well have been too much for a man whose head was already full of doubts. The boat was not only leaking, it was arguably in danger of falling apart if asked to survive the heavy seas of the Southern Ocean for months on end.

The whole of the next month was the beginning of what Crowhurst became infamous for – drifting and hiding in the South Atlantic. A glance at the map of his progress during January shows his race was over. Yet he stayed at sea, slowly heading away from land, plotting what had now unequivocally moved from exaggeration to fraud. The statistics speak volumes. For all of January, he averaged little more than 15 miles a day, an average speed of well under one knot. He spent much of his time undertaking a mammoth exercise to add credibility to his fake voyage; collating weather reports to coincide with the route the public still thought he was sailing. He would be able to say what the conditions had been like despite not being there at the time. The forecasts, transformed into descriptive accounts, would add weight to his official logbook.

There was a risk of being recognised by a passing ship but the odds were in favour of being dismissed as just another yacht. The evidence points to Crowhurst having long since stopped flying the international signal flags, MIK, which requested that a vessel's position be reported to Lloyds of London. He had six sets on board so each one could be refreshed and the signal could be flown throughout the voyage. Only one set was ever used and even it still had fold creases. Unlikely though it may seem now, Crowhurst was reported to Lloyds only once, and that was when he was flying the first set of flags just a few days after he left Teignmouth.

Increasingly, though, there was a danger that someone would notice that his radio transmissions were coming from the wrong areas. On 19 January, he said he was going to have to shut down the radio. He sent a brief telegram – knowing it would become a press release – to Rodney Hallworth, saying he was now sealing the leaking hatch above the generator. That would mean there would be no power for his radio. He said he would transmit when possible, indicating he might do so when closer to Australia.

Before the 'shutdown', he sent another message, this time to his sponsor Stanley Best, in which he exaggerated the damage to the boat. Crowhurst was trying to get Best to drop his legal right to ultimate ownership of *Teignmouth Electron*. He said the boat was 'ill found' and the 'float frame smashed'. Best did indeed drop his contractual right.

In those final telegrams, Crowhurst also gave one of his rarely claimed precise locations. He said he was 100 miles south east of Gough, a South Atlantic island in the Roaring Forties, just below Tristan da Cunha. It was a wholly bogus position, of course, as his actual position was relatively near Rio de Janeiro, but it was specific by previous standards. It was a risky move on Crowhurst's part because it actually showed him as having gone backwards on his fake route by more than 1,000 miles, bearing in mind his last claim was that he was 'somewhere off Cape Town'. However, he need not have worried. The reporting of this telegram became at least as absurd as the earlier mix up over the island of Trindade, which had propelled him spectacularly beyond even his own exaggeration. The wording in this new telegram was '100 SOUTHEAST GOUGH'. During transmission over what were often less than clear airwaves, it was transcribed as '100 SOUTHEAST TOUGH'. Hallworth assumed his man was having a 'tough' time and reckoned he must be round the Cape of Good Hope. Yet again, conspiracy combined with cock-up to put Crowhurst preposterously ahead of even his own make-believe progress.

Hallworth was increasingly exasperated by the lack of hard information from Crowhurst. He was used to spelling everything out. He wrote stories in a way that any reader, no matter how intellectually challenged, could understand without needing to draw too hard on their own imaginations. Hallworth took pride in getting to the heart of a story and serving the whole picture. It is easy to imagine the frustration he must have felt when he was trying to spin his man into the newspapers. Not only did he have a mere fraction of the story, but most of the facts he did possess came without an explanation. So when Crowhurst said the boat was damaged, Hallworth knew the public would naturally want to know why. He had a solution to his dilemma. He made it up. He took the few facts and embroidered them into something far more interesting.

Now the public was being told that 'a huge wave smashed over the stern of the vessel damaging the cock-pit'. It was all so dramatic that 'Mr Crowhurst had to take down all his sail for about three days while he carried out emergency repairs'. Hallworth had simply invented a scenario to help explain the radio shutdown.

That shutdown was to prove highly significant in the subsequent reporting of Crowhurst's race as it was his last contact for almost three months. Instead of his race now becoming a mystery, it was assumed that he was making good progress, based on the last mythical position and the mythical average speeds. The vacuum of information became a minor inconvenience. Crowhurst's imaginary race took off, building and building across the Southern Ocean. Every report was based on estimates that were themselves based on the nonsense of the final communication of 19 January.

If Crowhurst was to have been exposed, perhaps the radio shutdown should have been the pivotal moment. However, it was arguably not as obvious a ruse as it may appear now. The need to seal the hatch was plausible, given that the leaks really did exist and had already been mentioned. They would inevitably be worse in the bigger seas of the Southern Ocean, which was where everyone thought Crowhurst was heading, if he was not already there. Furthermore, there was a precedent. Knox-Johnston's radio transmitter had been out of action from almost exactly the same stage of his voyage. On the whole, the shutdown was treated more as a reason to be concerned for Crowhurst's safety than a sign that he was up to no good.

The only doubters were the same two men who were already puzzled by Crowhurst's erratic progress: Francis Chichester and the *Sunday Times* adviser, Craig Rich. Speaking 40 years on, Rich says news of the radio did ring alarm bells despite the specific circumstances. 'Out of radio contact was an unlikely story. I was suspicious in my own mind and I spoke to some of my colleagues about it. It was a nagging suspicion at this stage. Just what is going on here? And if you had water in your boat affecting the generator you would be bloody daft to carry on all the way through the Southern Ocean. Remember this was before Cape Town, where he could have stopped.'

There is always a risk that anyone who was involved in the Golden Globe story, and speaks about it now, is being wise long after the event or even goes so far as wanting to rewrite history. Certainly, nobody working at the *Sunday Times* during the race comes out of the Crowhurst story terribly well. It is very easy to see how Craig Rich has spent the best part of a lifetime repeatedly answering one simple question: why did you not spot that Crowhurst was cheating? However, it is clear that Rich's trust in Crowhurst had been sorely tested early in the voyage by the sudden claim of the 24-hours distance record. Tomalin and Hall admitted in their book that Rich had expressed considerable surprise at that claim. They described him as sceptical.

So it is logical that Rich, on hearing the news of a radio shutdown, began to take a closer look. He drew up a table, solely focusing on Crowhurst, of projected timings for when he was likely to reach Cape Horn. There was a range of predictions, based on average speeds. Rich intended to use the table to compare with Crowhurst's claimed rounding of the Horn, when it happened. 'I did slowest, fastest and most likely date at Cape Horn, just for Crowhurst,' he says. 'I created that table because of the radio shutdown.' Months later, it was to become a key tool in the private assessments of Crowhurst's actions.

Both Craig Rich and Sir Francis Chichester kept their suspicions in the background. Curiously, the two men did not meet until the year after the race, when they had lunch together, so their doubts during the race were expressed independently of each other. The closest Chichester came to publicly saying that he believed anything was wrong was when he used ambiguous language about Crowhurst.

His most interesting assessment of the race was in a lecture to the Royal Institution of Great Britain at the end of January 1969. He said his own voyage had made him realise that the greatest hurdle was not only Cape Horn, infamous for its storms and shipwrecks, but the entire 12,500 miles of Southern Ocean from where the yachts entered the Roaring Forties off Africa. Severe storms and wall-sided waves could be met any time.

Although hampered by the lack of information on all four sailors' progress, he said what he thought of each of the four men, and rated their chances of success. On Robin Knox-Johnston, he thought it would be a miracle if he sailed back to Falmouth without having to stop somewhere for repairs. He assumed, understandably, that Knox-Johnston was making very slow progress without a self-steering system, and so he said Bernard Moitessier was the most likely winner.

Chichester's comments on Nigel Tetley and Donald Crowhurst sounded routine at the time but, with hindsight, involved a careful use of words. He started by saying both were brave men for risking sailing trimarans single-handed in heavy seas. He said: 'Without continuous expert helmsmanship, I think a multihull is at a serious risk, in the vast seas and strong winds liable to occur at any time in the Southern Ocean, of being bowled along on the surface like a piece of this-tledown and of ending upside down.'

Then he stopped talking about the two men together and, after listing the recent multihull casualties, said: 'However, Lieutenant Commander Nigel Tetley, in *Victress*, shows signs of being a master seaman, and there is no doubt that he has done extremely well so far … Anything can happen at sea, and with remarkably good luck he could be the winner if both the leading yachts have to pull out of the race.'

It was a glowing tribute from the grandfather of single-handed sailing, and it was in stark contrast to the few, dismissive words that he then said about Crowhurst. 'He has claimed some fast bursts of speed … but his average speed has not been fast – 101 miles per day – and at his last fix south of the Cape [of Good Hope] on 10 January, he was about 8,800 miles behind Moitessier, so he does not seem a likely prize winner.'

The careful listener or reader will have detected that Chichester still doubted the 'claim' of a speed record. However, there was not so much of a hint of any questioning of Crowhurst's general progress. Chichester was indeed happy to refer to a Cape of Good Hope position 'fix' which had been reported in the *Sunday Times*, complete with latitude and longitude, but never actually happened. It was the newspaper's extrapolation of Hallworth's extrapolation of Crowhurst's false information.

Perhaps there was snobbery behind Chichester's comparison of Tetley and Crowhurst, an inclination more towards the naval officer than the town councillor. It is impossible to know the extent to which Chichester was influenced by his first encountering of the Crowhurst name – the man who wanted to sail

Gipsy Moth but about whom none of his friends had heard.

Chichester's speech to the Royal Institution was about more than the individuals in this one challenge. Indeed, the setting and sense of occasion were almost more interesting than what he said, considering that the Institution was created in the year 1800, with a mission to engage the public in scientific debate. Here, in its Georgian headquarters in Albemarle Street, Piccadilly, London, Sir Francis Chichester was invited to give the Friday Evening Discourse, a formal event founded in the 1820s by no less than the chemist and physicist Michael Faraday, most famous for his work with electricity. The very fact Chichester talked about the Golden Globe in such a grand and formal setting was a demonstration of the event's place in society.

In many respects, this Friday Evening Discourse was an interesting sign of the times. Chichester finished by touching on gender: 'On the oceans, no doubt women will one day be trying to circumnavigate the globe all alone, and no doubt some will be excellent. But how many women have pulled off great explorations of their own? Generally speaking, women rebel against solitude. The male animal inclines to solitude: that is why, so often, he is the loner.'

The Golden Globe race had been under way for eight months. It was increasingly making an impact.

7 : **TURN LEFT FOR HOME**

Robin Knox-Johnston led the charge for the most significant and feared point in the race. He heard the radio network 'Voice of America' say that the Chilean navy had been asked to look out for a 'damaged ketch' battling towards Cape Horn. If Christmas had been a time for contemplation, New Year was a time for quite startling anger. Knox-Johnston was doing better than Chichester had estimated, but not as well as he wanted. He thought he should have arrived at Cape Horn by now but instead, 1,500 miles away, he was again battling against winds coming from the east. Once more, he was haunted by thoughts of Moitessier enjoying the normal, prevailing westerly winds not far behind. He wrote in his log book that his mood was murderous and he would turn insane: 'What the hell is wrong with the bloody weather anyway? From the Cape of Good Hope to Aussie I had two days of easterlies. Since New Zealand I've had over 20 days of them ... I can do absolutely nothing and that makes me furious. Why the hell don't they mark this stretch of ocean as having variable winds instead of westerlies?'

As Knox-Johnston did at last get closer to the Horn, he began to prepare *Suhaili* for a potential battle, although he knew only too well that the mystique surrounding this notorious landmark was only partially deserved. True, the seas and wind could be the most chaotic on earth but, as with the rest of the Southern Ocean, the conditions depended on the fluctuating chain of eastward-moving weather depressions. It was perfectly possible for the weather to be calm. Nevertheless, the wise seaman assumes the worse. Knox-Johnston decided that the cumbersome scaffolding rig that had once housed the long-since redundant self-steering system was now weakened and had become a hazard. He cut it away with a hacksaw and dumped the whole contraption overboard, noting his position, 48° 23'S, 97° 35'E, for posterity's sake. *Suhaili*, he thought, felt more comfortable in herself, rather like an old lady taking off a too-tight corset.

For all the recognition of the Horn's varying conditions, during the final two days of Knox-Johnston's approach the elements were conspiring to create a classic rounding. The barometer showed the pressure was dropping in a way it had not done before. Knox-Johnston admitted he felt scared. A bitingly cold wind built up to storm force ten. Then the barometer rose and the wind eased off. Then it fell again. Throughout this uncertain period, Knox-Johnston was distracted by a series of problems, one of which involved a hair-raising crawl along the bowsprit – a ramrod-style pole that extended out of the front of the boat. It was the first time he wore his safety harness in more than three months. The other issues were turning into a long list.

They included a damaged jib sail, a new mainsail split down the middle, the gooseneck connection between the mast and boom broken again, and two very painful wrist burns caused by hot porridge.

On 16 January, Knox-Johnston decided to stay up through the night to look out for land, specifically the island of Diego Ramirez, about 60 miles south of Cape Horn. The blisters on his right wrist had now been rubbed away, exposing raw, weeping flesh to the elements, which now included squalls and particularly painful hailstorms. Even when he covered his wrist with a bandage it still throbbed painfully. A radio report on the BBC World Service said the full-scale Vietnam peace talks were delayed because of a wrangle over the shape of the conference table. Knox-Johnston was not impressed. He drank a quarter of a bottle of whisky, seeking comfort from the cold and the pain of his burned wrist.

It was a good time to check the remaining alcohol stocks and he found, to his relief, that he still had six bottles of whisky and four of brandy. He had consumed 14 bottles of spirits and calculated that he had been drinking at the rate of one bottle every 16 days. The good news was that he had 40 per cent of his alcohol stock remaining for the final third of the voyage.

On the evening of 17 January, *Suhaili* was directly south of the Horn. Knox-Johnston celebrated by opening a tin that had been sealed for seven months and contained a fruit cake made by his Aunt Aileen. It was in perfect condition. In the logbook, Knox-Johnston simply wrote: 'YIPPEE!!!'

Where was Bernard Moitessier? He had started the

race nine weeks behind Knox-Johnston. A simple calculation showed that for each third of the route he needed to close the gap by three weeks simply to catch up and finish at the same time. Down the Atlantic to the bottom of Africa he did indeed bring Knox-Johnston's lead down to six weeks but the voyage to Australia and New Zealand was less productive for the Frenchman. He clawed back less than another week, so by Christmas, off New Zealand, Moitessier was a little over five weeks behind. He would have to close the gap to no more than three weeks by the time he reached Cape Horn. Knox-Johnston's loss of a self-steering system and the endless days of frustrating easterlies meant the Frenchman had every chance of succeeding.

However, after Moitessier's drunken Christmas night, his attempt to catch up got off to a bad start when the wind direction changed without him realising. The boat altered course on its own, to adjust to the wind, and started heading straight for the coast of New Zealand hidden in the mist 15 miles to the north. Moitessier explained how the alarm was raised. He said a group of 25 porpoises, swimming side by side, repeatedly passed down the starboard side of the boat from the stern to the bow. When they got to the bow, the whole group suddenly veered and rushed off at a right angle to the right, as if to tell him that that was where he should go. When he realised something was wrong and did indeed turn to the right, a big black-and-white porpoise jumped ten or 12 feet in the air in a fantastic somersault, with two complete rolls, bursting with joy as if to say 'The man understood what we were telling him.' Two porpoises continued swimming off the bow of the boat for a total of five hours, as if they were ordered to stay until *Joshua* was out of danger. Moitessier was wonder-struck.

It was a typically bizarre story from the Frenchman. Whether it happened precisely as he described or was the product of a fertile imagination, he was profoundly affected, saying he now felt a certain peace for the first time and that he knew he would succeed in the voyage.

Now past New Zealand, the way was clear for him to chase down Knox-Johnston and win back more than a fortnight, reducing the overall lead at Cape Horn to three weeks. Yet that was not how Moitessier described his feelings. Instead, to him, clearing New Zealand meant he was, 'free on the right, free on the left, free everywhere'.

Moitessier's voyage was full of contradictions. No sooner had he spoken of his freedom than he was making a tactical decision that was clearly designed to increase his chances of winning yet would undoubtedly bring a rise in stress levels. He chose to stay well south of the 40-degree parallel. In doing so, he would benefit from the stronger winds there and the distance travelled would be shorter because of the earth's shape, but the downside was an increased risk of hitting an iceberg. It was the same dilemma Knox-Johnston had struggled with a month earlier before eventually choosing to take a chance with the iceberg limit.

Moitessier had in fact been fretting over the issue of how far south to go for some time. Long before the voyage even started, he wrote to 15 members of the International Association of Cape Horners, an exclusive group founded in Brittany in the 1930s and still going strong today. Now, decision made, he reassured himself by re-reading all 15 letters. Only three mentioned seeing icebergs and all were encouraging.

Moitessier made fast progress, consistently clocking up daily mileages close to 150. Exceptionally favourable weather saw him halfway to Cape Horn. Even the sun was shining. For five straight days he sat naked in the cockpit practising yoga, which he had taken up to shake off the rhythm of European living that made him tired and nervous. A stomach ulcer he had been 'dragging around' for a decade stopped giving him any bother. An annoying back pain disappeared. His appetite returned. Moitessier had seldom felt healthier. It was all in stark contrast to how he felt when he rounded Africa for the start of the Southern Ocean leg. He now realised that he had then been at rock bottom, in a dangerously low physical and mental state. Now, although he had a wild appearance with his almost shoulder-length hair and out-of-control beard, he had found what he called an 'indefinable state of grace'.

Even when the weather turned, it came from the right direction. Whereas Knox-Johnston was being frustrated by having to zigzag into untypical easterlies, Moitessier was bowling along in a straight line. Being a few weeks behind, and therefore in a different part of the same ocean, was making all the difference.

There was a difference, too, in workloads. Knox-Johnston constantly paid for his decision to set sail quickly in an under-prepared boat. He was in effect running a mobile workshop as he relentlessly battled to hold everything together. Moitessier, on the other hand, had used his extra two months in port to buttress

Joshua ready for the hard times ahead. The pay-off, or not, was that the Frenchman now had more time to think. He wondered how long the peace he had found would last. It was all very well pondering about sun, sea and clouds, but if he was to contemplate the whole of life he also had to think of the side he did not like. He called it the 'other world', where man had been turned into a money-making machine to satisfy false needs and joys. Now, just as when he passed Africa and dreamt of turning left for Mauritius, he dreamt of prematurely turning left again and sailing not for home, but for the Galapagos Islands. He could be there in a few weeks. 'But it would be too soon,' he wrote. 'I have not really found my Ganges yet, and would blame myself for the rest of my life; it would be as if I had not even tried.'

Moitessier then reined in his free thinking, urging a concentration of mind. 'Until the Horn, don't look beyond *Joshua*, my little red-and-white planet made of space, pure air, stars, clouds and freedom in its deepest, most natural sense,' he wrote. 'And completely forget the world, its merciless rhythm of life. Back there, if a businessman could put out the stars to make his billboards look better at night, he just might do it. Live only with the sea and my boat, for the sea and for my boat.'

Moitessier kept up the rapid progress towards South America. In the final two days running down to the Horn, he enjoyed an adrenaline-filled surge in speed during which he knew he was playing a dangerous game by keeping a lot of sail up. *Joshua* was coping well and Moitessier did not want to break the rhythm. He surprised himself by urinating inside his foul-weather clothes, a 'delicious warmth' running down his leg. The wind dropped down to between force six and seven, in time for the momentous rounding of Cape Horn on 5 February. Yet the moment was something of an anti-climax for Moitessier. He fell asleep and missed it, having failed to hear his alarm.

He had taken 42 days to sail from New Zealand, a considerable improvement on Knox-Johnston's 60 days. The gap between the two had indeed come down from nine weeks at the start to just three, although neither man knew for certain how the other was doing. With one-third of the race remaining, Moitessier was likely to reduce the lead to zero: the two men were on track to arrive at England's south coast at the same time. Incredibly, after what would be ten months of sailing, the Golden Globe was heading for a dead heat between the young Briton who left recklessly early because he knew his boat was slow, and the better-prepared Frenchman following on a faster boat.

When Moitessier did wake up, he assumed he was too late to see Cape Horn. He knew bad weather was coming and he was anxious to head up past the Falklands Islands, 500 miles to the north east. The Frenchman did not feel out of danger. Passing the voyage's most infamous landmark was not as complete an experience as might have been expected. Indeed, Knox-Johnston had felt the same, although it was Moitessier who expressed the sentiment most eloquently. He wrote: 'A sailor's geography is not always that of the cartographer, for whom a cape is a cape, with a latitude and longitude. For the sailor, a great cape is both a very simple and an extremely complicated whole of rocks, currents, breaking seas and huge waves, fair winds and gales, joys and fears, fatigue, dreams, painful hands, empty stomachs, wonderful moments and suffering at times.

'A great cape, for us, can't be expressed in longitude and latitude alone. A great cape has a soul, with very soft, very violent shadows and colours. A soul as smooth as a child's, as hard as a criminal's. And that is why we go.'

Under the moonlight and almost ten miles away, Moitessier did in fact briefly see the rock face that is Cape Horn, and marvelled at how it looked as hard as a diamond. He went below, turned up the oil light and felt his little world glowing softly. He wondered about the finish line 10,000 miles away in Plymouth. It felt so much closer, but 'Plymouth' did not feel quite right for this Frenchman brought up in Asia and never quite sure where home was. Somehow, leaving from Plymouth and returning to Plymouth now felt like leaving from nowhere to go nowhere.

Moitessier had now sailed for more than six months without news of the other men in the race. He wondered where Knox-Johnston was and whether he really had been the man the fishermen off Tasmania had mentioned. He worried, again, about Nigel Tetley in his multihull, regretting that Tetley had spurned his advice to take a saw for cutting a way out of a capsized hull.

Four days after rounding Cape Horn, Moitessier sailed close to the Falklands Islands' Port Stanley lighthouse. He tried to attract attention with a signalling mirror so that everyone would know he was safe and well. He failed to get a response and sailed on, tired and dejected.

In fact, Moitessier had been seen, although initial reports confused him with Knox-Johnston, who, unknown to everyone, was now 1,500 miles to the north, approaching the trade winds below the equator. It was only when the red colour of the hull was revealed that everyone knew it had been *Joshua* and not *Suhaili*. It was great news for the friends and family of Moitessier, but worrying for those who were concerned for Knox-Johnston. He had not been heard of since New Zealand, almost three months earlier.

The transition from Southern Ocean to Atlantic was a strange one for both leading men. They were both affected psychologically by the greatest landmark on the whole voyage. They had remarkably similar thoughts; both hesitant in turning left for home after Cape Horn. It was obvious that Moitessier had the potential to be unpredictable and unconventional. It was less likely that Knox-Johnston would do anything other than sail flat-out to win the race. Yet the Briton's first impulse was to keep going east, almost, he said, as if to cock a snook at the Southern Ocean. The manner in which the two men reacted to their own individual uncertainty was as different as could be. Knox-Johnston snapped out of this mini-crisis because he was drawn to modern comforts such as hot baths, beer, steaks – and women. For Moitessier, modern life was the problem. Far from drawing him north, he was repelled by it. In this one shared experience, the two men emerged as very different characters.

In fact, there was a geographical helping hand to shepherd potential wanderers onto the 'right' path. To immediately continue east from Cape Horn was easier said than done. In order to go round the Horn, the sailors had needed to drop down to 56 degrees south of the equator, into the so-called Furious Fifties. Once round, the sensible thing to do was quickly head north east past the Falkland Islands and back up to the 40-degree parallel and out of the iceberg zone. For Knox-Johnston, this direction encouraged increasingly positive thoughts of home. He was back on the straight and narrow. For Moitessier, it provided two weeks of thinking time. He was exhausted. Rounding the Horn had been full of nervous tension. Now he used this time, in which the route was dictated by geography, to give his mind a rest.

On 18 February, Moitessier reached a metaphoric crossroads, passing the dotted iceberg line on the chart and onto the 40-degree parallel. What happened next was a huge turning point in more ways than one. It had been hinted about. A few days earlier he had said he would soon be able to steer east to the Cape of Good Hope but that, surely, was an idle fantasy, comparable with his earlier dreams of turning towards Mauritius or Galapagos. It ranked with thoughts such as Plymouth being nowhere to nowhere. To truly mean it would be sensational.

He did mean it. Moitessier turned right, and began to head on round the world to the bottom of Africa for a second time, with the breathtaking objective of staying firmly in the Roaring Forties and sailing at least halfway round the world again.

Incredible. After coming so far, after so many trials and tribulations, Moitessier was now turning his back on the chance of success. At the very least, he knew he was probably on target for the fastest voyage and the

£5,000 he had always intended to snatch with a theatrical air of contempt from the newspaper men who wrote the cheque. Now he simply did not care. He was not going 'home' and he was not ready to stop.

Moitessier's own account of this unfathomable act was spectacularly matter of fact. This was how he told the readers of his book *The Long Way*: '*Joshua* is now clear of the broken red line marking the iceberg limit on the pilot chart. No more risks, no more watches; just take it easy, heading east towards the Pacific.'

Then, for a while, he carried on writing as if nothing had happened. His voyage was continuing, only to a non-specified finish. He wrote as before about the others in the race and about the wind and the sea, but soon he was also asking what sailing round the world meant, as the horizon was eternal. Round the world, he said, went further than the ends of the earth, as far as life itself, perhaps even further still.

As he sailed across the South Atlantic, instead of up it, his mind wandered, as if in a desperate, slow-motion search for the answer to life. His childhood in colonial French Indochina repeatedly came back to him; stories such as his Chinese nurse saying the earth could not protect the god in us unless we respected both the earth and the god.

Moitessier had made a momentous, life-changing decision yet he was not in a mood for the finer detail. He was experiencing a transition from racer to gypsy traveller. There would be no definite target, no finish line. He would sail past Africa, again, and then Australia, again, and then he really would turn left, either for the Pacific island of Tahiti or the Galapagos Islands.

There was a problem that crept into his mind; his family. Images of his three stepchildren floated before his eyes. He overcame any guilt by deciding that God knew he loved them, and now all the world's children were his own.

One moment Moitessier would seem to have an answer for everything; the next, he would be filled with doubt. After almost two weeks of heading east, the thought of how Francoise and the children would respond to him simply sailing on in his own world was now one he was struggling with. Would they understand that the rules of the game could gradually change, that the old ones had disappeared in *Joshua's* wake to make room for new rules of another order? He wrote: 'I do not know how to explain to them my need to be at peace, to continue toward the Pacific. They will not understand. I know I am right, I feel it deeply. I know exactly where I am going, even if I do not know. How could they understand that? Yet it is so simple. But it can't be explained in words, it would be completely useless to try ... This is something I just can't express: it would take hours and hours by the fireside.'

Then, suddenly, Moitessier decided he was giving up. By that, he was referring to his new challenge of sailing on round the world. His version of 'giving up' meant he was back in the race, or at least back heading in the right direction. He was tired and his spirits were up and down. It was also bothering him that not only would his family struggle to understand if he went on, they would go for perhaps another four months without knowing whether he was dead or alive. And there were other reasons to head for Europe. He wanted to see his mother, he wanted to share the 92 reels of film he had shot on the movie camera, and he wanted the mountain of equipment that he had left – to save weight for the race – in Plymouth. On 28 February, still far out in the South Atlantic, he steered north.

Little more than a day later, everything changed again. Moitessier turned east, Tahiti-bound. He said that heading north had made him sick at the thought of getting back to the snake pit called Europe, and he knew he could not trust himself not to continue racing to pick up the *Sunday Times* prize. The closer he got, the more disgusted he would become.

His mother would not worry. Her high spirits and rich inner life would see her through. Francoise and the children could take it too.

This time, Moitessier meant what he was doing. His language became angry as he railed against the modern world that he had grown to hate, with a damning critique for which he was to become famous. He wrote: 'I am really fed up with false gods, always lying in wait, spider-like, eating our liver, sucking our marrow. I charge the modern world – that's the Monster. It is destroying our earth, and trampling the soul of men.'

Moitessier was not simply resigning from a race or, for that matter, finding himself. From his early days as a child, he had a level of contempt for many things around him. Now he had a message. He was aware, but dismissive, of the charge of hypocrisy. Yes, he said, he did understand that the modern world had given him his beautiful boat, but it was because of that same world that he felt the need to have the boat and take off.

On 19 March he was off Cape Town, for the second

time. He had decided that he ought to make contact with the outside world. Now that his race was over, there was no reason why he could not have gone into the harbour but instead he waited outside, using his signalling mirror to attract the attention of a patrol launch. He fought against a burning desire to stop for a few months, recalling a quotation that said there were two terrible things for a man: not to have fulfilled his dream, and to have fulfilled it. As he prepared a plastic jerrycan with audio cassettes, camera film, ten reels of movie film and his log/diary, he felt free, free as never before. Again, he reassured himself that the children and Francoise would understand. There was enough material in the can for his publisher, should anything happen to him, to write a book so that his family's future would be financially secure.

Curiously, using a loudhailer, Moitessier warned the launch crew not to come too close to him. The *Sunday Times* reported that he had shouted the warning as he did not want to break the race rules. They were, however, close enough to talk, and Moitessier asked about the others in the race. The skipper was unsure of the details and said he thought four had been wiped out but he did not know their names and, no, he could not say if one was a trimaran.

One missing ingredient from the can was an announcement or explanation of the apparently irrational decision to sail on around the world. Since the last sighting at the Falkland Islands, the world had assumed he was heading for the equator in pursuit of Knox-Johnston and glory. Indeed, the French were planning all manner of celebrations for a presumed triumphant homecoming. There would be a massive maritime escort led by the French navy and there would be a national decoration, quite possibly the Légion d'honneur, the highest recognition for service to the country, created by Napoleon in 1802.

So Moitessier knew a form of words was needed. He wrote a letter for the *Sunday Times*. He chose to have it delivered separately from the book material; presumably hoping word of it would reach London more quickly than a package routed through diplomatic channels. Immediately after the transfer of the jerrycan, he turned towards a British Petroleum tanker, called *Argosy*, which had just left the harbour. Its captain, Ronald Friendship, knew all about the Golden Globe and the chase to the finish line. Like everyone else, he assumed *Joshua* would be near the equator and was amazed to see the yacht here at Cape Town and right up next to his ship. Moitessier, who he said looked as fit as a fiddle, was aiming a catapult at his bridge. The Frenchman, with one confident shot, fired off an announcement to the world. Moitessier's race was eccentric to the end.

His letter said: 'In a few words, my intention is to continue the voyage, still non-stop, towards the Pacific Islands, where there is plenty of sun and more peace than in Europe. Please do not think I am trying to break a record. 'Record' is a very stupid word at sea. I continue non-stop because I am happy at sea and perhaps because I want to save my soul.'

What a way to go. It was an astonishing rejection of everything the Golden Globe race stood for. '*Save my Soul*' dominated the headlines. The *Sunday Times* reported that Moitessier was almost alienated from terra firma and had mentally turned into an aquatic creature, in love with the sea and his boat. It was a seemingly ridiculous interpretation, yet perceptive. Perhaps the paper was now beginning to understand this man of strange ways. As for Moitessier, he said the story was now between only him and *Joshua*. It was, he said, a great love story that did not concern the others any more.

A single-track, potholed country lane winds its way up a gentle hill through small fields of grape vines. The rough and ready charm of working countryside suddenly transforms, in the blink of an eye, to a rustic suburbia. On both sides of the now tarmac lane, mature front gardens serve to both hide and yet show off the luxurious villas behind. Their plots command a lofty vantage point a few miles inland from the sea of the Côte d'Azur in Provence.

Forty years have passed since Francoise and her children were abandoned in a blaze of publicity. She is now almost 80, and has settled back home in her native countryside, less than half an hour's drive west of Toulon.

Visitors to the terracotta-painted villa must duck under the fan-shaped leaves of a huge palm tree positioned eccentrically a few feet from the front door. She answers with a flourish and the enthusiasm of a woman who likes to keep an open house. It is an early indication that Francoise Moitessier was never one to be easily crushed.

She leads the way into the sprawling, single-storey building, and into a large lounge furnished with the formality of a Regency state room. Ornaments and family photographs bedeck the countless small occasional tables. The cool floor tiles lead out to a sweeping terrace where it is obvious much of life is led. There is money here, and a sense of regulation and discipline. It is a surprising setting for a woman who was known in her own right for a travelling lifestyle on the ocean waves. It is winter now, and Francoise stays indoors, heading for a side room away from the stiff formality of the rest of her home. She is small, yet robust, and although she is swallowed up by a voluminous sofa she sits forward as if ready for action, cigarettes close to hand.

Francoise is immediately engaging, funny and full of life. She produces piles of paperwork and photographs from the Golden Globe chapter in her life, proudly holding up a black-and-white image of her wrapped in Bernard's arms. She is ready to talk. She is smart and quick-witted. She knows perfectly well what is coming, what the line of questioning will be.

An elderly man, supported by a walking stick in his right hand, comes in to say hello. His name is Georges-Edouard de Cazalet, a banker. He is Francoise's husband. They were married almost 20 years after the Golden Globe, when she was 57 years old. They met when they were both sailing and he is, it turns out, a major fan of the Bernard Moitessier story. He soon leaves, making himself scarce as if to give Francoise space to talk.

She rattles through the well-worn highlights, having spent a lifetime in this sailing-crazy country being asked how it felt to be dumped unceremoniously by a public hero. She has always been allowed by journalists to speak with a degree of superficiality. Now, perhaps, at a late stage in her life, she may lower the defensive wall that she began building within hours of news of the Cape Town letter breaking.

At that time, she told the French daily newspaper *France-Soir* that she could not explain her joy in knowing that Bernard continued to live in peace, a free man in the universe he had chosen. 'You can neither advise nor order Bernard,' she said. 'I knew that when I married him.' It was a sensational response to the cruellest of domestic dramas; vintage Moitessier. The man himself could not have been more philosophical.

The theme was taken up again years later with Francoise writing that Bernard had taught her the preciousness of life and introduced her to a wonderful world of peace, silence, sun and stars.

Now, sitting with her memories and souvenirs cluttering the coffee table, she is quick to repeat what she has often said over the years: she had been married to Bernard for eight years before the Golden Globe and she knew him well enough to realise he would not sail back to Plymouth. She tries to control the conversation by keeping the emphasis on Bernard, and away from her and the children.

However, it slowly becomes clear that, for all the brave and undeniably magnificent words, Francoise was indeed, as one would expect, profoundly affected by what happened. She does not retract any of her praise for Bernard, but she is ready to complete the picture. She describes the day she was told the news of the catapulted announcement.

She was living in Mantes la Jolie, a suburb north west of Paris on the south bank of the River Seine. Money was tight, thanks to Bernard's round-the-world voyage.

Professionally, she worked as a radiographer's technician and she had accepted a job in the suburbs because it came with accommodation. So, by day she worked for a doctors' practice on the seventh floor of a tower block, and by night, she lived in an apartment on the floor above. The two sons from her first marriage, Emmanuel, 16, and Hervé, 15, were at boarding school. The daughter, Beatrice, 18, lived in the apartment and was at home on the fateful day.

It was a weekend. Four motorbike policemen from the Gendarmerie knocked on the front door. They were holding their helmets and a letter from Bernard. He had written it in a hurry and catapulted it along with the letter to the *Sunday Times*. The policemen handed it over before making their excuses and hurrying away. Francoise recalls the moment vividly. 'It was not an ordinary thing,' she says with masterly understatement. 'I can picture myself in the flat. The letter was in an envelope.

'It said: "Darling, I don't have the courage to come home. We will meet later. We will meet later and you will be waiting for me." It was just one page, very quickly written.

'I remember my daughter was at home and she said to me, "What are you going to do?" She wept for two days. She adored Bernard.

'I said, "We are going to carry on living." I had my work. I was not going to cry. I had three children. What are you supposed to do? You have to carry on living. I probably did not sleep properly for three nights. I didn't sleep much, because I was anxious. I was feeling anxious and I could not sleep.

'I always knew Bernard's voyage was not going to

happen like everybody thought it was going to happen. But I didn't expect that exactly.'

The next day, the story was splashed on the front pages, setting off a media frenzy which was to run and run. *France-Soir* already had a pre-race deal with Bernard and Francoise. *Paris Match* put him on the front cover and published an eight-page photo special. A radio station broadcast part of the audio tapes that Bernard had thrown to the harbour launch in his jerrycan. On the one hand, excited French journalists were writing of Moitessier's 'noble gesture' in which they said he had turned his back on anything that could diminish the human value; on the other, Francoise was having to cope with rejection.

'All the big newspapers were talking about it,' she says. 'All of France knew about it. I couldn't go out. It was unbearable. Even the taxi drivers would ask me questions. Everybody would ask me questions. It was very difficult for me.

'Journalists came and they took pictures of us at the flat. They were taking pictures of the children. It was very difficult. It was quite unbearable. It was horrible. I was feeling horrible. I remember I was always on the phone and at one point I even thought of changing names. Changing my name!'

Francoise does not complain of the journalists or their behaviour. She accepts it was a huge story and that any embarrassment was something she simply had to cope with. In fact, she talks of the kindness everyone showed her, agreeing that they saw her as a victim. 'They were more than kind. They were very nice. They probably felt a little bit sorry for me. They probably wanted to protect me. It wasn't only the journalists. People would come up to me in shops.'

So, did she feel humiliated? 'Yes, certainly, certainly, because it is not a normal thing to do – because what he did wasn't normal.'

Francoise is a proud and thoughtful woman and later she reflects on the question of humiliation and decides it deserves a more subtle answer. 'I didn't think I was being humiliated, because I knew Bernard and I knew his character, because it was not his intention to humiliate me. He thought of his own pleasure. He was happy at sea and did not want to stop. What was terrible was to be exposed by the media, to always be at the front and being interviewed about it.'

Media storms have a habit of going away as quickly as they arrive. A story is the flavour of the month, and then the circus moves on. Not so with the Moitessiers. Bernard's decision not to stop but to carry on halfway round the world again served simply to keep the story running, despite his pleas for it not to be seen as a record attempt. It was three months before Bernard finally ran out of steam and pulled up in Tahiti on 21 June 1969. In all that time, no one, including Francoise, had been able to talk to him.

The day after he arrived in Tahiti, *France-Soir* put a senior journalist and Francoise onto a plane. It was to be a peculiar reunion after all that had gone before. 'Of course he had changed,' she says. 'You cannot be the same after 303 days but with me he was the same. It felt like we had left each other just ten days earlier. He wanted to know everything that had happened while he was away. He wanted to know about the children. We were not on the same level. He wanted to know about the children and I wanted to know about the trip.'

Francoise stayed for a month but then had to return to work. Bernard decided he would remain in Tahiti to write the book of his Golden Globe voyage. He had already thought of the title, *The Long Way*. Instructions for his publisher to reserve the title for exclusive use had even been left in the jerrycan that he had thrown to the Cape Town harbour launch, despite his rejection of the modern world. It was agreed that Francoise would make a film from the reels that were in the same jerry-can. Bernard said they would both be finished within a year.

Perhaps, with hindsight, it was obvious that things would not go according to plan. Francoise was expecting an unconventional time but was not ready for what was to come.

She travelled to Tahiti several times, while they worked on their individual projects, but could never stay long because of the children. She managed to get the time off work only by pretending to be suffering from depression, a plausible consequence of the couple's very public circumstances.

Francoise realised Bernard was being unfaithful. She says it was not a great surprise as it had been happening throughout their marriage. 'I have to admit that he always had affairs because all the women used to fall in love with him. He was a womaniser. But he was kind with me. We were very happily married. He was "having it off" occasionally, but our relationship was steady and he would always come back to me. Our relationship was very strong and I didn't really care what was happening on the side. It was infatuation, maybe.'

Francoise takes a break in the conversation to leave the room and have a cigarette. When she returns, she has an impish grin and half mutters that maybe not everything she says should be published in a book. It seems that she wants to both protect the reputation of a man who has had a remarkably good press and wants, at long last, to just tell it as it was, warts and all.

The one year which was set aside for writing the book and making the film became two. In early 1971, Bernard wrote an enthusiastic letter to Francoise saying he was fine-tuning his last chapter and was ready to come home for a family gathering in the south of France. They all met in preparation for his arrival. They waited for two weeks, but Bernard did not turn up and there was no word from him. Francoise was upset at the sight of her mother-in-law, disappointed and sad.

Several months went by, still with no word. In July, Francoise wrote to say that she needed to confirm a programme for screening the film she had put together. She had a contract to show it at the Salle Pleyel concert hall in Paris, and asked for a reply by return of post. Still she heard nothing.

In September, Bernard's editor called on Francoise. He had just returned from Tahiti where he had picked up the last chapter of the book. He told her Bernard was cutting her off financially. Francoise's response was to laugh. In the entire two years she had received not a penny. Unknown to Francoise, Bernard had come up with another bizarre decision. He had decided to give all the money he made from the book to the Pope. He felt *The Long Way* needed to carry the same weight as the voyage itself. If he accepted royalties, it would be tantamount to erasing the meaning of the entire voyage. He wanted the Vatican to use the money to help rebuild the world.

Then, in October 1971, as Francoise coped with the extreme disappointment of Bernard not turning up for the screening of their film, she received a letter from Tahiti. It was eight pages long and breathtaking in its audacity.

Bernard announced he had met a woman called Iléana and she had given birth to their son, Stephan. Francoise could not believe what she was reading. She had no idea her husband's philandering had gone beyond playful indulgence. She had not taken seriously the message that he was no longer intending to support the family, as it made no material difference. Their marriage had been unconventional from the start and could not be judged by others' standards. For all the living apart, she still regarded Bernard as her husband and herself as his wife. Now, in this long, rambling letter, she was learning of another woman and a son.

The letter became more brazen. Francoise stared at it in utter disbelief. Bernard was now asking for help with clothing the baby. He asked if she could send wool for Iléana to knit clothes for little Stephan. She wanted not just any old wool, but soft Angora wool. He had not been able to find any in Tahiti, so could she send some?

Francoise has said little about this letter over the years. In 2004, in France, she published an autobiography called *60,000 Miles of Sailing*. It concentrated on her voyages with Bernard before the Golden Globe and on her own in later years. The remarkable, life-changing, eight-page letter was dismissed in a couple of lines but now, sitting on her sofa, Francoise is agitated and admits it caused her considerable pain. 'I was incensed. I was incensed,' she says, repeating herself vigorously as she leans forward, flicking her shoulder-length hair away from her eyes.

She talks of the letter as if it was written yesterday. 'He was asking for Angora wool because he couldn't find any for the poor little baby's clothes! The mother should have taken care of that! Why was he asking me?

'It was the first time he told me about the baby. He could have told me a little bit earlier. Luckily, I had finished the film, otherwise I would have dropped everything.'

Did she feel betrayed? 'Betrayal, yes, of course. I felt hurt. Any woman receiving this kind of letter would.'

There is an obvious question to put to Francoise, and it is: just when did she regard her marriage with Bernard as over? She finds it an extraordinarily difficult question to answer, not because of hurt, anger or emotion, but because she simply cannot work out when the time was. To many newspaper readers it was when Bernard was off Cape Town and declared he did not have the courage to come home. Books and articles have since been written saying it was after the reunion in Tahiti. The mistake, perhaps, has been that ordinary people have tried to assess and judge an extraordinary couple.

Francoise was furious about the child but blamed the mistress rather than her husband. 'He had an affair with her but he told her he was married. He told her: "I can't marry you." The son was born and then he felt responsible. I was angry. I probably still am. He didn't hide his marriage. She knew it all along.'

So, she does not feel anger towards Bernard? 'No. All the women he had affairs with "had him", in a way. He wrote to me to say, "I am not in love with this woman but I am feeling responsible for the kid." I loved him. He was my husband. I didn't have anything to do with her.'

But he was cheating. 'I knew from the beginning he was the kind of man to have affairs. It was my choice to stay with him or to say stop and quit.'

Even after the eight-page letter, Bernard made the trip to Paris and stayed with Francoise. She gave him an ultimatum. 'Bernard used to come and see me. He would come back to Paris as if he left yesterday. He would put his things in order. I was getting a bit angry. Then I said now you have to choose. Take your son and bring him and I will take care of him. I said I will be very kind to your son if you come here, but now you have to choose between Paris and Tahiti. I tried to draw a deadline.

'He said ok, ok, and he went back to Tahiti and he came back and went back and it carried on. He couldn't leave his son, and the mother probably would not have let him take the son to Paris. He could not forget about his son either and leave a cheque with the mother.'

In the meantime, Francoise was running the business side of newspaper deals and the film that she had made at considerable cost. 'I expected him to do all the film presentations but he never turned up. It cost me a fortune and he never gave me a penny. I had to make up all the money. I had to manage on my own. It is why I spent five years doing film showings, to get the money back.

'I took care of so many things, of newspapers, of editors, of everything. I was taking care of all the contracts for him. I had put some money aside. I didn't want him to accuse me of taking advantage of all that money from the contracts, so I had started a blocked account where I put all the money.

'When he came to Paris he went to the bank and took all the money without telling me. I had no money myself because I had a lot of expenses. The bank had informed me that my husband had taken all the money out of the bank.'

Bernard also withdrew the royalties from his book, which had sold more than 100,000 copies in three years. The Vatican, unsure of why the money was being offered, had declined to take up the gift.

Surely, at this stage, Francoise had begun to think less of Bernard? 'Yes, yes, I certainly felt less of him,' she says, resigned to accepting that the man who taught her so much, and whom she so admired, was undoubtedly flawed.

'We didn't divorce at first. Bernard told me: "I will never divorce you – we get on so well. We will always be happy to meet each other again." I tried to get a divorce for six years. I had a team of lawyers. It happened eventually.

'Friends at that time told me to lead my own life. I carried on working, sailing and I had my children around me and a lot of friends. I was busy all the time. I didn't stop living. I lived my own life like I meant to. I confronted the events and carried on. I had my own boat and did what I wanted.'

In 1977, Francoise set sail from La Rochelle. She spent four years sailing to and around the Far East.

'I was always so much in love with the sea – I used to get so depressed when I came back from travelling. That meant I could understand Bernard perfectly.

'I do not regret the Golden Globe happening – it was

an amazing thing. I only regret that we got separated. The racing itself I do not regret. Round the world had never been done before – it was Bernard's dream. Even before the race was announced he was planning to go round the world. I asked him to wait one year for my children to finish school, so we could go together, like we had done before.

'Bernard said he couldn't wait. He couldn't help himself. He was very selfish. He should have waited for me. It was quite hard for me because I was in love with him. It was very difficult but I had a family to raise. I knew he was selfish when I married him.

'He succeeded in sailing round the globe one-and-a-half times and I was happy for him.'

In Tahiti, Bernard led an increasingly unconventional life. He was hugely offended when he was labelled as a hippy, in *Paris Match*, by the then young and upcoming sailor Olivier de Kersauson, after the two men met in Tahiti. He responded with a long letter of complaint.

He spent much of the rest of his life on the move, travelling around Pacific islands, the United States, Vietnam and France. He separated from Iléana and his child, and campaigned for the planting of more trees around the world. Friends calculated that he wrote more than 600 letters to newspapers, magazines and prominent figures including Ronald Reagan, Margaret Thatcher, Francois Mitterrand and the Pope, all in an effort to improve the world.

In 1994, Francoise received a telephone call to say Bernard was in Paris, dying of cancer. The man she was married to in 1986, Georges-Edouard, spent a day finding out which hospital he was in.

'I telephoned Bernard. He said, "Who is this?" I said, "Francoise." He said, "Which Francoise?"' She laughs loudly at the memory of this poignant moment, 25 years after the Golden Globe. 'He hesitated, then suddenly realised it was me. Then he asked when I would be coming. I said I would turn up. I was a bit afraid of going to the hospital on my own because it had been such a long time since we had seen each other. I took my daughter. I am glad I did.

'He said he felt sorry for all the trouble he gave me. I said we should forget about it all. Now it was over and belonged to the past, and we were meeting again.'

Bernard was two months away from death and he was allowed to spend time, under the care of a nurse, at the Paris apartment owned by his latest partner. Francoise and her daughter went to see him, and the complication of his tangled private life rose to an untidy climax. Iléana and Stephan, the Tahiti love child, turned up at the apartment. Francoise was not expecting this awkward gathering. 'I didn't know she was going to turn up. I was trying to be polite. She didn't stay for long. I saw Stephan her son for about a quarter of an hour. We were told to expect Stephan to be back for dinner but Bernard said, "No, he will not turn up." In my head, I was thinking about Iléana. I despised her. I saw her as a lower person. I just said "Hello" or something. It was difficult. In my mind, the last time I had seen Bernard was when he was young. We knew each other since we were in our late 20s. We lived together until 45. When I saw him again it was a terrible shock. As soon as we started talking, it was as if we had never been apart. There was no gap of time. This was more important than Iléana. She didn't matter to me. She was of no importance. The important thing was to see Bernard before he died.'

Of Francoise's three children, only her daughter Beatrice was reunited with the man they knew as a father. The oldest son, Emmanuel, died in an accident when he was 30, just as he was planning to visit Bernard. The youngest, Hervé, 15 at the time of the Golden Globe, was profoundly affected by what he saw as abandonment of his mother and the family. He became a psychiatrist after studying for 15 years. Francoise believes he wanted to understand more about Bernard. Hervé has two adult sons and lives in Toulon, near his mother, yet even in his mid 50s he will not talk about Bernard Moitessier.

'All my children loved Bernard,' says Francoise. 'For my children, it was terrible. If we talk about Bernard, Hervé leaves the room. Still, now. It is impossible to talk about him. His own natural father didn't really care, and for him Bernard was his father. When Bernard left, he was waiting for him to come back. He wrote wonderful letters to Bernard but Bernard did not understand. Hervé wrote a ten-page letter about many things, like religion, being on his own, and Bernard published the letter without telling him. Hervé never accepted that and never forgave him.

'Hervé was always very straightforward. He could not understand because he could see we were happy together. He could not understand.

'He always wanted to do psychiatry right from then. Did that help him? If I could ask him! But it is impossible still to talk about Bernard. Maybe one day.'

8 : DOWN TO THREE

Moitessier's catapulted message off Cape Town meant that the first man home would now undoubtedly be Robin Knox-Johnston, barring mishaps, and assuming he was still alive. His rounding of Cape Horn had gone completely unnoticed in January. In itself, that was hardly surprising but it contrasted disappointingly with the precedent set by Chichester's voyage two years earlier. Chichester was famously photographed from a media spotter plane, battling through a storm off the Horn. It became the iconic image of his adventure. The public was not to know how difficult the photograph had been to obtain, with a perilously overloaded light aircraft having to be flown out to sea four times before Chichester was spotted 20 miles from land. The plane had been hired for the *Times* newspaper group by the journalist Murray Sayle – the same man who would later be dispatched to Toulon to persuade Moitessier to enter the Golden Globe. It was a swashbuckling affair, typical of the era. Sayle had bypassed a pool arrangement, in which 30 other Fleet Street journalists organised a presence on a British frigate that was trying to locate Chichester. After hiring the plane, he had to find a Chilean pilot who was prepared to fly low in gale-force winds. There were four men on board and at one point, as they swapped seats to get the best pictures, the fuel supply was accidentally kicked off. They recovered from that farcical moment only to lose the use of one engine as they approached the landing strip back in Chile. However, they had the photographs and the world saw Chichester at this critical point in his voyage.

In mid January 1969, Knox-Johnston went round the Horn unnoticed, missed by the Chilean navy vessels that had been asked to look out for him. With his radio transmitter still out of action, his last known position was outside Otago harbour at New Zealand on 20 November 1968. There had been not a word or a sighting since.

Once round the Horn, he hoped to attract attention at the Falkland Islands, as Moitessier would later do, but the wind was unfavourable and he was blown too far to the east. He was worried about his family not knowing if he had made it through the Southern Ocean but he was also worried about losing time to Moitessier. It would have taken two days to work back against the wind to the Falklands. He knew that could mean the difference between winning and losing, so he pressed on and hoped he would come across a ship.

Three months on from the last sighting, there was still no sign of the young Briton. The headlines became pessimistic. Now, 'fears were growing'. The staff at his sponsor, the *Sunday Mirror*, admitted there was real concern that their man was dead, although they couched their fears in softer terms. They wrote: 'Even those with most faith in him, his parents, his friends, sometimes ask themselves – being realists – the inevitable uneasy question: will he ever be seen again?' All the newspaper talk now was of the superhuman strain he had been under in his fight against gales, sharks, a knockdown, broken radio and failed self-steering.

At the same time, the end of February 1969, the *Sunday Times* was sticking to an earlier prediction that Moitessier would finish on 24 April.

It was a period in which the papers had little idea of what was actually happening in the race. In fact, Moitessier had just turned east for Cape Town and Knox-Johnston was steadily moving north towards the equator, dealing with sunstroke by making a wide-brimmed hat out of an old piece of canvas he had to stiffen with paint, and getting irritated at news of General de Gaulle insulting the British ambassador in Paris over the Common Market. That news had fired up an indignation he put to good use, pushing *Suhaili* through a squall he would normally have eased back on. He reckoned de Gaulle was responsible for him opening up an extra five miles on Moitessier.

As he crossed the equator, Knox-Johnston suffered one of the biggest frights of his voyage – a medical scare that threatened his life. What he thought was agonizing indigestion had developed into a permanent pain in the middle of his stomach. He looked up his symptoms in the *Ship Captain's Medical Guide* and was alarmed to read that he might have appendicitis. When the pain shifted, reinforcing his self-diagnosis, he became seriously scared and looked on a chart for the nearest port big enough to have a hospital. It was a thousand miles away at the mouth of the Amazon. That would take at least ten days, by which time he could be dead. He decided there was no point in heading towards help. He continued on course for Falmouth, knowing that if the diagnosis was correct he was a dead man, but if it was incorrect he could still win the race. Far from feeling sorry for himself, Knox-Johnston was almost more concerned by his lack of seamanship in not planning properly for such an emergency. He should have included antibiotics in his medical kit and he should have had his appendix removed before he set sail. His life was in grave danger and yet he was embarrassed by his own negligence. He was hugely relieved a week later when the pain disappeared.

Again, the outside world had been oblivious to the drama on board *Suhaili*. Four months from the last sighting, there was still no word of him. Knox-Johnston had seen only one ship since New Zealand. It had been too far away to attract attention. At the end of March, he was in fact well into the north Atlantic and almost where the *Sunday Times*'s calculations estimated he would be. To everyone at home, however, the situation appeared very bleak. It was not helped by the news of Moitessier's withdrawal from the race. The Golden Globe was beginning to feel like an adventure too far.

A huge international operation to look for Knox-Johnston was set up in the approaches to Portugal's mid-Atlantic islands, the Azores. A NATO fleet of 30 ships, including eight from Britain, was on exercise in the area and was asked to keep a lookout for *Suhaili*. The British naval attaché in Lisbon helped obtain Portugal's co-operation. Azores islanders and fishermen were alerted in radio broadcasts. Pilots on the daily long-range patrols from the United States air-force base on the island of Terceira were asked to watch out.

Knox-Johnston and his by now battered boat were nowhere to be seen. It was looking very much as if he had been claimed by the heavy weather of the wild Southern Ocean.

He had been missed simply because he was slightly further south west than had been expected. As he got closer to the Azores, he started to come across merchant ships and did all he could to get their attention. Many were simply not keeping a proper watch and failed to see him. On at least two occasions he was seen but ignored; a demoralising blow for someone with formal training in the ways of the sea. In one case, he even fired an emergency rocket flare into the night sky. The ship briefly responded to the follow-up message on his signal lamp but then sailed on. To ignore a distress flare, without so much as investigating the problem, was beyond belief to this master mariner.

On the evening of Saturday, 5 April he at last made contact with a ship; the British Petroleum tanker *Mobil Acme*, which was on voyage from the River Thames to Texas. In a brief conversation by signal lamp, the officer on watch agreed to report his position to Lloyds, and wished him good luck.

He was 500 miles west of the Azores. It was the first sighting of Knox-Johnston for four-and-a-half months. Within three hours, Lloyds of London were contacting his parents with the news. The *Sunday Times* rang the family home in the early hours of Sunday in a frantic rush to get the story onto that day's front page. His mother, Mary, was quoted as being tremendously relieved. His father, David, said: 'Tremendous. This is tremendous news. But I have never thought at any time that he would not turn up. He's too damn good a sailor. He told me when he left Falmouth that he would be back on April 14. Now he's only going to be five days late. That's quite incredible.'

The *Mobile Acme* had added to its Lloyds message: 'Standard of signalling excellent.' That was good news for those on shore who were hungry for any sliver of information. It suggested that their man was functioning well.

Knox-Johnston was jubilant that he had at last made contact. He was even more delighted later when he heard that his professionalism had been praised. He returned the signalling compliment when he wrote his book of the voyage, pointing out that both he and the ship's officer on the bridge probably went to the same signal school on London's Commercial Road.

There were just 1,200 miles to go: two weeks if the prevailing winds continued; but there were two major questions in Knox-Johnston's mind. How close was Moitessier and had *Mobil Acme* reported his position? Such was the isolation brought about by a failed transmitter that he was blissfully unaware of Moitessier's drama off Cape Town and had no idea that his own sighting had caused immense excitement within hours. So, five days later, he was anxious to attract the attention of another ship, which was passing close enough for him to read the name: *Mungo of Le Havre*. At first, the ship carried on but then, most unusually, it turned round to come back. Knox-Johnston used his foghorn to signal the number of a radio channel and, with the two in such close range, his transmitter worked properly for the first time since the knockdown at the bottom of Africa. Now, for the first time, he was told that Moitessier was going round again. The rival who had been closing in for the best part of ten months was no longer in his wake. *Mungo*'s crew was French and it was clear that they knew about the race and they knew who they were talking to. They provided a latitude-and-longitude position, which coincided neatly with Knox-Johnston's own calculations. Once again, he was proud of his maritime prowess.

Later the same day, another French ship steamed over to *Suhaili* and sounded three blasts on the horn. The news was out. Robin Knox-Johnston was little more than a week from home and making history, and those around him knew it.

With a new-found confidence in his radio transmitter, he tuned into an international high-frequency circuit used by the GPO (General Post Office). It had been a fruitless task for months but now, closer to England, he got through to the monitoring station at Baldock in Hertfordshire. His radio call was linked into the telephone service and directed to the family home in Kent. His brother Mike answered the phone. After all the months of worry, there was an ecstatic reaction to hearing Robin's voice. His father was out of the house, but Robin spoke to his mother and sister Diana. The family confirmed the news that Moitessier was out of the race. Any thought that the French crew on *Mungo* had been up to no good was now dispelled. Knox-Johnston was delighted that all three remaining competitors were British. He was told Nigel Tetley was off the coast of Brazil and Donald Crowhurst was thought to have just rounded Cape Horn.

The homecoming arrangements were in full swing, with members of the family already descending on Falmouth. Close family would be basing themselves on the Isles of Scilly and would be motoring out to meet him. A small team of supporters, including the *Sunday Mirror*'s reporter, was already ensconced in the Marine Hotel in Falmouth and would be motoring out in a former rescue launch.

Knox-Johnston's solitude was well and truly over. He no longer saw himself as a sea creature. Now he was a sailor again with the simple task of getting home in a week or as quickly as he could. He celebrated with a whisky bottle, taking a swig for himself, pouring one over the stern and sacrificing another to Shony, one of the British gods of the sea.

Fleet Street's sense of competition and rivalry was stoking up. A series of newspaper boats were in the Scillies and Falmouth watching for any move from the Knox-Johnston family boat or the *Sunday Mirror*'s launch. Progress on *Suhaili* was erratic in frequently light winds but, with an estimated five days to go, it was agreed in a radio call to the *Sunday Mirror* that Knox-Johnston would give future positions in a secret code that had been set up before the race. This was necessary as anyone could listen to the transmissions; indeed, all the newspapers did. Knox-Johnston was grateful for his sponsor's support and felt they thoroughly deserved as much exclusive coverage as they could get. He was more than happy to co-operate.

The hope was that he would arrive in Falmouth on

Sunday, 20 April. The supporters' launch was aiming to find *Suhaili* on the Friday or at dawn on Saturday. A spotter plane would also be looking for him.

On Friday 18, news came that the launch was being 'tagged'. Knox-Johnston was enjoying the cloak-and-dagger operation. He wished he was the hound rather than the hare but it was, nevertheless, great fun. The sailing was the frustrating part. He was stressed from light winds and having to avoid ships and a fishing fleet. There was too much activity for it to be safe to sleep.

Shortly after midnight on Friday, a small ship appeared to slow and then stay about half a mile behind *Suhaili*. Another, smaller, boat moved in quickly to do the same. After so long with the sea to himself, Knox-Johnston was ill at ease and he watched the two vessels' lights anxiously. They stayed half a mile off. He challenged the crew of the bigger vessel with his signal lamp, asking who they were. The reply was *Queen of the Isles*, the name of the Isles of Scilly boat being chartered by his family. The smaller boat was the *Sunday Mirror*'s Falmouth launch. In the western approaches to the English Channel, Knox-Johnston had been found. No one knew how to handle this highly charged moment. The friends, family and supporters had nervously held back, not wanting to crowd their man. He had, after all, been examined by a psychiatrist before setting sail and would be re-examined on arrival: they knew he sounded sane and normal in his recent radio calls, but there was still an air of uncertainty. All the doubts and questions about whether a man could sail round the world non-stop were just as relevant now as when the race was starting. Indeed, if not more so.

Queen of the Isles moved in and the down-and-out-looking *Suhaili* was lit up by camera flash bulbs. Struggling with a rising wind, Robin was able to shout to his mother and father. It was the first time they had spoken directly for 309 days. He described it simply as a wonderful moment.

The Falmouth launch, with his friends from the *Sunday Mirror* on board, waited respectfully until daylight. The team had discussed how to handle this reunion and agreed that they would allow Robin to speak first. That way, if he was tense at being amongst people, they could gauge how he was. It was an agreement that produced another delightful moment. Knox-Johnston was waiting for someone else to break the silence. The two boats drew closer and closer as everyone stood grinning at each other. They were only 15 yards apart when Knox-Johnston could stand it no longer. His first, historic words were aimed at his publisher, who was on board the launch and who had helped make his voyage possible by paying an advance for a book. He shouted: 'I see you're still wearing that same bloody silly hat.' The publisher threw it into the sea.

During the next two days, the two support vessels continued to stand guard as the winds conspired to delay Knox-Johnston's triumphant return to Falmouth. On Monday, 21 April, he saw Bishop Rock lighthouse off the Isles of Scilly. He still faced one more night at sea but now he was close enough to land to be joined by all manner of craft, whether on the sea or in the air. His location had long since ceased to be a secret. Indeed, the newspapers' boats had to work together at one point when *Suhaili* was separated from her escort in bad visibility. Press photographers were now hanging out of helicopters. A Coastal Command plane made half a dozen low-level passes. Small craft had motored out of the Scillies. A Royal Naval Reserve minesweeper, HMS *Warsash*, steamed round to *Suhaili*'s stern and flew the international signal for 'Welcome'. Knox-Johnston almost burst with pride as *Warsash*'s commander carefully manoeuvred right up to *Suhaili* for his crew to let off an almighty cheer. Knox-Johnston spotted his three brothers among the crew. From then on, *Warsash* took up station ahead of *Suhaili*, as if to clear the way to Falmouth for this very British hero.

On the last day of this marathon voyage, Tuesday, 22 April 1969, the convoy grew hour by hour. The Falmouth lifeboat, in full regalia, added a splash of colour. Then Knox-Johnston saw a vessel that would have meant little to the waiting crowds but meant a great deal to him. It was the tug boat, *St Mawes*, named after the town opposite Falmouth, but which had a past working life in East Africa for the company British India. Here and now, it was representing Knox-Johnston's adult life. British India had been home since he left school. It was the company that had trained him as a seaman and which had encouraged his round-the-world voyage by willingly granting extended leave. Now the tug was being chartered by British India especially for this homecoming. It had even been painted in her old colours, with two distinctive white bands on a black funnel, and was flying the company flag. Many familiar faces were on board, including his first captain at sea. Knox-Johnston had been carrying his own identical company flag and now was the time to hoist it.

At 3.25 pm, he crossed the finish line into Falmouth harbour to the sound of a cannon firing and an estimated quarter of a million people cheering. The first people to board *Suhaili* were from Her Majesty's Customs and Excise. The senior officer famously quipped: 'Where from?' and Knox-Johnston replied: 'Falmouth.'

It was a famous victory that turned Robin Knox-Johnston into a household name. He was every inch the all-conquering hero and was quickly dubbed the Edmund Hillary of the seas. The papers were soon writing of his new-found stardom. The *Sunday Times* predicted he would make £100,000 in his first year home.

Sir Francis Chichester was on hand to greet Knox-Johnston in Falmouth. Everyone was keen to get the two men together for a proper conversation as quickly as possible. First, there was an official reception followed by a party that ran through the night until six in the morning, and then another full day of engagements. When the two men were brought together, Chichester could not help but admire the younger man's stamina. Their conversation was published in a vast spread in the *Sunday Times*, entitled: 'A dialogue: The old man of the sea and the new young hero'.

Chichester began by saying that at the start of the race he did not think Knox-Johnston would make it, if only because his boat looked vulnerable. He was hugely impressed by the young man's resourcefulness in strengthening the cabin top when it shifted in the knockdown off the bottom of Africa. Many of the stories were coming out for the first time including, even, the extent of the self-steering problems. Chichester was almost beside himself with amazement when he found out how early on *Suhaili* had to be sailed by balancing the sails, describing this new information as 'extraordinarily interesting'.

Chichester brought up the subject of Moitessier and, in doing so, raised a question that would go on to vex Knox-Johnston for the rest of his life: who would have won the Golden Globe if the Frenchman had stayed in the race?

Moitessier's retirement did not impress Chichester. He told Knox-Johnston that he too felt an urge to continue after Cape Horn but he did not approve of Moitessier giving way to this feeling. 'It's not fair to the other people in the race,' he said. 'Once he was in it he should have stayed in it.' It was Knox-Johnston who pointed out that Moitessier could not have intended, when he set out, to continue sailing, as he would not have bothered to go to Plymouth for the start.

French claims of a moral victory irritated Chichester. He told Knox-Johnston: 'You wouldn't know, but in France they were saying that Moitessier gave up when he had the race in the bag. This is quite wrong. I worked out that if he'd kept up his average speed to the Horn, he would have got in two-and-a-half days before you, but since that's 8,800 miles away it is ridiculous to say that he had the race in the bag.

'It's like saying a horse would have won the Grand National if he had not fallen at Beecher's Brook.'

The theoretical mathematics of the two sailors' progress was of only limited use in determining who would have been home first, as the average speeds varied during the different phases of the race.

Craig Rich, advising the *Sunday Times*, was the one person who constantly updated his calculations as the race progressed. He still has the exercise book in which he did the sums; he can see that in November 1968, at around the halfway mark, he came up with specific finishing dates for both men. Knox-Johnston was passing New Zealand while Moitessier was behind in the distant approaches to Australia. Rich estimated that Moitessier would catch up and overtake Knox-Johnston on the home stretch up the Atlantic, finishing on 24 April. It was an estimate that barely moved in the ensuing months, such was Moitessier's consistency of speed. Knox-Johnston was expected to finish a cruel week later, on 30 April.

However, Rich's estimates demonstrate the shortcomings in judging passage-making speed under sail. Black-and-white dates and times give a false sense of precision when, in reality, there are too many variables. Indeed, the perils were demonstrated perfectly by Knox-Johnston right at the end of his voyage when what was supposed to be the final four days stretched frustratingly into five. If the last days could deliver a 25 per cent delay, it is easy to see how timings for the entire ten-month voyage were nigh on impossible to pin down. Rich knew this, of course, but had to satisfy Fleet Street journalists who were ever-hungry for plain, identifiable facts. His paymasters were not comfortable with ambiguity.

Knox-Johnston surprised Rich, Chichester and everyone else by making remarkable progress despite the limitations imposed by the lack of a self-steering system. By finishing on 22 April, he beat Rich's estimate by one week and, more importantly, beat the estimated time for Moitessier by two days.

No wonder Knox-Johnston, 40 years on, still feels peeved at an often-held assumption that Moitessier would have won the Golden Globe.

At the age of 70, he is an old sea dog out of Central Casting. If a child was told to imagine what a sea captain who sailed round the world looked like, he or she would come up with Sir Robin Knox-Johnston. He is big and powerful; handsome in a mature, rugged way with his grey beard and healthy, craggy face. He has a handshake that is both gentle and not to be messed with.

He also has a reputation as a grumpy old man when it comes to certain things in life, such as new technology on sailing boats, or the suggestion that Moitessier would have won in 1969.

At first, he talks about the race mildly and politely, as if trying to stifle an understandable boredom of an event that happened so long ago. Indeed, he admits: 'I suppose I do in a way tire of talking about the Golden Globe. I would much rather talk about what I want to do tomorrow. That is interesting. This is history.'

There is no trace of hostility or rudeness. He admits to his tiredness only when specifically asked if four decades of Golden Globe questions have perhaps become a little tedious. Knox-Johnston knows the Golden Globe has shaped his life and he is happy to oblige, although he says glory and riches were not his motivation for sailing round the world.

'I didn't do this for plaudits. I didn't do it to be famous, or for money, because there wasn't any anyway,' he says. 'People don't really understand there wasn't any wealth in it. That is a journalists' invention. None of us made vast amounts of money.'

Knox-Johnston was awarded a payment at the end of the race but gave it away; receiving only a trophy that he later presented to his old school in Hertfordshire. 'The only money I made was from selling the book and magazine articles. It took me a long time to realise I should charge for lectures.

'I keep my private life very much to myself. I didn't respond to deals with the *Hello* or *OK* magazines. I didn't go seeking glory.

'The book has been published in eleven languages. It ticks along. I get a cheque from time to time. I couldn't live on it but it pays for my smoking.'

There is modesty in Knox-Johnston. He has carved out a successful career in the yachting world, co-owning the company that runs the Velux 5 Oceans round-the-world race – a modern version of the Golden Globe – and the Clipper Round The World Yacht Race, in which amateurs form the crews.

So would Moitessier have won if he had not dropped out of the race? 'I would have been two days ahead,' says Knox-Johnston, torn between knowing that is too close to call and realising that people want precise answers just as the *Sunday Times* did during 1969. 'He was not speeding up. I was speeding up. He wasn't. I was getting faster. But even ignoring that, if you take our averages up to that point, mathematically I would have come in ahead.

'No one ever listens. Only the other day I saw something that said Moitessier was winning when he pulled out.' Knox-Johnston swears under his breath, his bushy beard muffling an expletive that exposes his frustration.

'I can't be bothered with it. It isn't true but there is no point in fussing about it. The *Sunday Times* is responsible. They wanted to maintain the excitement [in the months when it looked as if Knox-Johnston would win] for the next question: would Moitessier get home the fastest against Crowhurst and Tetley?

'It rankles me that a newspaper like the *Sunday Times* slightly twisted it to make their story, and the French, who hate admitting that they are not winning, always maintained he was beating me when he pulled out, which is not true.

'What the French wouldn't admit was that I was three weeks ahead of him at Cape Horn, and they can't accept that. So I keep getting this thing that Moitessier was winning when he left the race. Well, winning what?

'So to that extent it rankles but there is nothing you can do about it. It rankles less now than it used to. It used to a lot.'

By now Knox-Johnston is positively riled. He is muttering and grumbling, and he laughs at himself for being so irritated. Yet it is obvious that he is consciously holding back, knowing that what he is saying is for the public record.

Curiously, the debate was played out between the two men themselves. Knox-Johnston reveals that Moitessier wrote to him to admit he would not have won.

They first made contact after the Frenchman heard that Knox-Johnston had empathised with the decision to sail on. 'When I first got back people said Moitessier must be mad. I said I knew and understood what he did, and he didn't need to explain it.

'I, too, was a sea creature at home in my environment.

I didn't really want it to be interfered with or interrupted. I said to people: "No, Moitessier is not mad." I had quite similar urges.

'He got to hear about that and I got a lovely, charming letter which I responded to, of course, and we kept in touch on and off.

'When an American magazine said Moitessier was leading when he pulled out, he corrected them. He wrote to me and said, "I'm sorry about this, Robin." He wrote, "I just want you to know that I have written to them and told them they were wrong."

'He always said he thought I would have beaten him back, but he would have won the prize for fastest voyage.

'He wrote absolutely charming letters and we met once. He was a nice friendly chap, as you would expect.'

Some of the men in the Golden Globe race had considerably more in common with each other than was generally recognised. Their backgrounds and characters were diverse, but it arguably took a certain kind of person to be drawn to this one adventure. Only they truly knew what it meant and what it involved, and that created a common bond and respect for each other.

9 : DUEL FOR FASTEST TIME

Knox-Johnston was right about the *Times* newspaper group wanting to maintain the excitement after he had finished. Indeed, the race's founders had always been planning for this moment, as they demonstrated when they had quickly introduced the £5,000 prize for the fastest voyage.

So now, this second prize was apparently being chased by two men, Donald Crowhurst and Nigel Tetley, who both appeared to be on target to convincingly beat Robin Knox-Johnston's voyage of ten months.

The world was still oblivious to Crowhurst's bizarre double life that was being played out in the south Atlantic. In the months that Knox-Johnston had been sailing for home from Cape Horn, Crowhurst had been hiding in a nautical no-man's-land. January's fairly aimless drift southwards became February's plod westwards towards South America.

On 6 March, the same day Knox-Johnston crossed the equator while fearing he had appendicitis, Crowhurst had a bizarre accident: he ran aground. It was just one twist in an extraordinary episode which had been in the making since he had turned towards land.

He had decided to take a massive risk and go ashore so that he could repair the increasingly leaking starboard hull. He needed wood and screws in order to stay afloat. However, there was no hurry. He was deliberately killing time. The more he delayed his secret landing, the less ridiculous it would appear if he was recognised and reported. He might be able to explain that he had to run from his last so-called position, which he had given as 100 miles off Gough Island – between South America and Africa. Crowhurst was not to know that it would have been an absurd explanation, thanks to Rodney Hallworth's misreading of the Gough telegram and subsequent announcement that his man was off the Cape of Good Hope.

Crowhurst appears to have chosen the landing site carefully, avoiding the large ports and towns. It is clear from his markings in the nautical guide book *Admiralty South America Pilot*, Volume One, that he studied hundreds of miles of coastline, eventually choosing a small settlement on a coastal dirt track, called Rio Salado, in Argentina. His running aground happened in the River Plate, off the small cluster of sheds and buildings that was Rio Salado. Considering his diligence in picking this spot, he was unlucky, not because he ran aground but because one of the buildings was a shack used as an outpost for the Argentinean coastguard to monitor traffic in and out of the river. A bizarre couple of days followed. The coastguard staff took Crowhurst's details, including his passport number, and carefully logged it all in their official notebook. It was rare for them to have a visitor of any kind, let alone an apparently eccentric British yachtsman, and they were keen to help. They used their jeep to drive him almost twenty miles up the coast to where he could get the materials he needed. There was, however, a dual purpose to the jeep trip. Rio Salado was too basic and cut off to have even a public phone, which of course was why Crowhurst selected it in the first place. The drive for materials meant the senior coastguard official would be able to use a phone booth to report this strange arrival to the regional office. Crowhurst was initially agitated when he heard the phone call would be made but he soon accepted it.

He was in luck. The regional officer on the end of the line was satisfied that there was nothing untoward and saw no reason to refer the matter further up the chain of command to headquarters in Buenos Aires. As a result, this flagrant breach of the race rules went unnoticed by the world. After two days of being fed and watered, and with *Teignmouth Electron* now strengthened, Crowhurst set sail again.

He had told his new friends in Rio Salado that he was winning a round-the-world regatta and was on the homeward leg. So, for a couple of days, he headed north east to maintain the charade of sailing for England. Once well out to sea, he turned south.

There is a tendency to believe that Crowhurst simply drifted in the south Atlantic, biding his time, before popping up months later. In fact, it was a nerve-wracking experience. There is ample evidence that he was ever-conscious of the risk of exposure. When studying his logbooks, Tomalin and Hall, working with Craig Rich, saw that he was plotting when and how to break his radio silence and reappear on the race route.

Sailing down Argentina's coast, usually out of sight of land, he knew he had more time to kill if people were to believe that he truly had sailed round the Southern Ocean and past Cape Horn. By heading south, towards the Falklands Islands and away from the shipping routes, he increased his chances of staying undetected. He would also be able to dip into the Roaring Forties and film the conditions that, so far, he had been describing with the use of his imagination rather than experience. He would even be able to film the Falklands, as if passing them after a triumphant rounding of the Horn.

His calculations of a plausible average speed and the distance to be covered from the start of his radio silence in January led to a target date of 15 April for his pretend rounding of the Horn. He would have to play out his secret existence for another month.

The radio silence, apparently throughout the Southern Ocean, had been explained by the claim of needing to conserve battery power because of the sealed generator hatch. But a call near the race milestone of Cape Horn would be expected. The logistics of that call – and the need to make it convincing - would be crucial if suspicions were not to be raised.

By heading south, Crowhurst was moving out of the shadow of South America and, on 21 March, he was able to pick up New Zealand radio weather reports. He tried to send a message to New Zealand or Australia but failed to get through.

Crowhurst had had plenty of time to think, and he used it now to come up with complex schemes so his true location would not be betrayed by this vital communication. At the end of March, with the Falklands on the horizon, he turned around from what was to be the most southern point of his entire voyage. He was still two weeks away from the date he had set for a fake rounding of the Horn but he now decided he needed to make radio contact before this key moment. Otherwise, it could be obvious that every single radio call before and after the January silence had been made from the Atlantic. A call that was apparently made from the Southern Ocean, on the approaches to Cape Horn, would reinforce the story that he had sailed round the world. To pull off such a trick, he set about creating a smokescreen of confusion.

In the meantime, Nigel Tetley, the only other man still in the race, was sailing around Cape Horn for real. True to form, his rounding on 18 March was understated and lacking in drama. He kept a safe 15 miles away from the infamous headland to avoid being swept by the currents in the event of a lack of wind. It was a wise tactic as he was indeed becalmed. Rather than becoming frustrated, he stoically turned the moment into a celebration. Out came another terrific meal: the best tinned meat, rice, dried onions and mushrooms and a bottle of wine. It was not a classic rounding of the Horn but it was vintage Tetley.

Unknown to Tetley at the time, Moitessier was off Cape Town writing his retirement announcement and preparing to catapult it the very next day, and the NATO search for Knox-Johnston was under way. The papers were saying Tetley was now the favourite to win the Golden Globe and, as Crowhurst's position was uncertain, he was also being tipped to make the fastest voyage. Suddenly, this quiet, no-nonsense naval officer was jettisoned from his position of making up the numbers to being a likely double winner. He was told the news in a radio call a week after rounding Cape Horn. Far from whooping with delight, he felt deflated. He had not met Knox-Johnston or Crowhurst but they were colleagues in this race and he was concerned for them. It was Moitessier's weird decision to drop out, and his comment that he was doing so to find his soul, that had the biggest effect on Tetley. He reflected on the character of a man he had got to know well, before the start, and whom he regarded generally as an astounding human being. It was only now that he began to understand the complete lack of rivalry Moitessier had displayed among their group of four in Plymouth.

Moitessier had said everyone who got round would have won, and now Tetley thought how right that comment had been. He had good reason to feel that way. Publicly, his own voyage to Cape Horn had been straightforward. Relative to the others, it had been conducted out of the limelight. However, Tetley had suffered his fair share of life-threatening scares.

Two weeks after the famous photograph with an absurdly normal Christmas dinner, he had run into violent, storm-force-11 winds with hurricane-strength squalls. He described awe-inspiring, spine-chilling waves marching towards *Victress*, seemingly intent on causing destruction. It was enough for Tetley to judge that it was too dangerous to carry on. He had offered a prayer of thanks for his survival and turned north for Albany in Australia, before later changing his mind and deciding to stay in the race.

On the two-week approach to Cape Horn, *Victress* was subjected to a series of high-wind batterings, one of which almost caused a capsize. The boat had performed a half cartwheel – narrowly avoiding the dreaded pitchpole – and for a few moments had teetered on the brink of disaster at an angle of about 50 degrees.

More storm-force winds smashed the perspex in the cabin windows, leading to a dangerous flood. The cabin top was weakened at its join with the deck, just as Knox-Johnston's was in his knockdown.

Most worryingly, structural joinery was beginning to crack under the strain. Tetley realised that, much as he loved *Victress* and admired her seagoing qualities, she was not robust enough for the Southern Ocean. He was hugely relieved to reach Cape Horn and to do so in calm weather. As he prepared the celebration meal, he patted *Victress* fondly and said: 'Vicky, we've made it!'

One week later, Tetley passed close to the eastern side of the Falkland Islands. What happened during the next 24 hours was extraordinary. It was missed at the time by those tracking the race and has never been picked up on in all the decades of the Golden Globe story being retold. Yet it was an episode that could have changed everything.

Tetley and Crowhurst came very close to seeing each other. Tetley, worried that he was still within the iceberg limit, had turned slightly to the west of north once he was round the Falklands. Of all the space in the southern Atlantic, he had inadvertently chosen to aim directly at where Crowhurst was coming from. On the night of 23 March, the two boats were heading straight for each other, with Crowhurst now less than two days' sailing from the islands. Ironically, Tetley wrote: 'That night, under snug canvas and with the open ocean ahead, I had my first peaceful night for several weeks.'

The next day, Crowhurst altered course dramatically. He had been heading directly to the Falklands for almost a week. Now he turned to his right and, for two days, sailed back towards Argentina. It was an apparently inexplicable change of course, although Tomalin and Hall thought it was caused by a storm that they said blew Crowhurst a hundred miles off course. Tetley did record that there was a gale on the night of the 23rd but regarded it as nothing unusual. He reefed his sails and stayed on his chosen course.

Forty years on, Eve Tetley reveals that Nigel later spotted the coincidence. From what Nigel told her, she believes Crowhurst picked up his Morse transmissions and was startled into an otherwise illogical change of course. By moving out to the west for two days he would have known he was taking himself away from Tetley's probable route.

On 26 March, Crowhurst turned around again and resumed his course for the Falklands. Tetley, clear of the risk of ice, was by now sailing for home, to the north east.

The two trimarans had come within a whisker of each other. Had Crowhurst's presence been revealed, it would immediately have been obvious something was wrong. Tetley's nature was to see the best in people. He was a generous man without a suspicious mind but even he would have had difficulty in explaining

Crowhurst's appearance. It would obviously have been odd that Crowhurst was heading south when the wind gave no reason to, but perhaps that could have been explained away. The fact he was in the south Atlantic at all could not. Crowhurst was supposed to be in the Southern Ocean, heading for Cape Horn with a probable arrival date of 15 April. If he had been seen by Nigel Tetley, the game would have been over. Crowhurst would have been exposed and one can only imagine the difference that would have made. Indeed, the race was shortly to develop in a way that had a profound effect on both men.

As Crowhurst turned from the Falklands to fall in behind Tetley, who was now five days ahead, he was refining the smokescreen he needed in order to make his dramatic reappearance. He drafted a message that said he was in a radio zone to the west of South America. He addressed it to Cape Town radio via New Zealand, knowing perfectly well that it would not be picked up in New Zealand but at least the final message would still have those instructions, and suggest he was coming from the right direction. It was all designed to be complicated, perhaps too much so, for he changed his mind. Instead, he crossed it out of his radio log and added a note saying: 'This will probably cause trouble at Capetown, won't send it.'

The scheming almost backfired on 9 April 1969. Crowhurst did send out a generic message that he transmitted several times, aimed on each occasion at a different listening station. There was no answer until, unexpectedly, Buenos Aires radio on the east coast of Argentina made contact and asked for his latitude and longitude. This was not a radio station he had aimed at and there was a great risk that people back home would wonder how the contact was made if he had been where he was supposed to be – approaching the Horn from the west. Crowhurst was evasive. He was anxious to give away as little as possible. He did send a telegram but that too was vague. He said little more than: 'HEADING DIGGER RAMREZ. WHAT'S NEW OCEANBASH-INGWISE'. Crowhurst was back to his cryptic ways.

Rodney Hallworth had heard nothing from his man for almost three months. There was no way of knowing for sure that he was even still alive. News of the Buenos Aires telegram came through as Hallworth was shaving. He quickly telephoned Clare Crowhurst with the good news and then set about working out precisely what this latest cryptic message meant. 'Digger Ramrez' obviously meant the small island of Diego Ramirez off Cape Horn. Crowhurst's telegram had also said 'LOG KAPUT 17697 28th', which Hallworth assumed meant the logline had broken on 28 March after 17,697 miles. That was enough to calculate an average speed and deduce Crowhurst would round the Horn on 11 April.

So it was that on 11 April it was reported that Crowhurst had probably rounded Cape Horn. The date was not what Crowhurst wanted. He had already decided that his target of 15 April was too early and could raise suspicions, so he had changed it to 18 April. Now Hallworth's optimism placed him at risk of exposure. Hallworth must have known the news was almost too good to be true, because he told the papers that his man might have sailed around the fringe of Antarctica 'to lop 2,000 miles off the journey'. He said Crowhurst had told a friend that he would take the shorter but more hazardous route if he was a long way behind.

Once again, though, there was an element of farce in the reporting of where Crowhurst was, and this time it was compounded by a correction. Several newspapers, with the help of the race organisers, reassessed the information and came up with a new date. Based partly on the Buenos Aires radio contact, they decided Cape Horn had been reached on 18 April. The confusion saved Crowhurst but the real reason he was spared serious scrutiny by the press was almost certainly that Robin Knox-Johnston was now on his final approach to Falmouth and was attracting all the attention with his heroic homecoming.

It was a different story behind the scenes. The two men who for months had felt uneasy about Crowhurst were asking more questions. They felt the apparent progress through the Southern Ocean was too fast. Francis Chichester was now in Falmouth for Knox-Johnston's return and he was expressing his doubts to the race organisers. Craig Rich, working for those same organisers, was doing the maths. He went back to the table of projected arrival dates he had compiled when Crowhurst announced his radio silence back in January. These figures were designed to be compared to Crowhurst's claimed date for rounding the Horn. Crowhurst had beaten even the most optimistic forecast by more than two weeks.

He had also beaten Tetley's time by a similar margin. This was the vital ingredient for the *Sunday Times*. They knew that after Knox-Johnston's imminent arrival there was a danger that public interest in the race would fade away. Keen to maintain excitement, they declared that the battle for the £5,000 prize for the fastest voyage was hotting up. Crowhurst, the man at the back of the field, was now the favourite. So remarkable was his progress that his finishing date had constantly been brought forward from an early estimate of November, which had been based on the first difficult two weeks. Now, not only was the town councillor tipped to finish on 8 July but, according to the *Sunday Times*, he 'could well be a fortnight earlier'.

It was heady stuff, considering that one week earlier Tetley had been declared the favourite. It all had a direct effect on the two men still in the race. Crowhurst was soon to become alarmed at the thought of the extra scrutiny that winning the prize would attract. Tetley was driven to risk pushing a boat that he should have been nursing home after the strains of the Southern Ocean. Far from the race becoming dull, it was about to enter its most astonishing phase.

It was some time before Tetley was aware of all the drama around him. He sailed up the south Atlantic believing that Knox-Johnston and Crowhurst were still missing and that he was still being tipped for both prizes. Knox-Johnston's out-of-the-blue contact with the tanker *Mobil Acme* off the Azores was on 5 April; Crowhurst's re-emergence was a few days later. Yet it was 17 April before Tetley heard the news. At the time, he was only ten days from the equator and had every reason to believe he would make it home and win, despite struggling to keep the boat together.

Victress was still leaking badly and was taking on a

disturbing amount of water every day. Tetley had decided that he could ease the strain by not following the old clipper route that swung out into the ocean away from land. He stayed close to South America, where the wind was more likely to be against him than coming from behind. It was an unusual choice but it was the strain of running from the wind in the Southern Ocean that had weakened *Victress*. He had the added complication of having lost his self-steering system off Cape Horn and was now balancing his sails as Knox-Johnston had been doing since Australia.

Tetley's reaction to the news that he was not alone in the race was a mixed one. He was relieved that the two men were still alive and he was even glad Knox-Johnston's victory would hive off most of the publicity. However, to be beaten by Crowhurst would be a different matter altogether. The ever-present comparison between the two men drew a competitive response. He did not want to lose to anyone in a similar boat.

The two trimarans were now pitched against each other in an apparent duel. Tetley immediately set about conducting a close-up survey of the areas of the boat he thought had suffered the most so far. He crawled deep into the confined space of the starboard hull to where he had heard the structural cracking sounds in the final stage of the Southern Ocean. His worst suspicions were confirmed. Most of the fastenings that held together the inner timber beams were in poor shape. Worse still, four frames had indeed cracked. Tetley judged that *Victress* would see him home but she would then be a write-off. He felt sad; thinking of how fond Eve was of the boat made him sadder still.

On that same day, Tetley allowed himself time to imagine the future after the race was over. His retirement from the Royal Navy had become official as he passed New Zealand. He had a plan for a new life with Eve, which they had discussed before he set sail from Plymouth. They would have a new, larger yacht built and would sail off to the Caribbean where they would charter it out to fare-paying customers. Now, sitting in the cockpit of the damaged and weakened *Victress*; he drew a preliminary sketch of his dream yacht: a 60-foot trimaran.

Several days later, Tetley closed to within 60 miles of the point at which he would cross his outward track, just below the equator. He would then have sailed round the world. Of course, such an achievement meant less than a true voyage to and from a port. Nevertheless, he would be able to claim the world's first circumnavigation in a trimaran. Excited by the approach to this milestone, Tetley threw caution to the wind. He kept up the pace, knowing that he had to sail faster than Crowhurst if he was to gain on his rival's elapsed time.

It was too much for *Victress*. There was an unusual splashing noise coming from the front of the boat. Tetley's senses, like those of most long-distance sailors, were tuned into a certain rhythm and motion of his boat, and it was immediately apparent that there was an interruption to them. He moved forward to investigate. A sizeable proportion of the boat's superstructure had disappeared. He looked more closely at the bow section of the port hull. The plywood was holed and split. He climbed through an inspection hatch and squatted inside the narrow confines. He was knee deep in water. Five structural frames were broken. He could feel the sides moving in and out like a concertina. Tetley stared at the damage that had been building up out of sight, and assumed his race was over. He spent the next hour studying charts in search of a safe harbour to head for. He decided on Recife in Brazil – the same port John Ridgway had retired to nine months earlier.

There were holes to patch up before he went anywhere. Tetley sawed off part of the deck so he could get to the damage. Now that he could see it more clearly, he realised he could strengthen the broken frames and beams with stainless-steel straps. It was possible he could do enough to keep sailing for England. He worked furiously all day in the stifling heat of the equator, keeping himself going with lime juice and spoonfuls of Marmite. He covered the biggest splits and holes with pieces of plywood in the hope that the gaps would not worsen.

Tetley knew that the damage to the port hull was too great to keep the sea out. There were simply too many leaks. His solution to this crisis was drastic. He drilled a series of cup-sized holes through the bow below the waterline. The theory was that *Victress* would be a floating colander – when the hull lifted up above the waves, the sea would drain away as fast as it came in.

It was an extraordinary way out of a potentially disastrous situation. Deep in the Atlantic, Nigel Tetley was quietly proving that he was from the same mould as Knox-Johnston. It was a hell of a place to start boat-building, yet his resourcefulness and instinct for invention were keeping his voyage alive.

A fresh breeze was blowing as he finished two days of feverish work. He set the sails for a sea trial and climbed back into the scene of his renovation work, once more crawling along the inside of the port hull to its bow. The conditions alternated between bath and shower but, crucially, the job appeared to be holding. The next day, Tetley reached the point at which he had completed a circumnavigation. He raised a glass: 'To Miss Vicky. Much abused, yet great-hearted to the end!'

Donald Crowhurst's response to apparently being back in the race was a peculiar one indeed. Far from being relieved by the breaking of his silence, he began to show signs of being deeply disturbed. What had started out as embellishment to mask poor performance, and save face, had long since got completely out of hand. During the race, Crowhurst had repeatedly read Einstein's *Relativity* and, in one of his logbooks, wrote a critique of the Nobel Prize winner's seminal work. Bizarrely, and to the consternation of those reading his logbooks after the race, he drew on parts of the text for deep cosmic significance. This was no joke. Crowhurst was deadly serious. He started a long period of obsessive writing that focused on man's place on earth. One page, which concentrated on what he called the 'Cosmic Integral', concluded mankind added up to a blank.

In short, Crowhurst was showing signs of mental unbalance. His condition was to deteriorate chronically but such was the nature of this race that no one else on the planet had any idea what was going on.

Crowhurst had, of course, plenty of time to think, and possibly too much time. After he had turned away from the Falkland Islands, he spent all of April slowly meandering north. He needed to work out when exactly his fake voyage would catch up with his real position, and it seems he decided the right place would be about

1,000 miles north east of the Falklands. After the 9 April telegram in which he indicated he was about to round Cape Horn, he went back to radio silence. Although he had let it be known that he was still in the race, he had a few more weeks of hiding in the south Atlantic to do.

The moment that Crowhurst could at last stop pretending he was somewhere he was not came on 30 April 1969. For more than five months he had, at its kindest, given a misleading impression about where he was. Now there was no need to worry about being seen or which radio station picked up his signals. He could be where he was, officially. It was a precious moment and a novel experience for Crowhurst. He responded with a new bullishness. He sent two hammed-up, theatrical telegrams. One was to Rodney Hallworth, saying he was heading 'pell mell' up the south Atlantic. The other, more surprisingly, was to the BBC newsdesk in London. It offered congratulations to Knox-Johnston for being the first home but it also hyped up his own apparent progress, saying accuracy in reporting the race demanded a distinction between first and fastest. With great gusto, he signed off as 'Outraged of South Atlantic'.

Curiously, for the next four days, *Teignmouth Electron* barely moved. It was only on 4 May that Crowhurst started to sail for home as if in pursuit of Nigel Tetley.

The chase did not last for long. In mid May, Crowhurst appeared to be having doubts as to whether he could pull off what had grown into a gigantic hoax. Aside from receiving personal telegrams telling him that Clare was very proud of him, he was beginning to hear about the plans for his homecoming: a celebration that looked set to rival that of Knox-Johnston. Hallworth sent a message saying; 'TEIGNMOUTH AGOG AT YOUR WONDERS – WHOLE TOWN PLANNING HUGE WELCOME – RODNEY'.

This news should really not have come as a surprise to Crowhurst, but the extent to which he thought about the consequences of specific actions at any point in his voyage, or indeed in the planning stage before he set sail, is not always clear. Certainly, at times, he thought through various scenarios with immense determination and cunning but he was often less perceptive when looking at the bigger picture.

It was only now that Crowhurst appeared to confront the reality of a heroic homecoming. If, as he had suggested in his mildly indignant telegram to the BBC, he did indeed win the race for fastest voyage, and its £5,000 prize, his logbooks would be scrutinised by the race organisers. His attempts early on in the voyage to run a fake logbook, with back-to-front celestial calculations of his position fixes, had proved unsustainable and short-lived. Without a credible record of daily fixes along the fake route, suspicion would instantly be raised.

All of the evidence points to Crowhurst having come to the conclusion that his dark secret of hiding in the south Atlantic would be exposed. His only way out was to lose to Tetley and finish the race for fastest voyage in a respectable second place. There would be no prize and, therefore, no scrutiny. Yet there would be no shame either. He would have succeeded where others failed. He would be one of only three men to achieve a single-handed, non-stop voyage round the world.

Slow speeds now, however, could be considered odd back home. There had been enough erratic progress without adding to any puzzlement. Crowhurst needed to be subtle in the manner in which he lost to Tetley. He began to pave the way for a change. On 16 May, he sent a telegram that said, 'GOING WELL FOR THESE PARTS – NO CHANCE OVERTAKE TETLEY – NOW PROBABLY VERY CLOSE RESULT'.

He slowed abruptly and soon the *Sunday Times* was adding a week to his estimated finishing date. Crowhurst had found a solution, of sorts, to the dilemma that he might be exposed as a cheat.

Or so he thought. Five days later the Golden Globe race was to take another of its extraordinary turns.

On 20 May, Nigel Tetley was riding out a gale. He had just sailed through the middle of the Azores islands at exhilarating speeds. Days like this gave him a chance of beating Crowhurst, although he always had a nagging feeling that *Victress* was being pushed too hard. Two weeks earlier, off the Cape Verde Islands, he had refused to let up despite heavy pounding of the boat on waves. Then he had decided that he had no time left for more repairs, such was his determination to win this mini-battle. He was prepared even to risk losing the port bow altogether. Internally, the rest of the hull was isolated from the front section, like a submarine with its bulkhead compartments. In theory at least, he could keep sailing. *Victress* would not be a pretty sight but he could still make it home.

Now he was past the last milestone – the Azores – and with the boat still in one piece. The wind was unusually strong for the time of year but Tetley was so used to gales that he did not bother to even mention the conditions during a routine radio call to London. It was only because of *Victress*'s vulnerability that he decided to play it safe and lower the sails. Drifting gently in the wind, he drew a line on his chart directly to Plymouth. Home was a mere 1,100 miles away. He had been at sea for eight months, defying the critics who said a trimaran could not make it round the world with just one person on board to watch for brewing trouble. Technically, he had completed a circumnavigation. Now he was only two weeks from the finish line and a glorious homecoming that would probably change his life forever, whether or not he wanted it too.

It was a nice thought with which to go to sleep and get badly needed rest.

At midnight, Tetley woke up, unsure as to what had disturbed him. Then he heard a peculiar scraping noise. Immediately, he knew that the port bow must finally have succumbed and fallen off. Still in his bunk, he turned a light on. Water was flowing into the cabin without an obvious explanation as to why. He dashed up to the deck and strained into the darkness to see what had happened. Where there should have been boat there was nothing. The port bow had indeed broken off but that did not explain how water was getting into the entirely separate main hull. Tetley looked more closely. Instead of drifting off harmlessly, the broken bow had turned into a weapon. With a stroke of appalling bad luck, it had somehow pierced its way through the main hull's side.

Back inside the main cabin, the water had already

risen six inches. Tetley knew instantly, without thought or self-discussion, that his race was over. There was no time to think what a cruel blow this was, only two weeks from home after eight months at sea. It was like a marathon runner tripping up in the stadium, like a climber getting to within a hundred metres of the summit of Everest, yet there could no tears or regrets. The priority was survival, and there was precious little time to ensure its success.

Tetley reached straight for the radio and broadcast a Mayday. He grabbed the life raft and heaved it up onto the deck. Already wading in the cabin, he snatched his logbook and some warm clothes. By the time he was in the raft, *Victress* was so swamped that her vigorous rolling had turned into slow-motion swaying, as if sedated by drugs. A line from the raft was snagged and Tetley was being pulled back to the sinking boat. He groped around in the darkness, crying out loud: 'Give over, Vicky, I have to leave you.' He cut the line and drifted off in the wind. *Victress*'s navigation light brightened suddenly, flickered and then went out.

The next morning, Tetley was spotted by the American Air Force. Later in the day, he was picked up by an Italian tanker on charter to British Petroleum and bound for Trinidad.

Eve was flown out of London's Heathrow airport by Music for Pleasure, ready for Nigel's arrival. As his tanker approached, she didn't wait for him to get ashore. She was taken out in a harbour pilot launch that manoeuvred alongside. Eve stood tall and proud on the foredeck of the launch and waved and shouted up to Nigel as photographers caught the moment. She caused considerable excitement, standing out among the soberly dressed men who surrounded her, as she leapt on board in her white mini-dress, shoulder bag and huge sunglasses. At first glance, Nigel thought she was wearing shorts. He had been at sea long enough for fashions and hem lines to change.

Nigel Tetley was stoically philosophical about the ending of his dream. If he was disappointed, he hid his feelings and instead talked of an increased respect for the sea and the mariners of old. He was more concerned about the trouble he was causing for those who had rescued him. He was yet to find out that there had been no need to risk everything by pushing *Victress*. He still had no inkling of the fact he had been racing against an opponent who was not what he seemed.

Donald Crowhurst heard about Tetley's sinking within a few days. In an instant, the strategy of coming second fastest was blown apart. It was inconceivable that he could lose two months in order to be slower than Knox-Johnston.

Crowhurst reacted oddly. He slowed down, but not with any apparent purpose or mission. He simply let the boat sail itself. Much of his time was spent obsessively trying to repair his radio which was now receiving but not transmitting. In the tropical heat, he sat naked, working on the electronics for 16 hours a day. He listened to BBC Test Match commentaries, and he made more tape recordings of his own, that appeared to be for eventual public consumption. Crowhurst was losing track of time. He was sailing slowly and was heading to the north west, but he appeared not to care.

Towards the end of June, he opted out. On 23 June,

Crowhurst took his last noon sight of the sun and from then onwards gave up on all navigation.

The next day, becalmed in the weed-strewn area known as the Sargasso Sea in the middle of the North Atlantic, he began writing a long, 25,000-word message to the world, sensing that he had only seven days to commit it to paper. He wrote a title: *Philosophy*.

He had a great theory that minds like his own were so advanced that they were free of normal physical restraints. He used a mathematical equation to prove that the need for physical existence was superfluous.

Tomalin and Hall described Crowhurst as scarcely sane when he started his writing, saying he lost control with each page until the end, when he was totally out of touch with reality.

Crowhurst was conjuring a way out of the impossible situation he had built for himself over the previous eight months. He argued man had evolved to a state where his mind could escape from his body. In other words, Crowhurst could free his own mind from his physical existence and float away.

He believed his theory was a momentous discovery in the history of time. He regarded it as comparable with the work of Einstein and it was he, Donald Crowhurst, who was writing it down for the world to see.

He wrote that he was the only man on earth who realised he could turn himself into a cosmic being, by his own intelligent efforts, but he had to get on with it before he died. It was as though he was beginning to see himself as a god.

Day after day, night after night, Crowhurst continued with his *Philosophy*. Such was his lack of awareness in all around him that towards the end of this disturbing week his clock had run down to a standstill and he not only had difficulty calculating the time, but also the date.

He eventually established it was 1 July and 10 am. He began the final phase of his writing. He created a margin on the left-hand side of his remaining pages where, as he set down each thought in the form of a list, he updated the time right down to the precise second. It was obvious that he was now on some sort of countdown.

His text was at times incomprehensible but it was building to a confession which came after more than half an hour of a tortured process in which he was still writing of God and cosmic beings. He wrote:

> Now is revealed the true
> nature and purpose and power
> of the game offence I am.
> I am what I am and I
> see the nature of my offence
>
> I will only resign this game
> if you will agree that of
> the next occasion that this
> game is played it will be
> played according to the
> rules that are devised by
> my great god who has
> revealed at last to his son
> not only the exact nature
> of the reason for games but
> has also revealed the truth of

the way of the ending of the
next game that
　　It is finished –
　　It is finished
IT IS THE MERCY

The precise timings in the left-hand margin became slightly confused during this passage but it was started just before 10.30 am and presumably, based on the previous rate, was finished within ten minutes or so. What happened during the next half hour will never be known. Tomalin and Hall speculated that Crowhurst waited in resigned agony, preparing himself for death and the cosmic explosion. If Crowhurst had finished writing, he changed his mind. He wrote 11 15 00 in the margin and committed his final, disjointed words to paper. This time, his countdown was given a final deadline:

11 15 00　It is the end of my
　　　　　my game the truth
　　　　　has been revealed and it will
　　　　　be done as my family require me
　　　　　to do it
11 17 00　It is the time for your
　　　　　move to begin

　　　　　I have not need to prolong the game

　　　　　It has been a good game that
　　　　　must be ended at the
　　　　　I will play this game when
　　　　　I choose I will resign the
　　　　　game　11 20 40　There is
　　　　　no reason for harmful

These were his final words, scrawled erratically at the bottom of a page. There was no return to the logbook in which he was writing. Indeed, there were presumably only a couple of minutes to his bizarre resignation from the game, whatever that meant, at 11.20 and 40 seconds. Or perhaps that is the time the last line was written?

Nine days later, on 10 July, the crew of a ship called *Picardy*, en route to the Caribbean, came across *Teignmouth Electron* drifting in calm weather with just one small sail up. As the ship's captain sent a boarding party to investigate, a crew member took a photograph of this mysterious boat. There was no one on board.

The news reached London that same day and the result was a media storm. This was a modern-day *Mary Celeste* mystery. The story was out so quickly that no one had been able to warn Clare. A police squad car arrived at Woodlands, the family home near Bridgwater, only to discover that she was out walking the dog. The extended family was preparing for Donald's triumphant homecoming and Clare's sister answered the door to the police. When Clare did turn up and was told that the boat had been found and there was no sign of Donald, she refused to believe he was dead. However, the scene was already being set for the impending media siege. The squad car was parked in the drive and local nuns, who had heard a news report, turned up to offer their support.

10 : A HOUSE BESIEGED

At the age of 75, Clare Crowhurst sits surrounded by books, piled chaotically on shelves that take advantage of all available wall space. Lying part-read on the window sill is Stephen Fry's novel *The Liar*. She is happy in the company of books.

This grandmother of five has spent most of her adult life hiding from the intense curiosity in the family name. At the time of Donald's disappearance, she gave one media interview only. It was to the BBC and she did it because she felt contractually obliged to. She then closed the door on all journalists.

Sitting in her large, comfy reading chair, she appears strong and healthy but fidgets a little nervously and struggles to clear her throat: the nerves not helped by the presence of this journalist, and the voice not helped by the fumes from a huge old wood-burner fuelled, on this winter day, by chipboard salvaged from a boatyard by her youngest son, Roger.

Unlike Francoise Moitessier, Clare Crowhurst has never been able to move on. There has been no man in her life since the tragedy of the Golden Globe. As she puts it, she shut down sexually in order to protect herself from more unhappiness. For one who spent decades repelling requests to talk, she is now astonishingly candid.

She makes no effort to convince herself, or to pretend to others, that she has come to terms with what happened 40 years ago. She is not able, even now, to stop thinking of Donald. 'I think I have thought of him every single day for 40 years.' Without being asked why, she offers her own explanation with an assertiveness that is filled with heartache. 'It is the feeling of regret,' she says, slowly. 'I think people just don't get away from the feeling that they might have been able to do something and they didn't.' The regrets over that last night in Teignmouth at the end of October 1968, when Donald was perhaps seeking a way out, seem never to be far away.

During the months of the actual race, Clare had little time to worry. She was struggling to manage Donald's electronics business at the same time as running a large house and family. The business was proving too much and it slowly ground to a halt. She says she failed. Customers were not receiving their orders on time, so the orders stopped coming. She had more success with their four young children. They tracked their father's apparent progress by moving a pin on a *Sunday Times* wall map in their playroom at Woodlands. Each move was based on Rodney Hallworth's press releases from his Devon news agency. As the months went by, and the pin became too static to maintain interest, Roger began to have recurring nightmares that his dad's boat was sinking.

That day on 10 July 1969, when the nuns and the police joined forces to defend Woodlands, remains a vivid memory. It was Clare's introduction to the media's insatiable appetite for a huge story. 'There was a police sergeant in the front hall and he had taken control of the telephone,' she says. 'I remember thinking this is so odd. Everything was out of my hands, in the weirdest way. He was a very nice man and was being very helpful but the house had been taken over. It was weird.

'Everyone was out on the front lawn. I remember telling the children the boat had been found and that we were very worried about their dad. I said we were going to go to bed now. I just wanted them out of the way of the people on the lawn.'

Clare refused to believe Donald was dead. She drew comfort from the fact that no body had been found. There was, strictly speaking, no evidence of death. But what was a comfort to Clare was a cracking mystery to the public. The *Mary Celeste* photograph taken by a crew member on the *Picardy* gave this mystery an impetus. So too did an error in the *Sunday Times*. In the second-to-last paragraph of a two-page spread entitled '*The Last, Tragic Voyage of Donald Crowhurst*', they said his life jacket was missing. They were wrong. They were quick to correct what was an innocent mistake but the damage was done. The conspiracy theorists now had enough to go on, even though *Teignmouth Electron* was found 700 miles from land.

The theories were not the sole territory of those who see deceit in everything. The chairman of Teignmouth Council at the time Crowhurst sailed from the town, Arthur Bladon, told the press: 'There is still a nagging doubt in my mind about the whole business. It all reads like a fairy story. In the first place the yacht disappears. Then it turns up empty after there had been no question of despondency. The mystery of the missing life jacket remains.'

A former business associate of Crowhurst's, Duncan Campbell, went further. He said: 'I think Mr Crowhurst may well be alive on an island somewhere, or he could have been picked up by a foreign boat. It is even possible that the last signal was not sent from the yacht itself.' Campbell said Crowhurst was happily married and not the sort of person to part with life easily. 'None of us believes he can be dead. We have not seen the end of the story by a long chalk,' he said.

Small wonder that the months ahead brought reported sightings of Donald Crowhurst. He was 'seen' in the south west of England, South America and a caravan in Scotland. A washed-up bottle containing a message, saying he was stuck on an island, was found on a beach near Cherbourg in northern France. At least one Fleet Street journalist was sent to the Cape Verde Islands. The reported sightings continued for years. Indeed, the disappearance of the former British government minister John Stonehouse in 1974, who faked his suicide by leaving clothes on a beach, created the atmosphere for a fresh burst of over-imaginative 'sightings'. Some were mistakes, others were cruel hoaxes.

Clare still has a letter from the man who said he saw Donald in the Scottish caravan. 'It is from a chap apologising profusely, called Henderson I think. It was an incredibly long and apologetic letter. The chap said, "I really didn't want to hurt your family." I got the apology about three months after the article was printed.' Incredibly, she blames Rodney Hallworth for that particular hoax. 'I only heard the background of it all

from somebody else who knew Hallworth who told me
he was behind it all. Apparently the hoaxer got a girl
pregnant and wanted to tell the nation but it was going
to cost several hundred pounds. Hallworth said, "I'll
finance this story if you say you saw Donald
Crowhurst." Hallworth was definitely behind that story.

'When the story was published, I said let's be practical. How is a man supposed to come out of the sea and
suddenly purchase a caravan in Scotland?

'There were mountains of post at the time. People
really are marvellous. They wanted to communicate
sympathy. There was tremendous, genuine feeling of
sorrow that someone interesting like that had died. But
why they instantly felt he had died never seemed clear to
me, because I thought there were lots of other alterna-
tives, but they must have been right.

'Certainly for years I thought he could have survived.
But I couldn't accept the fact that he would have
survived and not come back and certainly not want to
be with his children. He absolutely adored his kids. The
possibility that he would have stayed away deliberately
you couldn't entertain.

'Your mind chases itself round in circles. I had time to
think a lot. The children were at school … Now, I think
he definitely died at the time. But how he died? I find it
impossible, knowing the person, to believe that he
committed suicide. I still find that impossible to believe.'

The enduring fascination in the Donald Crowhurst
story meant Clare and her children could not escape
from it and get on with their lives. Woodlands was a
large house surrounded by trees and bushes. It became
a difficult place to be.

'The place was full of journalists and that appalled me,' says Clare with considerable force. 'The situation was totally out of control. They were coming through the drawing room windows. Some of them even tried to come through the bedroom windows. There was a feeling that Donald was in the house. Because the house was large, they felt that he was there. One night I was drawing the curtains, I don't think it was more than a week after the boat was found, and something made me pull them back again and there were two journalists in the garden.

'This was a quarter of a mile from the main road. It was dark down there. There were no lights. It must have been quite scary for them, actually. We had a particularly vicious goose. It's a pity it didn't do its job,' she says, able to smile about it now.

'I remember one journalist actually saying to me, "We don't like being lied to, he's living here isn't he?" You just shut the door on them.

'I became so odd about the way I dealt with them when it was still going on a considerable time later. There was a big greenhouse where I grew a lot of vegetables and very often I would be up there when journalists would arrive, see me in the greenhouse, and start chatting and asking questions. I would slowly manoeuvre myself down to the house, in the front door and then close it. There was no way of closing them out of the greenhouse.' She laughs as the memories of how farcical it all was come flooding back, but it is painfully obvious that it was not a laughing matter at the time.

'This went on for years afterwards, literally years. They would approach the children,' she says with some disgust. 'I must admit that I felt really hounded for years. It wasn't me they were interested in. No, they were convinced Donald was living in Woodlands. There is no doubt about that.'

The 10 July discovery of *Teignmouth Electron* without Donald on board was shocking enough, but it took almost two weeks for the true story of his voyage to come out. Everyone, including the *Sunday Times*, Rodney Hallworth and Clare, still thought he had at least sailed round the world. Three days after the boat was found, the *Sunday Times* launched a 'Donald Crowhurst Appeal Fund' for the family, starting it off with a £5,000 donation from the paper. Robin Knox-Johnston was widely praised for insisting on giving the £5,000 he had won for having completed the fastest, as well as the first, voyage.

Bizarrely, *Teignmouth Electron* was on the way to the Caribbean, the crew of *Picardy* having used an on-board crane to lift the boat onto its deck. Hallworth quickly went to London to sell the exclusive rights to the logbooks – which he arguably had no right to do – on the assumption they would tell the story of a great adventure around the world. Clare had no idea that that was what he was doing.

The *Sunday Times* was the highest bidder. With no time to lose, Hallworth and the paper's Nick Tomalin and a photographer jumped on a plane. They arrived in time to be waiting on the dockside at Santo Domingo in the Dominican Republic to meet the *Picardy* on 16 July.

Hallworth was immediately taken aside by the captain, who had read the logbooks. The captain persuaded him to rip out, for the sake of the Crowhurst family, the pages that suggested suicide.

Only the next day, on reading the logbooks more fully, did the team suspect that Crowhurst had never even left the Atlantic. That changed everything, and Hallworth owned up to the missing pages. The team flew back to London for an urgent editorial conference.

Craig Rich, the navigational advisor, received a phone call directly from the paper's editor, Harold Evans, asking him to come in immediately. Rich remembers the moment well. 'I was ushered into his office with a legal person, Ron Hall and Nick Tomalin. Nick was unshaven and had come straight off the plane with the logbooks.

'Harold Evans turned to me and said, "There are the logbooks, there's an office, go through them and, as soon as you can, confirm he hasn't gone round." I said I knew he hadn't gone round. He said, "Tell me that the logbooks support what you are saying." Twenty minutes it took me. He never went into an easterly longitude. It was simple. I could tell he hadn't gone round and I had a rough idea where he had gone just by glancing at the latitudes and longitudes.

'Then Harold Evans said a strange thing. He looked at me and said, very slowly, if we didn't disclose this, did I think people would find out? I said, "Christ, you want me to say absolutely nothing about this for the rest of my life?" He said that was what it would amount to.

'I think he either wanted to protect the family or he thought it might reflect very badly on the *Sunday Times*, encouraging the guy to go to sea for the money.

'It was left as "Thanks for your comments," and once they had decided what to do they would be in touch. I went home and didn't even tell my wife because Harold Evans asked me not to!

'Ron Hall called me the next day and asked if I could spare a week or so. They sat on it for ten days and in that time they got me up there and I extracted latitude and longitude for every day as quickly as I could over a couple of days. From that I did a very basic version of his actual route. Nick and I were together in an office working alongside each other, although I never realised what a great story it was. They kept it absolutely quiet until they were ready to make a statement and hold a press conference.'

During those ten days, Clare Crowhurst had a highly emotional time. It was Hallworth who broke the news to her that Donald had not left the Atlantic and that he was suspected of committing suicide. He did it in such a clumsy, bulldog manner that she has never been able to forgive him.

Hallworth and Clare always had a strained relationship. Much of it was personal and, even though he has long since passed away, still is. 'Rodney Hallworth and I had this animosity which had existed right from the beginning. As soon as we met up he used to say, "Kiss." I hated being kissed by Hallworth, I must admit. I think it built up from there.' She laughs at how petty that might sound now. 'In some ways he was a funny man. Looking now at old pictures of him I'm surprised he doesn't look bigger. I thought he was gigantic. But I was much smaller then. Roger used to take the mickey by stuffing cushions up his jumper. He'd put on a deep voice and say, 'I'm Rodney Hallworth,' and he'd struggle through a door. He seemed absolutely gigantic then.'

It is difficult to tell if Clare is being sidetracked by memories tumbling back or if she is deliberately changing the subject, to avoid reliving the moment

Hallworth blundered into the house, blurting out the news from the logbooks.

'Even now I don't like talking about it. It was such an incredibly cruel thing to do. He was tactless, more than tactless, he was cruel. But I suppose it is silly to expect more.

'The solicitor was already beginning to ask questions about how the *Sunday Times* knew more than we did. I had completely forgotten about the logbooks. It never occurred to me that someone would go down, get them and sell them. I was beginning to absorb this as well as all the rest of what was going on. I knew they existed because I bought them in the first place.

'It is just the feeling that there was this powerful man, there was this family, and he was just so incredibly cruel. Basically that's it.

'I think most people think I don't like talking about it because of the religious aspects of suicide, but I don't think so. I truly don't feel that anyone should have to continue living if they really feel that life is awful. I certainly would not have any strong feelings about ending my life if I didn't have children who would suffer if I walked out of it now. I was brought up a Catholic but I have absolutely no feeling for religion and I truly feel that if your life is impossible you should be able to just walk out of it, so it isn't that. I don't think there is anything to come after. I think this is it. What you see is what you get.

'It was basically boiled-up anger. In fairness to Rodney, he took the whole brunt.'

No one saw how Donald Crowhurst died, or how he came to be separated from *Teignmouth Electron*. However, the 25,000-word *Philosophy* and the countdown to, 'I will resign the game,' obviously point to Crowhurst stepping off the boat. Tomalin and Hall went as far as describing what he probably did in the final two minutes to what they regarded as a deadline, 11.20 am and 40 seconds. They pointed out his chronometer was missing. They believed he timed his every move as he sorted his papers in the cabin, ready for discovery, and then climbed up to the stern to jump into the sea along with the chronometer and a fourth logbook that they believed was a totally false record of the faked voyage. The papers he left behind were enough to tell the true story.

It is fair to say that Tomalin and Hall's book, commissioned by Harold Evans and backed by the full resources of the *Sunday Times*, was so comprehensive that everything that has since been written or filmed about the Crowhurst story has been at least influenced by it. That, for Clare, is at the heart of the problem in people understanding her views today. Thanks to Tomalin and Hall, it is well known that Donald Crowhurst had a strange childhood, was a young maverick, became a slightly batty inventor, was a social climber, an accident-prone weekend sailor and an all-round underachiever who took on an almighty challenge that he was not up to. Everything written about him since, including this book, effortlessly paints at least part of that picture, but on what evidence? Clare Crowhurst does not recognise this man. It all comes back to Tomalin and Hall's book.

She despised *The Strange Voyage of Donald Crowhurst* and has taken decades to accept its value. 'I really hate the *Sunday Times* book,' she says, defiantly.

'I read the manuscript once, well, the first night when

Nick Tomalin brought it down. I stayed up all night reading it when the children were in bed. I thought, "This is absolutely horrendous." The whole thing was done very badly, I think. When Nick Tomalin came round the next morning I said I had burned it. He said, "That's no good, we've got another copy." Of course I knew he would have another copy but I thought I couldn't resist the chance to shock him.' She laughs loudly at the memory of her indignation.

The authors wrote that publication was approved by Clare Crowhurst, whom they described as the heroine in the story. 'They muddled that together,' she says. 'My solicitor was making all sorts of threats. It was all too late because Hallworth had sold the logbooks to them. He had no right to go down there, because I had already said to him, "Donald needed a press agent, I don't." [She had already dispensed with his services.] But he went off down, saying nothing to me. He got the logbooks and sold them to the *Sunday Times* and tried to keep quiet about the whole deal. But of course my solicitor was on to what had happened. He had to go through a very lengthy argument with their solicitors to get any money back for me. But there it is.'

Clare was so outraged by the book that she wrote a stinging and highly critical letter to the *Times* shortly before it was due out on the bookshelves. The letter was published on 10 July 1970, coincidentally a year to the day after the empty *Teignmouth Electron* was found. In it, she placed on record that she did not have the power to stop the book, and she accused the authors of smearing her husband's character. She wrote: 'Nicholas Tomalin said on the radio that he got to know Donald better than his own wife, but I feel that this was not the true Donald he got to know but a shadowy image that was moulded to fit into his theory that all heroes are neurotics. They are not. I have written this solely to preserve what I consider to be the true character of my husband so that in the years to come my children and my friends will not be able to reproach me for letting this book be published without any word of protest. Having done this, I would ask that I may be permitted to sink into anonymity and be free from the glare of publicity which controversy sometimes brings.'

The plea for anonymity was wishful thinking. However, Clare's greatest concern was the legacy of the book and the effect on her family.

Speaking now, she says: 'I would definitely have done anything at that stage to stop the book. I thought it was going to be disastrous for the children. They were so young. I thought it was very unfair to do that book at that time, in that way.

'There was a copy around the house for a while. But my mother-in-law asked to borrow it and I never got it back and I never bought another copy.

'I think I am ambivalent about it now. Looking at it in a sort of abstract way, I can appreciate that it is a powerful book. You are a journalist and you write something which people are going to want to read, and it is basically true, let's face it. But you can put emphasis here and emphasis there. And you can change a scene. A change of an adjective can make a huge difference. I accept it happened.'

The night reading the manuscript in bed was truly shocking. It was the first time that Clare saw much of the detail of what had happened. She was reading the story of the gradual demise, and descent into madness, of the man she loved.

Craig Rich recalls how painful it was even for him, a dispassionate observer, to read the logbooks and, in particular, the 25,000-word *Philosophy*. He says: 'I found going through the logbooks to be a tremendously emotional experience. I was there for six weeks doing all the calculations down to the nth degree. It was very emotional and it is something which has lived with me all this time.

'I'm a seafarer and this guy was on his own. I was living with it in a way. Originally, when I was doing the calculations on whether this guy was a crook or not, I had no personal knowledge of the man. I'd never met him. But then I read the logbooks properly. I was getting the impression of what he was like. I was reading the words of a dead man who probably committed suicide and I could see that he was deranged. I was only 29. To a large extent, sailors are simple people. They've led fairly sheltered lives. I had not been exposed to that sort of thing: someone going mad. I found it quite shocking. I felt it was a bit like intruding into somebody's life because he had poured it all out, you know. I found it quite uncomfortable, quite an emotional thing.'

Any reader of Crowhurst's logbooks did not need to be young and sheltered in order to be shocked. The *Sunday Times* journalists were as baffled by the mental aspects of the story as they were by the concepts of latitude and longitude. They were soon joined in their office by a psychiatrist from the Department of Mental Health at the University of Bristol. He was Dr Glin Bennet and he was there to help them understand what was happening to Crowhurst as the months passed by at sea.

Bennet had a fair amount in common with Crowhurst, aside from being the same age and having a young family. Not only did he sail, but his boat was a multihull and he kept it at Exmouth in Devon, five miles along the coast from Teignmouth. Bennet was gripped by the Crowhurst story the day it was revealed in the *Sunday Times*, and he quickly contacted Nick Tomalin, offering to help decipher the many cryptic comments in the logbooks.

Now, still living in Bristol at the age of 80, he admits that the story took hold of him. His third child was born the day before it broke, but he says he felt he had to find out what had happened to the man at the centre of this great mystery.

After helping the *Sunday Times*, Bennet was in a unique position to write a paper for the *British Journal of Medical Psychology*. His obsession with the story stretched to calling on Clare Crowhurst at Woodlands, a fact which to this day Clare remembers with some irritation.

She says: 'I had a real row with Glin Bennet at one stage because he was dropping into Woodlands, just chattering away. I didn't realise he was writing a paper on it. I was absolutely livid. I said, "I don't want to see you any more." So I didn't see him again after that.' Clare laughs as she complains that Bennet still has her leather briefcase.

Bennet's interest in the Crowhurst story survives to this day, and it can be easily explained. Indeed, an opening remark in that paper, published in 1974, says it all: 'It is perhaps the most completely documented account of a psychological breakdown … This was a breakdown on a heroic scale with the Atlantic Ocean as the arena. The steps towards the final disintegration proceed with the remorselessness of a Greek tragedy …'

Speaking now, Bennet is reluctant to over-complicate the diagnosis. He says: 'I don't think he was paranoid. I still don't know where I would put him. His judgement was impaired in a state of high anxiety and fear.

'The log was classic psychotic writing, psychotic as in losing grip but not with a paranoid element.

'His judgement was clouded after the issues of the first few weeks. He was adversely affected by stress, although we didn't use the term stress so much then. After pretending to round the Horn, the whole thing moves from just being out of his depth to classical tragedy.

'He went mad. He felt he had the power to create God. At that point there was little difference between living and dying.'

Bennet, as a sailor himself, was conscious at the time that he thought Crowhurst had damaged the sport's reputation.

'I am more sympathetic towards him now,' he says. 'He was an ordinary chap who had got ideas beyond his capabilities. He was hooked into a fantasy. He wandered into the world of heroes and failed. He couldn't bridge the gap between fantasy and reality.

'I felt very much for Clare. She had a terrible time. She was totally unprepared for this sort of thing.'

It was not to get any easier for Clare Crowhurst and her young family, and they were just part of the Golden Globe fallout.

11 : SINKING FEELINGS

Life for Nigel Tetley was strange after his Mayday sinking so close to home. He had come within a whisker of eclipsing Robin Knox-Johnston and being hailed as the new Sir Francis Chichester, yet now he was back to where he started: a man in his mid forties retired from the Royal Navy.

There was a brief flurry of media activity when he and Eve arrived back in the United Kingdom from the West Indies, two weeks after he abandoned ship. Nigel held a press conference and was photographed on the roof of London's Carlton Towers Hotel, flanked by none other than Knox-Johnston and Chichester. The two great men were showing their recognition of Tetley's achievement in getting as far as he did. It was a point lost on the press. The simple, undeniable fact was that two of the men on the roof had finished their voyages and the one in the middle had not.

The *Guardian* newspaper was typical in running only a brief article, placed as far back as page 13. It was headlined '*Sinking feelings*'. The introduction was brutal, saying one thing had become clear: there was one club for people who had sailed round the world and another for those who had not. While Knox-Johnston and Chichester had been feted as heroes who had won money and fame, the paper pointed out that all Tetley would get was a painting of his boat.

He was quoted as saying he had sunk because he pulled out all the stops after hearing Crowhurst was still in the race. 'You have to face your own thoughts,' he said. 'It was a very deep experience ... I have no real feeling of having failed or having dipped out in any way.'

And that was that.

It was, by anyone's calculation, an anticlimactic end to what had started out as the dream of a lifetime.

If the return to normal life was a sad one, it was to become far worse. It was to end in a terrible tragedy which no one saw coming.

Initially, Nigel and Eve Tetley picked up where they left off. The Golden Globe race had separated them for almost a year. It had felt an eternity for a couple who had lived together as husband and wife for only two years and had known each other for only one whirlwind month before that. They now had each other back but their only home, *Victress*, was gone.

The priority was to have a new boat built. The sketch of a 60-foot trimaran which Nigel had drawn at sea as he dreamed of the future, prophetically just weeks before sinking, needed to be turned into reality. Money was tight but there was an unexpected boost when the *Sunday Times* awarded a £1,000 consolation prize for coming so close to finishing.

Work began at a boatyard in Sandwich in Kent, north

east of Dover. It was a tortuous 300-mile drive from Plymouth, so Eve resigned her job and, during the following two years while the boat was being built, she taught at a succession of schools never more than 30 miles from the boatyard, in Folkestone, Deal and Sandwich. Together they wrote Nigel's book *Trimaran Solo*. Eve typed the manuscript and helped with the maps and drawings. She wrote an appendix outlining the lists of food and how she approached the issue of stores for a long voyage. However, *Trimaran Solo* was the driest of all the books published and was not a commercial success.

The new boat was called *Miss Vicky*: the pet name they had used for *Victress* and which Nigel had raised a glass to as he turned her into a floating colander. Now a name from the past was taking them into the future.

In the latter stages of building, Nigel and Eve were able to move on board and moor in the River Stour at Sandwich. They were getting back to the lifestyle that had made them so happy before the race. Nigel was seeking sponsorship for a transatlantic race that would take the boat geographically closer to their dream of Caribbean chartering.

There were moments when Nigel enjoyed some recognition for his Golden Globe voyage but they were few and far between, and they possibly caused more harm than good. He was invited by the Royal Navy to give a lecture at HMS *Sultan*, an engineering shore base in Gosport, on the west side of Portsmouth harbour. Robin Knox-Johnston went along to listen, as did the Portsmouth greengrocer, Alec Rose, who sailed after Chichester and finished a round-the-world voyage just as the Golden Globe was starting. Rose, like Chichester, stopped in Australia. He also stopped in New Zealand. Rose's voyage was remarkable but Tetley had arguably achieved more by not stopping for repairs. Yet it was Rose who was knighted the day after he arrived home.

At the lecture, something happened which would have left Tetley in no doubt that the division between success and failure was cruelly unsubtle. It was a minor moment, insignificant to most, but it was spotted by Knox-Johnston. He describes it 40 years on: 'The place was full of commanders' wives. After Nigel finished speaking, they all got up and he was just cast aside as they tried to get to "dear *Sir* Alec".

'I saw the hurt on his face so I went up to chat to him. That was how we got to know each other. We had hardly met at that stage. I wonder how much of that he put up with. How much more of that, "Yes, but you didn't succeed." It was a very remarkable voyage and he never really got the credit for it.'

No one will ever know to what extent Nigel Tetley was affected by the public's failure to see beyond his voyage in absolute win-or-lose terms.

One Wednesday in February 1972, he failed to come back to *Miss Vicky* on the River Stour. He had been at the boatyard as usual that morning. A friend said he had received a letter from a national company turning him down for sponsorship.

Eve had an appalling two days in which there was no word from Nigel, and little clue as to his whereabouts. His bicycle was found outside the local railway station, adding to the mystery and to Eve's distress.

On the Saturday, 5 February, a sixteen-year-old boy was walking in woods near his home in Ewell Minnis in the countryside outside Dover, 15 miles from Sandwich. He came across the body of Nigel hanging from a tree.

The news was broken to Eve.

The Dover coroner and the police set about trying to build a picture of Nigel's last few days, appealing through the media for information from anyone who might have seen him.

The *Dover Express*, under the headline, '*Police probe last hours of man who sailed to fame*', printed a description: five feet ten inches tall, a full beard, wearing a blue windcheater and corduroy trousers, yachtsman-type half-length Wellington boots and carrying a blue-and-white bag. The paper added that he might have been wearing a Cossack-style fur hat which had been in the bag.

In death, Nigel Tetley's Golden Globe voyage did suddenly make the national newspapers for the first time since the brief mentions of his homecoming press conference. The *Guardian* now put him on the front page with the headline, '*Sailor dead*'. The *Daily Mirror* said: '*World-race sailor Nigel found hanged*' and the *Daily Telegraph* said: '*Solo world yachtsman found dead*'. The *Telegraph* reported that a friend, who was not identified, said he had been depressed and that the final blow came in the sponsorship rejection on the morning he disappeared.

It looked as if Nigel had committed suicide. The logical assumption was that the inability to attract new sponsorship was part of an overall sense of failure. It seemed as if, for all the stiff-upper-lip stoicism, Nigel

Tetley had not truly got over his desperately bad luck in sinking so close to home. Perhaps the subsequent revelation of Crowhurst's cheating, and the realisation that he had not needed to push his boat so hard, compounded the misery.

It was not that simple. There was no suicide note and, at the inquest in Dover three weeks after Nigel's body was found, it was revealed that there was a sexual nature to his hanging. Eve was at the inquest and it was in this public forum that she learned the shocking news for the first time. Sitting in front of the press and public, she suddenly and completely unexpectedly realised the inquest was discussing what Nigel had been wearing.

The police revealed he had taken some of his regular clothes off and placed them at the foot of the tree. A constable then listed a variety of women's underclothes Nigel had put on: a white suspender belt and stockings, and a corset over his head like a hood. He had tied his wrists behind his back. A pathologist suggested Nigel had died during a masochistic sexual exercise.

It was a phenomenal shock to Eve. She simply had not been prepared for what she was hearing. She had been distraught during the days Nigel was missing and was then overcome with grief when his body was found. For Eve, simply the loss of the man she loved had been too much to cope with. Now, from nowhere, there was another, unfathomable dimension.

It was all far too much for Eve to absorb. She told the inquest: 'All this about stockings and things is incomprehensible to me.'

The coroner said the evidence did not point to suicide. He recorded an open verdict.

The story was back in the papers, local and national, and this time the coverage was dominated by the lurid details of precisely how Nigel had dressed up.

It was an atrocious backdrop to his funeral, but there were many supporters who were determined not to let their friend down. Robin Knox-Johnston and Chay Blyth were among the mourners at a crematorium outside Dover. A Royal Navy chaplain conducted a service with special naval prayers as Eve rested a simple spray of freesias on the white ensign covering her husband's coffin. The workers from the boatyard left a blue-and-white floral tribute in the shape of an anchor.

Philip and Mark, the teenage sons from Nigel's first marriage, were there. Eve had got to know them well during school holidays when they lived with her while Nigel was at sea. That day at the end of February 1972 was the last time Eve saw them.

It is difficult to imagine a more abysmal end to what had started only four years earlier as such a wonderful love story and true-life adventure.

In the following years, the finer points of a coroner's open verdict were lost on the public. The notion of suicide was easier to understand than masochism. It stubbornly remained the public's preferred theory, to the extent that it became common currency.

Decades on, the death of Nigel Tetley is still written about in books, magazines and on the internet as suicide. Even in whispered conversations based on the embarrassing details made public in 1972, an assumption is often made that Nigel Tetley killed himself. It is an assumption based on neither the evidence or the coroner's verdict.

It is easy to see why Eve retreated to Alderney, the most northern of the Channel Islands. At just five by three kilometres, it is smaller and more down to earth than its higher-profile neighbours Guernsey and Jersey. Ferry services are infrequent. The airport is little more than a field with a small, 1960s, prefabricated building complete with a 'knit-while-you-wait' box for passengers to make squares for charity blankets. Everything about the island appealed to Eve. She especially liked the idea of its tiny population of just two-and-a-half thousand.

Eve has lived here for 30 years. She says, only half-joking, that it has been her hiding place, her sanctuary.

The people on the island rarely ask her about the Golden Globe. Everyone knows and regularly sees each other, as they almost all live in the island's one town, St Anne. In spite of this, or perhaps because of it, there is genuine respect for each other's privacy. So Eve is able to enjoy living in a Victorian cottage she has rented for 17 years, off one of the narrow cobbled streets that lead to the town's old cattle market at Marais Square.

Her avoidance of the past goes only so far. She has reread *Trimaran Solo* perhaps 30 times. The book is close to hand now.

'For a while I was reading it once a year, or thereabouts,' she says. 'This was the time I didn't like talking about it. I didn't mind having a quiet read to myself. It was all right because the book is about the happy bit and doesn't include the unhappy bit. So that was all right.

'My life with Nigel was only four years, which isn't very long, is it? It was – what's that awful phrase? – quality time. It ended so abysmally awfully. That is why it is too painful. Something so good to have ended so badly is just awful.'

Now she has come to the conclusion that, at the age of 68, it is probably good for her to talk, although there is an unnerving sense of experimentation in this decision.

The time during the race was not as exciting and glamorous as might be expected.

Indeed, it was surprisingly normal. Eve carried on teaching in Plymouth and looking after Philip and Mark. She got most of her information on the race by walking to the local newsagent every weekend to buy the *Sunday Times*, just like everyone else. Occasionally, she would get a phone call from the paper to tell her of a radio message from Nigel. It was all considerably more dull than even close family had expected.

Nigel's mother insisted on visiting during the Christmas when he was at sea. It was a visit that Eve saw as more of an inspection. 'I think she thought I was leading a vicariously glamorous life as the wife of a famous husband,' says Eve, giggling at the thought. 'She seemed bitterly disappointed that we weren't. I had the impression that she didn't like me much, I'm afraid. Maybe she thought I was a bit common, coming from the north of England and being a schoolteacher ... I may have misjudged her completely,' she adds unconvincingly.

That same Christmas produced one of the most heart-rending moments for Eve – the photograph of Nigel eating a grand dinner all on his own, deep in the

Southern Ocean. It was the picture in which Nigel had held up the tankard Eve had left on board as a Christmas present. 'I thought it was very sad,' she says. 'He had done his best but it is always so sad to see someone having made an effort for Christmas and they are all by themselves, whether in a boat or a house or flat. You open your presents, drink your champagne and that's it.

'I remember seeing the picture and thinking, "That beard!" He was clean-shaven when he left me. I just thought, "Oh, poor Nigel, all by himself," which of course he had been for months but it made it come very close. Poor soul, he's all by himself, trying to be cheerful. Look at that smile. What a beautiful man.'

Eve uses every opportunity to praise Nigel, as if countering his airbrushing from the race's history. All these years on, she has immense pride in Nigel's achievement and especially the style he displayed in keeping *Victress* going when taking on potentially disastrous quantities of water. Far from being unnerved by the memory of his drilling holes to let the water out as well as in, she speaks with the delight of an excited teenager: 'Isn't it wonderful? There's a man who knows what he is doing. How crazy. How crazy can you get?'

It all went wrong, of course. Nigel's attempt to be the fastest round the world failed. In the following months, as the truth about Donald Crowhurst's story unfolded, Eve became angry that her husband's dream had been snatched away because someone had been cheating. Nigel was upset too, but in a very different way. He had more sympathy for Crowhurst.

Eve reveals that Nigel began to avoid the subject of

Crowhurst because he realised it made her so angry. She makes no secret of the fact that her anger has barely subsided in all these years.

'Had it not been for Crowhurst, Nigel would have plodded home cheerfully,' she says. 'He certainly wouldn't have bust her up as he did. He would have chortled home gently ... He didn't want to lose to someone in a similar boat. Crowhurst is why he sank. The fact that it was caused by someone cheating ... that is horrid.

'What was the rhyme we were told when we were kids: "Tangled web we weave when once we practise to deceive"? The first lie led to all the rest.

'Nigel was very upset about the Crowhurst end, very upset. I think he probably felt, "There but for the grace of God I could have gone." It wasn't so much the cheating but the going bonkers, the effect of the solitude ... I just think he was so sympathetic to Crowhurst's predicament. Perhaps sympathetic is not the right word, but understanding. I had no time for that.

'He didn't like talking about Crowhurst at all. Really, really didn't at all. He didn't like the fact that I hated Crowhurst so much. Hate, hate, hate. We didn't talk about it much, once he realised.'

Eve laughs loudly, almost as if she realises her anger of days gone by is as sharp as ever. Under her breath, she utters an expletive to describe Crowhurst, and then she smiles.

Her life would have been very different if Nigel had not sunk. His voyage would have been the fastest and he would have returned home a hero, perhaps eclipsing Knox-Johnston as a public figure. A knighthood would have been inevitable and 'Sir Nigel Tetley' and 'Lady Tetley' would have been the darlings of the world of sailing, much as Sir Robin Knox-Johnston became.

Eve has no time for such rumination. She laughs at the notion of 'Lady Tetley'.

The trauma of Nigel's very public death left Eve simply having to get on with life. The new, unfinished trimaran, *Miss Vicky*, was still her home but she did not want to stay in the Dover area. Once again, the young Robin Knox-Johnston came to the rescue. He had astutely been harnessing his Golden Globe fame to carve out a career in the commercial world. He bought an old boatyard on the Solent's River Hamble, a mile downstream from where Blyth and Ridgway had prepared their boats four years earlier. By partnering with the Rank Organisation, he developed it into a new marina, Mercury Yacht Harbour. He offered Eve a berth for *Miss Vicky*. He was obliged to put it through the books to keep Rank's accountants happy but he charged only a nominal rent despite the boat being a huge 60 feet long and 32 feet wide.

For Eve, Robin Knox-Johnston was offering a lifeline. To this day she speaks of him in glowing terms. 'Robin told me I could live on board. Up until then that berth had not had water or electricity but Robin spoiled me rotten and had them laid on. I lived there and got a job teaching in the local school.

'He was just such a support. He always comes across exactly how he is, straightforward. 'Mr Straightman'. It's very easy to mock that. When he lived in Hamble he was a verger in the church, did all the right things and always wore the right clothes. He is that sort of person. I wouldn't dream of knocking him. He's such a lovely bloke.

'I haven't seen Robin for donkey's years but if I needed his support he would be here like a shot. I know he would. He is that sort of man. For all that it was a long time ago, I still regard him as my friend.'

Eve rebuilt her life during four years living at Robin's marina. In her mid 30s, she met and fell for an older man from New Zealand. The age gap of almost 20 years was much the same as with Nigel. This time, instead of a Royal Navy officer she had fallen for a former test pilot of RAF Vulcan bomber planes.

She was soon unintentionally pregnant with her son, John, who was to be her only child. John was only two months old when they motored across the English Channel to Alderney in a small cargo boat piled high with furniture. The boat was owned by none other than Robin Knox-Johnston, who was on board to help them.

When they tied up alongside the high concrete quay at Braye Harbour, the low tide meant there was a precipitous climb up a ladder to the top of the wall. 'I was holding John in a carry cot and I was looking up at this horrible bloody ladder,' says Eve, physically recoiling at the memory. 'I was saying, "Oh, my God," and "How do I get up that?" Robin just took the carry cot, put the handles between his teeth and shot up the ladder.' Eve laughs loudly at how, once again, the hero of the Golden Globe had come to the rescue.

That was the summer of 1977 and, after Eve returned briefly to collect *Miss Vicky*, she and Robin lost touch with each other.

Eve did not marry the father of her child and the relationship was short-lived. He returned to England. She stayed in Alderney with her young son but once again she was homeless. She had no money. However, she did still have Nigel's dream boat.

She moved back on board and tried to make ends meet by cleaning and gardening for islanders. She boosted her meagre income by selling the results of painting harbour views but it wasn't enough to pay for a mooring. Instead, she had to anchor out in the middle of Braye Harbour and trust that the anchor would hold firm. Islanders would watch with some bemusement as Eve struggled every day to row ashore in a rubber dinghy. The only surprise when she eventually gave up living on Nigel's boat two years later was that it had taken so long.

She has never sailed since but she does still paint and is a member of the Alderney Art Club.

To this day, Eve wonders to what extent Nigel was disappointed by the failure to finish his voyage and the lack of interest in his story. 'I am sure in his heart of hearts he must have been, but not overtly so,' she says. 'He would never let on because he was that generation of stiff upper lip. He would never ever let it show if he was disappointed. He never showed it to me.

'He didn't seem to be different after the race. He seemed to be as sane as ever. Yes. But no one can look inside someone's brain. I think that's why I love reading so much. I have always got something heavy on the go but I love a good novel because it is a little window into someone else's way of thinking, isn't it? Who has a window into someone else's mind? I don't think anyone has.'

The memories of Nigel's death are still terribly raw. Eve tells the story of him going missing as if it happened yesterday. Her desperate attempt to find out what was going on was in itself a traumatic experience. She went to their bank to see if Nigel had withdrawn any money. Despite sharing a joint account, they wouldn't tell her.

Eve's voice is full of exasperation, as if she is inside the bank now. 'I just left in tears. How could you not let me know? It is just as much my bank account as his. It's funny how little things like that create, um …' She falls silent, unable to finish her sentence.

'For many years after Nigel's death I couldn't even talk about it. I couldn't or wouldn't, for 15 or 20 years. I'd just, you know, well up and get really tearful.' Eve pauses and is visibly fighting back the tears now. But she insists on continuing, almost as if this is a hurdle she feels the need to get over. She tries again, several times, and on each occasion there is a frustrating, agonising struggle for words but she does not want to change the subject.

'I still get, a bit, you know. It just seems to me that Nigel's death is so unexplained, completely staggering. I was staggered. I knew nothing … Friends had just whipped me up and the first I knew of how he had died was at the inquest. Bloody hell. It was all so unlike Nigel.'

Eve's eloquence has deserted her. There are no words to explain how she felt then and how she feels now.

With hindsight, there had been a hint of what was to come at the inquest when the police visited the boat, but Eve had been in no state to pick up on it. 'One of the first questions a policeman asked me when it was established Nigel was dead was: "Are any of your clothes missing?" I thought what a funny question. I went into our cabin and he said, "What about underwear?" I had no idea why he was asking that.

'Well, in those days, because we weren't well off, I had one suspender belt and one pair of stockings which were still there. It wasn't a question of a whole drawer of things, and I have never worn a corset in my life. Where did all these bits come from? You can't hide anything in a boat. Where did they come from?

'There was a psychologist who was saying he was obviously doing it for kicks, for sexual amusement. I thought; hang yourself from a tree? Well, I don't know.'

Eve struggles to make sense of it all just as much as she did at the time. She says there were no problems in their relationship and regarded it as solid as before Nigel left to sail round the world. Regardless of the official verdict at the inquest, she sometimes wonders if perhaps Nigel did commit suicide, but she thinks not. 'He was too brave for that,' she says. 'I was so distressed at a youngster having found his body. He would never, ever, have inflicted a vision like that on some passer-by. However, if it was suicide then I begin to understand why the church sees it as such a sin because it puts so much on the people left behind. Such a load of "What did I do or not do?"

'What was he doing in Dover, for God's sake? We never lived in Dover. The Dover connection is just a mystery. The whole thing is a huge mystery.'

Even the passage of time has failed to clear up the questions and doubts in Eve's head. She speaks in a manner that suggests she has no confidence in ever finding answers.

Eve was painfully aware after the inquest of all the inevitable gossip triggered by the coverage in the newspapers, although no one spoke directly to her about it. She never got the chance to talk properly with Philip and Mark about their father's death. 'I have actually not seen them since the funeral,' she says. 'I don't know why. I suppose bad associations. I don't think they blame me. I don't think so, no.

'I think they went to their mother. Nothing since that day. Nothing. Again, it is hurtful, isn't it? These are the boys I looked after while their father was away.

'I haven't tried to contact them. I thought, well, if they don't want to know they don't want to know. I have not heard anything about them since the day of the funeral. I have no idea where they are.'

Eve's life had crashed in on itself and there was yet more grief to come. The publicity led to a shock she simply was not expecting. 'It was the next really, really hurtful thing,' she says. 'I went up after the funeral to my parents. My father met me at Durham station. He said, "I don't want you talking about Nigel's death. I don't want your mother upset."'

Eve is again visibly shaken. 'I wouldn't have minded if he had said I could talk to him about it, because as a policeman he was not going to be fussed by anything that had happened.'

There is an irony in Eve not being allowed to talk about Nigel's death at the time, and yet not wanting to talk about it for decades afterwards.

Time has not been a successful healer. In some

respects it has made matters worse. Eve has been irritated over the years by the Donald Crowhurst story overshadowing the efforts of her husband and the other men in the Golden Globe race. Without Nigel by her side to keep her emotions in check, her mood has not been helped by the money directed at Clare Crowhurst 40 years ago, and the sympathy over the years since. 'Poor Clare, people say, and yet she's in a bloody fine house. I'm thinking well, you know, how about having your home sunk beneath you and finishing up with a lot of nothing. Nobody ever said, "Poor Eve."'

In a state of agitation, she whispers sarcastically, "Poor Clare" again. She pauses to regain composure; realising decades of simmering resentment are getting the better of her. 'Anyway,' she says, taking a deep breath. 'Don't be nasty, Eve. Don't be a cow. Tut tut.' She laughs at her lack of self-control.

The truth is that Eve Tetley has so rarely had this conversation that she has been learning how to handle it as she has gone along.

Clare Crowhurst has battled for 40 years to keep the family's story out of the public eye. She has long since grown weary of invitations to co-operate, and almost always turns down any approach.

Yet, despite her rejections, there has been a remarkably long line of creative projects inspired by Donald's hoax: poems; British, French and Soviet Union films; several plays in the USA and Canada; an American opera; a Tacita Dean art installation short-listed for the Turner Prize; and songs by half a dozen rock bands.

The newspaper letter that Clare sent in 1970, lashing out at the *Sunday Times* book and pleading that she be permitted to 'sink into anonymity' can safely be regarded as having failed.

She wrote of the children in that same letter. At the time of the race, they were mercifully young; James was 11, Simon eight, Roger seven, and Rachel five. However, the relentless interest in their family name meant there was no escape as the years went by. Clare put all of her energy into trying to control events and guiding her children through the minefield of growing up with their father's story.

Of all the four children, Simon's upbringing was the most privileged. He won a scholarship to go to Millfield School in Somerset. It was Britain's most expensive public school, occupying a grand house originally owned by the Clark shoe family. Simon became a boarder just over a year after his father disappeared.

Clare was able to stay in Woodlands with James, Roger and Rachel only because of the *Sunday Times* appeal fund. After Max Bygraves and Arthur English starred in a celebrity concert for the fund, she asked for it to be closed down, saying there were more deserving causes. Knox-Johnston, who had donated his £5,000 prize before it was known Donald Crowhurst had faked his voyage, insisted that his money should stay in the fund for the sake of the children. Clare has always been grateful for Knox-Johnston's donation, regarding it as extraordinarily generous. The fund total, £15,000, was twice the value of Woodlands. Although it meant the family had a financial cushion, Clare took in lodgers and ran a bric-a-brac market stall to help make ends meet.

At the age of 48, Simon, now a research technician and father of two, sits in the large kitchen of his Victorian townhouse on Cambridge's inner ring road. On the old family-sized table he has placed a large package that he clearly intends to refer to later.

His father's story is never far away. The *Sunday Times* book that is so despised by his mother exists here in several languages, including Norwegian. One of the photographs of the wreck of *Teignmouth Electron* taken in the late 90s by Tacita Dean, for her Turner prize entry, is on a wall upstairs.

Sitting at the table, Simon is intrigued to hear that Eve Tetley has been talking about the race and her loss. He immediately wants to know more, and soon it becomes clear why. He has spent most of his life feeling guilty about Nigel Tetley's death.

'I still do,' he says. 'I feel awful about the extent to which my father was to blame for what happened with his circumnavigation. I would apologise abjectly to Eve or anybody else for what he did in that respect.

'I think Nigel Tetley deserved more credit for what he achieved. He had done so well in the race. That is what people forget. He had come so close to completing it.

'It is a pretty grim thing to be responsible for and I think my father would have felt awful about it when he realised the potential role. Up until that point, well, okay, he had actually done some things a lot of people would have condemned him for but he could always say it didn't hurt anybody. It was even just a joke. But after that, that would have brought it home to him that it wasn't a joke and what he had done had potentially lethal consequences for someone else. Being in a highly stressed frame of mind, anyway, I think that was what finally took my father over the edge.'

Simon is relieved to hear, for the first time, that an open verdict was recorded at the inquest into Tetley's death. He too has grown up with the misconception that it was officially suicide. However, always conscious of the manner in which people have simplified his own father's tragedy, he is immediately cautious. 'You can't disentangle one thread from another necessarily. In a way, people like stories to fit into templates they have in the back of their mind. That way they can pigeonhole it and forget it. But it is often more complex than that – multi-dimensional.'

There is nothing casual about Simon's use of language. He is deliberate and takes time to think, choosing his words carefully. There is a sense that it all comes from the dark days that hit his childhood home in July 1969. Recalling those days now, he can see the nuns who appeared at the top of the drive and he can see his mother only minutes later scooping him up to go to Roger's bedroom and sitting them both on the bed. 'She said the boat had been found and our father was not on it. Then she broke down in tears ... We didn't know he was dead. But I think from that point we knew something very serious had happened because of my mother's reaction. We were trying to tell ourselves he might be found.

'The search was called off pretty early on when they started looking at the logbooks. We couldn't understand that as children at all. We just thought why are they stopping looking? Of course, by now they had looked at the logbooks and come to the same conclusion most people do.'

In the year after his father's disappearance, Simon only once saw the logbooks in the study at Woodlands. It was little more than a glimpse and he failed to understand the true nature of their content. He went through his teens knowing that his father's voyage was fraudulent and that there was considerable public interest in the fact, but not knowing the depth of the story and what happened to his father's mind.

Clare was trying to protect her children and deal with the issue as best she could. Talk was far from banned, but it was conducted on a limited basis.

One aspect of the story that was not discussed in the family was the *Sunday Times* book. Simon says it still has not been and, indeed, he is surprised to learn that his mother was sent the manuscript and burned it the next day. To this day, he still occasionally learns of new twists and turns in the family story.

As a child, he knew a book was published but was too young to register its significance. His mother's refusal to keep a copy in the house meant he soon forgot it even existed. It was a convenient arrangement, and understandable that his mother should see it as shielding him and his brothers and sister from considerable pain. Within the covers of that piece of detective work lay the full horror, in agonising detail, of their father's awful breakdown.

However, it was inevitable the full story could not stay hidden forever. At some point, each child would come across *The Strange Voyage of Donald Crowhurst*. In Simon's case, it happened when he was 16 and the moment will live with him forever. It was the first day of the sixth form at Millfield and it happened in the school grounds in an old building, reminiscent of a log cabin. It was a library dedicated to history books, and one of the privileges of doing A-level history was that he was now allowed to use it.

Simon sits up at his kitchen table as he describes how he went into the library in search of a book on King John. 'I remember it vividly. It is the sort of thing which sears itself on your memory.

'The library was quite basic, really. It was completely lined with books and bound copies of historical journals. I went in and there, not on the top shelf but on the second shelf down, was this book: *The Strange Voyage of Donald Crowhurst*. The name jumped out at me. It was bound in white with the letters in black. Just as you can hear your name in a crowded room when someone says it, well, I just instantly saw it.

'It was like a little electric shock. The first thing I noticed was the quotation about schizophrenia [a mention dropped from later editions] at the beginning. It was like an adrenaline rush from the start.'

Simon, as a new sixth former, did not have borrowing rights at the library. He was a mild-mannered, polite and well-brought-up young man so it did not even occur to him to help himself to the book and smuggle it out. So bewildering was this discovery of the book that he did not want to draw attention by asking staff if the rules could be bent for what was obviously an exceptional case. So, here he was, heart racing, enquiring mind in overdrive, with the story of his father suddenly gushing out and becoming more complicated by the minute. Yet he had to break off from his frantic reading, put the book back on the shelf and go back to class.

His head was spinning. For days, the start of every lunch break, every tea break, signalled a rushed walk back to the odd cabin that was the library. He would quickly, but discreetly, reach up for the book, take up his position at a table and pick up where he had left off in the 269 pages that documented, and commented on, his father's story.

'I would just be in there continuously, reading it until I got to the end. No one knew what I was doing. There were other people there but they weren't interested in what I was doing. To them, I was just poring over a book. I was absolutely riveted. Things that people had said dropped into place. It wasn't as though I didn't know anything about it but it hadn't been formed into a kind of coherent narrative, whereas this book was doing that. I read fairly fast so it took only a few days, and then I read it again. I got to the end and started again. I had to go back to class each time with this turning in my mind, and through the night as well.'

Simon's discovery of the book that was in effect banned from home could have been an explosive moment in family circles. If ever one of the children was likely to confront their mother with demands for answers, this was surely the time. He chose to keep quiet. He told no one. He certainly did not phone home and tell his mother. Instead, he bottled it up inside and used his new-found information to try to make sense of it all. It is a quest that continues to this day.

Clare was unaware that he had seen the book until many years later, when Simon agreed to be interviewed by the *Daily Telegraph*. It was the late 1990s when the artist Tacita Dean focused, literally, on the wreck of

Teignmouth Electron, a project that interested Simon. He agreed to talk to several newspapers and he spoke about the possibility of his father committing suicide. No one in the family had talked publicly like this before. Clare was both shocked and angry. She had given the logbooks to Simon, who wanted to study them at home in Cambridge, and now she demanded their return.

Clare laughs as she tells the story of scolding her grown-up son, but she admits Simon's public comments created tension in the family; a tension that had perhaps been beneath the surface for 30 years.

She says: 'Simon is a little bit troubled. It bothers me. He was very keen that I start talking. He feels the whole thing has been too secretive. I was really just trying to protect the children, I think. I truly believe that is what I was trying to do but Simon feels it has all been treated too quietly.

'It's difficult isn't it? People have different approaches ... I think we have all learned to cope, but Simon's attitude is different from mine. There is no doubt about it. I appreciate that. There's no row but there has been a certain tension. I think his feeling is that everything should be available to journalists. They should read everything and everything should be wide open. I think why the hell should it be? Some things are private, but then I think back, and there was nothing in my parents' family that I felt I had ever to be secret about, so I try to think about it from Simon's point of view.

'He does feel very strongly that I kept too quiet about the ancillary aspects of the end of the race, but they were very small children and I didn't feel they were able to cope with the details.'

Clare's use of the phrase 'ancillary aspects' avoids spelling out her husband's demise, but she admits she is referring to what she describes as his madness and the faking of his voyage. She says she struggled with the questions of how and when to tell the children.

'I think in a way it is awfully difficult to say, "Today is the day I tell them." I think if the children asked me questions, I answered them. But of course they didn't know the questions to ask. I was completely clueless about that. I think I talked probably a bit more to James, the oldest boy. But there it is, you know. You get some things wrong with kids.

'I was very lucky in my childhood. I should have appreciated more how losing a father is for children because I had a really brilliant dad. There it is. There it is … I think, because Simon was away at school, he might have been a bit left out, actually, left out of the small talk at home.

'But I must admit I truly don't think I ever discussed the suicide aspect with them. That's probably terribly remiss of me. I have tremendous guilt problems.'

Clare talks as if she is punishing herself. Yet there is no manual on how to bring up a family with the unique background of the Crowhursts. As the children grew up, she put a great deal of energy into fighting off media attention. She made such an almighty fuss about BBC plans to repeat a programme featuring Donald, that several executives visited the house. She complained it would be a disaster for one of her sons who was due to sit exams. To her amazement, they agreed to drop the programme. It was a rare victory.

Clare has found her own ways of escaping from the

attention. As the children reached their late teens, she travelled alone, spending a great deal of time wandering around Europe.

She sold Woodlands and left Bridgwater in the late 80s and immediately went to extreme lengths to find solitude. She travelled to Australia. The excuse, if one was needed, was to visit her brother in Brisbane, but Clare was soon wandering around the outback. It was as if continental Europe had not been enough. She fell in love with what she saw; a vast wilderness with few people. There was no one who talked about round-the-world yacht races. No one knew who she was and no one asked questions. The Crowhurst name meant nothing.

She had already spent 20 years hating those awful moments when people would come up to her and ask to know more about the story. Her tactic was always to wriggle out of the question somehow. She would divert the conversation as if dealing with an overly inquisitive child. The technique usually worked but having to engage it frequently was wearisome. Occasionally she would be caught out by the sheer audacity of an approach, such as one around the time in 1990 when she was buying a ticket at a theatre in Devon. 'The woman selling the ticket said, "Crowhurst, as in Donald?" I said, "Yes," and I must have said it very dryly because she looked up and she said, "You're not, are you?"'

'I thought that was the end of it and I went off into the theatre and sat down. She came trotting in and she said, "Tell me one thing, if he came back now, would you have him back?"' Clare laughs at the brazen nerve shown by her inquisitor.

'I felt it was such an extraordinary question to ask someone just out of the blue like that. I said, well, with the proviso that we are now very different people, I would just have been glad he had survived.'

She laughs again, still surprised that she actually answered the question. The entire exchange, so long after the Golden Globe, was a measure of how the conspiracy theories had taken hold and made the Crowhurst name so fascinating. There was little escape.

In the Australian outback, Clare found a solution. Deep in the gold prospecting belt, 200 miles inland from Brisbane, she came across an old settler's cottage. It was surrounded by a hundred acres of its own land. There was nothing but bush, kangaroos and wild pigs. Using some of the money from the sale of Woodlands, she bought it for £20,000 and completed the deal so quickly that she moved in a week after seeing it. She still owns it. It is a bolthole she would be reluctant to lose.

'I love being absolutely alone there. I go for six months at a time. I love the isolation. I love sitting out on the veranda, having kangaroos coming up for bits of bread. At night, underneath the house, I can hear wild pigs rooting.

'I take a tape player and a recording of *Under Milk Wood*, or something like that, and play it very loudly. I'd love to stay there but I love my grandchildren more.'

Clare's permanent home is an old three-storey house in the centre of Seaton, a fishing village turned Victorian seaside resort in Devon on the south coast of England. It is an hour's drive south of Bridgwater and, perhaps surprisingly, less than an hour along the coast from Teignmouth. Clare came here by accident. The house was originally bought by Roger for his wife and two children. He later sold it to his mother and now, separated from his wife, he lives in a flat on the top floor from where he runs an underwater surveillance business.

It was Roger who as a six-year-old had had the nightmares that his father's boat was sinking. He has never spoken publicly about the Golden Globe and almost certainly never will. He answers the phone for his mother and shows no hostility to enquiring journalists. There is no display of irritation at being asked if he would be willing to speak; indeed, he sounds close to laughing at the suggestion. He politely declines.

Sitting in the ground-floor living room, Clare reveals that Roger is upstairs but there is no way he will come to talk. 'It is loyalty to his dad. He and Simon are very good friends but they have a totally different approach to it all. Roger really doesn't think the ancillary aspect of it is that important. He just feels the overall tragedy was what mattered, that his dad should have been there and he wasn't.'

Roger, apparently, looks very much like his father, to the extent that complete strangers occasionally approach him.

Both Roger and Rachel did, as teenagers, discuss the family story with their mother. Rachel, an occupational therapist, lives with her husband and daughter only five minutes' walk away. She regularly calls into her mother's house.

The eldest of the four children, James, was 11 when their father's boat was found. In the archive television pictures, he stands taller than the others, being a significant three years older than Simon.

As a young man, James bought a reel-to-reel tape recorder so he could listen to the audio recordings his father had made at sea. The ever-curious Simon asked his older brother what was on the tapes. The answer was that they contained little of value, as their father had used the recordings to talk about anything other than the voyage.

James dreamed of restarting his father's business, *Electron Utilisation*. His A-level results were not quite good enough for his first-choice university, Southampton, so he went to Sheffield. Just like his father before him, he studied electronic engineering.

At the age of 22, eleven years after his father disappeared, James was returning books he had borrowed from a friend. He was outside the university on his motorbike, pulling out onto the road, when he was hit by a hire van travelling in the opposite direction.

He was killed instantly. A decade on from the family's high-profile disaster in the Golden Globe, the Crowhursts were thrown into a second tragedy.

Clare talks about the accident in a manner which suggests she is doing so only because she does not want her eldest child to be forgotten. The words do not come easily. 'I think you just go from day to day,' she says. 'A child is, in some ways, worse because you really don't expect to bury your own child, or cremate your own child.

'I have no feeling that I want a tombstone, somewhere to go to, none of that. Maybe that is something to do with his dad, that I have no memorial or anything.'

Clare wonders how much James knew about his father's story. 'I have chopped that around in my mind and I honestly can't remember talking a lot to James about it either. I always had the feeling that if one of the children asked me a question I would answer it as honestly as I could, but I just don't remember the subject coming up much.'

The years in which the children grew up at Woodlands, without their father, were bewildering ones for Clare. 'It's very difficult to say you thought one thing or the other,' she says. 'Your mind chases itself round in circles. I had time to think a lot. The children were at school and in fairness we had enough money to live on because the *Sunday Times* money and Robin's £5,000 made a big difference.'

As a result of her former job at the BBC's monitoring station, Clare knew Morse code fluently. At home, with the children at school, she was hearing it in her head. She tried to decipher it but it would make no sense.

Helping the children deal with the tragedy of the Golden Globe was made more complicated by her own confusion. She had too many questions spinning around. Why did Donald not hole the boat and call for help? Why did he not say he had to drop out for repairs? Or if he wanted to kill himself, why did he not sail into the Southern Ocean and die a hero? For many years, she searched for answers in the three A4-size logbooks. She kept them in the study. They were not locked up or hidden away but were left out for easy access. In the first year, she would open them every week.

'I used to regard them as vital,' she says. 'I used to go in the study and just read bits of them. For years afterwards, I used to dip into them and try to understand what was going on in his mind. It was just a case of going into that room and dipping in. Then I found I was getting incredibly morbid about it all. It is very easy to become morbid, actually.'

At the time, Clare was reluctant to accept anybody else's interpretation of what happened to Donald. 'I was absolutely convinced he was still alive. For years I was convinced that he would literally surface, I must admit. You can call that bonkers, if you like, but people perceive things differently.'

Even now, after decades of contemplation, Clare's opinion wanders as the question of suicide nags away. She says: 'I think I accept that he had a mental breakdown and he was under tremendous stress. I think I accept that a person who is going through a breakdown is a very different person. The person who went to sea, I couldn't even begin to imagine would have a mental breakdown. I really couldn't.

'He did change. There is no doubt about that. But I think you don't change fundamentally, actually. Maybe I'm wrong?'

So, has her view on whether Donald committed suicide altered at all in all these years? 'I think maybe my mind refuses to accept it. I suppose it is possible but I still think it is very unlikely and it is much more likely to have been an accident. He just fell overboard.'

Clare cites possible scenarios for an accident, such as a hole in the webbing between the boat's hulls, and the stern light being out of its socket as if he was trying to repair it. 'Nobody believes me because they prefer the other theory. He was due to have a talk with the BBC man that day. They made an appointment to talk. I think it could have been a confession that he would have got worked up about. I think the possibility of a confession is a very strong one but nobody listens to that.'

Clare is well practised at privately disassembling the case as put by Tomalin and Hall. Possessing the determination of a defence lawyer, she has a confident response to each piece of evidence.

Hence the missing chronometer that Tomalin and Hall believe Crowhurst held as he jumped overboard at the end of his countdown could have been thrown overboard at any time in a rage against the sea.

The claim that he also took with him the fourth, fraudulent, logbook is disputed by her counter-claim that there never was a fourth logbook.

No question, no detail, no piece of the jigsaw is a surprise. Clare has carefully considered it all, over and over again. She says, boldly, yet with a politeness that shows both tolerance and resignation: 'You won't change my mind now.'

She does accept that the *Philosophy* countdown at least points to Donald taking his own life but believes the very last line contradicts this theory. 'The line, "There is no reason for harmful ..." was very peculiar because there is no way he would regard suicide as not harmful. Suicide is harmful, isn't it?

'It is knowing the person concerned. It is so difficult to accept he would think that was a way out. But then he became a very different person, I accept that also. I suppose that is why my life has been lived in this sort of haphazard way. I think one half of my mind says it must be and the other half says no.'

She remains irritated when people assume Donald committed suicide but she does acknowledge that even her children now all believe that is probably how their father died.

Simon treads very carefully when asked to confirm that he believes his father deliberately stepped off the boat to kill himself. He says that, on the balance of probabilities, it is hard to come to any other conclusion.

He says: 'I think my mother believes I swallowed the line in the book. I know Tomalin and Hall tried to dovetail things so it kind of looked like a logical progression from Crowhurst the batty inventor to batty sailor or something like that. I wouldn't 100 per cent endorse the perspective taken in the book on everything. Probably part of the problem is that it is so good at biblically reconstructing scenes that by the end of the voyage people read it as if that is not reconstruction but as if somebody was there recording it, which they weren't. That can be a problem.

'You are never going to have photographic documentation of what happened at the end of the voyage. The temptation is to resolve it in terms of certainties but in anything where you are interpreting evidence you have always got to think, "Well, I could be wrong." I could be wrong about my way of seeing it. Maybe there is another way. If that's what my mother feels, then fine. That's ok. I would never want to stop her from saying that is what she felt.'

Mother and son are speaking a few days apart and more than 200 miles from each other. One is in Devon and the other in Cambridge. Both, from time to time, suggest it would be wise to seek a second opinion from the other. Simon knows the story of his father's voyage inside out, so when he hears anything he has not known before, he picks up on it immediately. It slows him down, as he visibly wonders if the new information changes his perspective.

He says: 'It is interesting that my mother spent so long looking at the logbooks. I hadn't realised that. I knew she had seen them and thought about them. I didn't realise she had looked at them so carefully.

'My father's death doesn't make sense in terms of what he was like before. She thinks about the person on land, another person. But a lot happened, enough to change somebody fundamentally and catastrophically. I think that is a lot even now for my mother to accept. Fair enough.'

Not surprisingly, the final pages of the logbooks are at the heart of the family's struggle in reaching agreement. 'How do you interpret those 25,000 words of the *Philosophy*? My mother does have a different take on it to me. She sees it as jottings, as ideas he jotted down almost as if they were casual thoughts and ideas. They seem to me to be a bit more intense than that.

'She believes he was thinking of announcing what had really happened. So "resigning the game" might mean "I'll give up this game and come clean about what I've done and haven't done." So she emphasises the line when he says, "It will be done as my family require me to do it," which I think for her is pretty well impossible to interpret as meaning he is going to kill himself.

'I don't think he did see it as killing himself. He saw it as a kind of transformation into another state of being. In that sense I don't see it as suicide either. He was thinking in a totally different realm by that stage. But there is also an element of guilt, of punishment there as well. So it is quite a multi-layered thing.'

Over the years, the Crowhursts have been asked several times if they would support attempts to bring the rotting wreck of *Teignmouth Electron* back to Britain. The boat was sold after the Golden Globe and was used in the Caribbean for racing and as a tourist boat, before being abandoned on the small island of Cayman Brac. It still lies on the south-west shore among palm trees between the beach and a road. It was bought in 2007 by an American artist, Michael Jones McKean, who described it as both an archaeological ruin and a destroyer of dreams. His plan, to create a full-blown replica of it lying in a dilapidated state, is one more project to add to the long list inspired by Donald Crowhurst.

Clare has not enjoyed, or even understood, all the attention. Her blessing has been elusive. The idea of bringing home the wreck of *Teignmouth Electron* has been especially repulsive, if only because she believes Donald may have been raging against the boat. 'That's why I have never supported people who have wanted to bring the boat back,' she says. 'I hated that boat. It was appalling. It was hopeless. But he didn't build it.'

Simon shares his mother's desire to leave *Teignmouth Electron* where it is, although he admits he would like to see the wreck for himself and that he even occasionally looks at it through Google Earth's satellite cameras.

There is pride in the Crowhurst family, whatever the public perception of the name. It is personified in Simon's placing of the package on his kitchen table. He has an air of impatience, like a child on Christmas day, as it sits unopened while more important matters are discussed. When the moment comes, out he pulls from a large padded envelope one of his father's original Navicators.

It is the invention that Donald Crowhurst was selling at the London Boat Show back in 1968 when the Golden Globe race was taking shape. This plastic device, the size and shape of a police radar gun, was what Crowhurst was known for when his entry to the race was announced. Publicly, it almost defined him. The boffin with the Navicator was easily seen as the boffin with the futuristic box-of-tricks computer.

Simon demonstrates how it was held like a handgun, with one arm outstretched. It was pointed in the likely direction of land and moved until it picked up a coastal radio signal. Then a compass bearing was read off from the eye-level sight.

Its grey, curving, plastic case would not look out of place on a *Doctor Who* set. It does indeed, as Simon points out as if he is selling them now, still look remarkably futuristic. Simon talks rapidly about how all the components were soldered and the assembling was done by hand, and how many of his father's evenings were spent testing them. He talks about how people loved the Navicator so much that for years afterwards they were asking for spares. Simon is not a sailor, but he knows this device inside out.

It is a genuinely touching moment. In the Navicator, the son has something tangible with which to identify with the father he was too young to truly know. No wonder he was eager to show it off.

12 : FORTY YEARS ON

The lives of those caught up by the Golden Globe have been inextricably linked for 40 years, yet few of the players in this maritime drama have talked to each other since the year of the race. The three 'Sea Widows' went their separate ways after the photo shoot on the River Thames, midway through the race. That was in January 1969, when their husbands and Robin Knox-Johnston were the only four still sailing. They have not met or spoken since. Instead, they have each gone to extreme lengths to find peace: Francoise Moitessier sailing to the Far East on her own; Eve Tetley seeking sanctuary on Alderney; and Clare Crowhurst buying her settler's cottage in the Australian outback.

Bernard Moitessier's funeral, in June 1994, was a strange affair. He was a bigger celebrity than ever, having recently published another successful book. Television crews and journalists were among the gathering at a picture-postcard harbour in Le Bono, a village five miles up the River Auray in Brittany's Gulf of Morbihan. The old boat, *Joshua*, was brought from a sailing school in La Rochelle and dominated the historic, stone quay underneath a 100-year-old suspension bridge. Family, friends and many of the women in Bernard's life threw flower petals onto the water as a last farewell. The service was followed by a social gathering. Francoise watched the people around her and felt too many did not truly understand Bernard and what he stood for. They were, she felt, too interested in a celebrity culture and its trappings. She walked out, sad that Bernard's life was ending with what she regarded as a circus.

'It is true that when we met again at the end of his life we felt very close. We had lost 20 years of our lives. It was silly, a pity.

'But I found a nice guy,' she says, referring to her later marriage and life after Bernard.

Unlike Francoise, Eve Tetley and Clare Crowhurst did not remarry.

Eve is content with her life of retirement on Alderney. She walks out of the front door of her terraced cottage, not stopping to lock it, and makes her way down the narrow street to the market square and her favourite pub. Two young women are ordering shots of alcohol at the bar. They are former pupils. One jokes with 'Mrs Tetley', asking if she thinks the other girl has dyed her hair too black. It is Saturday night, and the bar and pub restaurant are full. Eve knows everyone.

'It is such a delight, such a delight, to walk down the street and say "Hello" to almost everybody,' she says. I'm a small-town girl. Durham was not a big city in my day. I love knowing everybody. It is comfortable.'

Despite living on a small island, Eve has rarely taken to a boat in the last 30 years. She almost always travels by air, if at all. One of the few exceptions was when she was visiting New Zealand, where her son lives. Off the south coast, she was on a steel-hulled motor sailor taking tourists to the Fiordland National Park. Eve knew only too well that she was more than 40 degrees south of the equator, well into the Roaring Forties. The weather was fine and settled, yet the swell of what is the only ocean with an uninterrupted path around the planet was awe-inspiring. She sat among the tourists with her thoughts of Nigel and his months battling through the Southern Ocean. She was struck by the vast emptiness around her and how there was nothing but a few birds. She thought of how strange it must have been to experience that day after day, month after month.

Eve still reads *Trimaran Solo*. She has a stack of old photograph slides from the four years she had with the one man who truly swept her off her feet.

As she waits for a crab dinner to be brought to her pub table, she is relieved that she has at last talked honestly and frankly about the dark chapter in her life. It has taken a long time, but she has reached a new milestone.

Eve has always been determined that the Golden Globe would not destroy her. For all the pain it has caused, she has soldiered on.

She says: 'I haven't let it ruin my life. I have enjoyed my life and got on with it. It has not defined my life.'

Both Eve and Francoise managed to find ways of dealing with the trauma. Clare admits she has been less successful. Her efforts have not been helped by the enduring fascination in the Crowhurst story, which Chichester described as the sea drama of the century.

After the early media storm and conspiracy theories, she thought the public would go away. 'I am still always amazed at the interest,' she says. 'I can remember when the *Sunday Times* was going to write the book, and Jim Barrington, my solicitor, said, "Look, they have got the stuff and we have got to go ahead with this because even if they don't make use of it now, everybody else is going to make use of it." He said, "It will all be over by Christmas. You won't hear another thing about it after Christmas." Jim, bless him, is now dead and it is still going on. I really do think it is time it was put to sleep.'

Clare has to stop and think when she is asked what sort of life she has had. She seems unsure of the answer. 'Simon says I never cheered up afterwards. He wrote in an article that he never really saw me happy again. It was really weird. I said to Roger, "Is that true? Am I a miserable old sow?" He said, "No, he didn't mean that." Roger is very protective of Simon. I understand that Simon has got to stand in his corner and state his case but I don't feel I have been a miserable old sow, you know. But you accept that children have got to be brought up by somebody who is reasonably lively and normal.

'On the whole, I lead a pretty normal sort of existence but what is a normal existence? My life has been comparatively straightforward. I was incredibly happy with Donald and I think that is the real problem. You always think, "Wouldn't it be lovely to just feel that happy again?" When I think of Donald, I think mostly about what a glorious time we had together. People say it must have been hard work for us with four children but it wasn't. Maybe I have a cloud-cuckoo attitude to it but it seems to me we had a glorious time.'

They are powerful memories, and Clare is in no mood to let them go. 'I think of him every single day, I think. Certainly several times a week.

'I haven't moved on. As the Americans would say, I need closure.' She laughs, but it is a nervous laugh as she admits that 'closure' is never going to happen. 'Not going to now, no,' she says.

When she is asked if her life has been shaped by the Golden Globe, Clare needs no time at all to think. She is immediately sure of the answer, and she delivers her response assertively. 'Yes, it has definitely been shaped by it. There is no doubt about that. It has affected my life to the extent that I think it has dictated it because I have been weird in some ways, I know. The business of not wanting to talk too much about it, you know. I hate it when people say, "Oh, do tell me what happened, I never understood it," and I always get out of that one.'

Clare gives the impression that she will use her dying breath to defend her husband. She still keeps his logbooks, close to hand in the mildly disorganized hallway, next to a towering Welsh grandfather clock which used to stand proudly by the front door in Woodlands. They are protected in an old, dark-wood box just a little bigger than their A4 size. She describes the box as a sort of coffin. The hardback covers of the three books are scuffed and worn to the extent that their once-sharp corners are now rounded. The damp air at sea has left the pages crinkled like old parchment paper, yet the tiny writing gives them the appearance of microfiche. On these sometimes water-stained pages lies almost the full story of Donald Crowhurst's disastrous last year. There is much to be unnerved by, yet Clare can see beyond the tragedy.

She leaps to Donald's defence at any hint of criticism. She has, though, in trying to come to terms with what happened, softened her response to other people's conclusions. She used to be outraged, but is now more prepared to accept that others may be right. On being told that Simon spoke of his father as being the architect of his own downfall, she bridles, and almost has to force herself to pause and reflect. Then, slowly, she says: 'I think for a son who is wounded by the lack of a father, that is fair comment, really. You have to regard that as fair comment, I think.'

When asked specifically if the Golden Globe's influence has been for the worse, Clare speaks deliberately and intensely. 'Definitely. Oh there's no doubt about it. It has been a disaster. I think it has been a disaster for the children even more, their father being missing which is, God knows, enough, but it has shaped their lives, without a doubt.

'It is sad. I think it is a wasted life in the sense that I didn't feel I could do anything in a way because you are carrying such an awful lot of baggage. Tremendous amount.'

Clare is referring not only to a lack of desire for another man in her life. She is afraid of making a fool of herself. 'I have always been inclined to write. I have always scribbled things out and made short stories. Simon says I'm a very good writer, actually. But there is absolutely no way I would present anything to be published, because I feel you are exposing yourself to more ridicule. I haven't thought of it like this before but I think it probably is ridicule.

'I am afraid of a lifetime of ridicule.'

Within Golden Globe circles, there has been a tendency not to interfere or to pry during the decades since 1969. This tendency has affected all those involved. No one discussed an agreement, or called for it. It simply happened.

One of the few lines of contact has been occasional letters between Simon Crowhurst and Sir Robin Knox-Johnston. It has been the only link between the family and the man who donated his prize money. For more than 15 years, Knox-Johnston and Clare Crowhurst lived a mere 45 miles from each other in Devon. Neither felt the need to make contact. They are both frequently asked about the £5,000 Knox-Johnston donated to the Crowhurst fund and which he insisted stayed there even after the scale of the hoax unfolded.

Knox-Johnston was not wealthy and he intended to resume his career in the merchant navy. The £5,000 was the equivalent of two-and-a-half years' pay, yet 40 years on, he plays down the extent of his generosity. He says he never expected to win the money because it was for the fastest voyage, not for being first home.

He says: 'When Donald Crowhurst's boat was found, I knew very early on that he had cheated. I was one of twelve who knew. I was very keen it was kept quiet because of the children. James was nearly 12 and Simon, nine. Lord Goodman [a leading London lawyer] said, "You can't."

'I wasn't giving money to a cheat. I was giving the

money to an unfortunate family who were going to be in an even worse plight now. Those children were going to suffer. They were going to get it at school. I just thought there is no change to the situation.'

In 2006, Robin Knox-Johnston and Clare Crowhurst did meet for the first time when a film, *Deep Water*, was being made about the Golden Globe. It was a simple and quiet meeting in which neither side was interested in making a fuss. 'There was nothing special in meeting Clare, because time has moved on,' he says.

Knox-Johnston downplays the meeting because he baulks at any hint that the Crowhursts are in debt to him. He sees the donation as done business, from another time.

The Crowhursts have always been uncomfortable at the way the public interest in Donald's story has overshadowed the achievements of Knox-Johnston and the others in the Golden Globe.

Simon Crowhurst says: 'I'm always embarrassed by it. My father was the one who messed up more than anybody else yet he is the one who gets all the attention.'

It happened again in 2007 when Knox-Johnston sailed round the world in the Velux 5 Oceans Race and returned home just as the *Deep Water* film was being promoted. 'Robin Knox-Johnston is someone who I could understand being very, very, angry with my father,' says Simon. 'It seems he can't escape from my father. Not only did about 90 per cent of the attention from the Golden Globe race go to him, but next time, when Robin is completely independently sailing around the world again, all everyone is talking about when he gets back is Donald Crowhurst! But he is so incredibly stoical, such a robust character. I have a great deal of admiration for him.'

Knox-Johnston is more interested in the future than in the past. He is delighted that his daughter, Sara, who was born when *Suhaili* was being built, met Simon at a screening of *Deep Water*. 'They sat next to each other during the film and just chatted, which I thought was rather nice,' he says.

Knox-Johnston's friends in the sailing world describe him as a much more subtle person than people expect. The Crowhurst donation is well known, they say; less so is the time he has given over the years for good causes and, in particular, sail-training charities. He believed in Ellen MacArthur long before everyone else and encouraged her to pursue her solo sailing dream, recognising that Chichester's Royal Institution speech back in 1969, in which women were said to rebel against solitude, belonged to another time.

His generosity continued even after his life savings were wiped out by the financial disaster of Lloyds in the 1990s. Knox-Johnston was a 'Lloyds Name'. He had what he openly describes as a miserable five years trying to pay off debts and secure his future, at one point having to remortgage his house. Yet during this time he still continued his charitable work.

He continues to sail, and once confided to a close friend that his love of being at sea was based partly on escape from the complications of life on shore. That friend also said he hates political correctness but is kind and tolerant of everyone.

He was dealt a terrible blow in 2003 when his wife, Sue, died of ovarian cancer. She was the same childhood sweetheart whom Knox-Johnston had moved to Bombay with as a young man and then divorced when they fell out over the building of *Suhaili*. Knox-Johnston says one of the best things he ever did in life was to remarry Sue in 1972.

They had been looking forward to retirement together and Knox-Johnston admits he felt bitter at their dream being shattered. It was what sent him round the world again in the 2006/7 Velux 5 Oceans, a single-handed race owned by his own company.

That was a remarkable affair. At the age of 68, Knox-Johnston, the first man to sail non-stop round the world single-handedly, was bridging the gap between an old generation of sailors and the modern Formula One racers. He himself had said that trying to compare the two eras was like comparing the bi-plane with Concorde.

No one understood the differences more than Knox-Johnston, if only because in the decades since winning the Golden Globe he had kept more than a keen and curious eye on the developing single-handed race scene.

The Golden Globe was such a peculiar and chaotic event that 14 years passed before there was another single-handed round-the-world race: the BOC Challenge in 1982. Knox-Johnston declined an invitation to take part but he did agree to be chairman of the race committee. This time, there would be rules. Knox-Johnston was not going to allow a repeat of the unruly Golden Globe. He insisted that every entrant had to sail a qualifying passage of at least 2,000 miles and, crucially, they had to do it on the same boat they would be racing. It is a requirement which still exists for most

events to this day, with varying distances, and its introduction was a direct result of the experiences of the likes
of Blyth, Ridgway, King and Crowhurst, who all floun-
dered on boats they did not know.

Ten of the 17 starters in that BOC Challenge finished,
a considerable improvement on the Golden Globe's one
out of nine. Knox-Johnston, as chairman, called a
meeting after the event. There would be another race in
four years. The maximum-length boat allowed would be
60 feet and there would be a series of design rules to
prevent too much safety being sacrificed for speed. The
rules meant that designers would have room to be
creative but that the boats would have enough in
common to make for exciting racing. The 'Open 60', a
boat designed and purpose-built for long distance solo
racing, was born.

It is the one-class boat which now dominates single-
handed round-the-world races. Knox-Johnston
continued over the years to play a part in the Open 60s
evolution, working closely even with a new rival race,
the Vendée Globe.

However, his role was always on shore. The news that
he wanted to go to sea and actually compete in one in
2006/7 was a shock to most.

Knox-Johnston became irritated that people thought
he was too old to cope. He had already noticed that as
soon as he had reached his mid 60s people had started
to treat him like a small child again. So, in open defiance
of the sceptics, he bought a second-hand Open 60 and
set out to prove them wrong.

Immediately, he found that one crushing difference
between sailing *Suhaili* and flying along in a modern

carbon-fibre boat was noise. Instead of the gentle swish of passing water, there was a constant bone-breaking vibration. *Suhaili* rarely went faster than 8 knots. Now he was doing up to 20. Everything, including him, seemed to shake, rattle and roll. He found it unsettling and worrying, and understood why some Open 60 sailors wore ear defenders.

During the race itself, he made headlines as a grumpy old man cursing modern technology. He never really came to terms with his chart table looking like the flight deck of an aircraft. *Suhaili*'s only electronic equipment had been a low-powered single sideband radio, and that had not worked properly for eight months. His Open 60 had no less than three satellite communication systems: Inmarsat Fleet 77 for phone calls, faxes, emails, internet and live video conferencing; Sat C for navigation warnings and race control position polling; and an Iridium satellite phone for communication in remote areas. Perhaps most startling for a man who is wary of computers, there was a laptop to control communications, including software for transmitting video and still pictures; another laptop loaded with software programmes for navigation and weather forecasts; and a third laptop to act as backup to the other two. There was also an electric autopilot with two control panels, radar, active echo transponder for detecting other vessels' radar, GPS, electric water maker, a chart plotter to display electronic charts and GPS positions, an RNLI emergency tracking system, depth sounder, wind gauge and distance log.

Knox-Johnston was quick to point out that almost every system had its own alarm for when it was not working properly. He took some pleasure in announcing that he once had four alarms bleeping loudly at the same time.

Those who were studiously watching how this man from the history books took to the modern stage took great delight in reading his 'bloody electronics' dispatches. He wrote: 'This was meant to be a sailing race, not an electronics obstacle course!'

Knox-Johnston was discovering that the two eras he was straddling were further apart than he had realised. Although following essentially the same route and enduring the same weather patterns, what *Suhaili* did in ten months the Open 60s do in three. The stress of the modern pace was a major challenge.

Despite the differences, Knox-Johnston in 2006/7 was able to race at the age of 68. He survived capsizing in the force-ten storm which created havoc among the fleet in the Bay of Biscay, and went on to finish fourth out of seven starters. But he swore he would never do it again.

Whole fleets of single-handed boats now race round the same 'course' set first by the old trade clippers and followed by Chichester, then non-stop by Knox-Johnston. In the 2008/9 Vendée Globe, the race closest to the Golden Globe's spirit of non-stop and without assistance, there was an unprecedented field of 30 skippers, all in Open 60s. Almost half of those men and two women had at least attempted the voyage before, which helps explain why the number of people who have sailed round on their own is only around 200. More than double that number have gone into space and more than ten times have climbed Everest.

Those who try it are no longer expected to see a

psychiatrist, as Knox-Johnston did before he set off in 1968, when people wondered if he would go mad. Incidentally, on return, friends said he had indeed changed, by mellowing and losing some of his natural aggression. The official diagnosis, though, was the same as on departure – 'distressingly normal'. Yet it is still, according to the man himself, one of the most difficult and hazardous challenges available.

In comparing the two eras, it is tempting to focus on the electronic gadgetry and boat speed. However, the race to be the first was not only about the voyage; it was as much a scramble to the start as a race to the finish. The professionals in the Vendée Globe will have planned their campaigns for years: indeed, in Les Sables d'Olonne, western France, watching the 2008/9 fleet leave was the 20-year-old British woman, Katie Miller, a Young Sailor of the Year who was inspired to recreate Ellen MacArthur's teenage voyage round Britain. She was in France to make vital contacts, with a dream of being on the start line not for the next race four years later, but the one after that, in 2016.

The professionalism of the modern day costs money. Sponsors of the new Open 60 campaigns have to spend up to £3 million just to build the boat, let alone run the Formula One-style team that surrounds the celebrity skipper. In 1968, Knox-Johnston's sponsorship amounted to 120 cans of Tennent's beer and a £5 voucher from Cadburys. If he had not struck a deal with the *Sunday Mirror* and a book publisher, it is unlikely he would have been able to go.

The truth about the Golden Globe race was that at least six of the nine adventurers set off in boats that were less than ideal, whether in design or in lack of preparation. Knox-Johnston's decision to rush off in a boat that he already owned, when it was in a questionable condition, looked wild and foolhardy at the time. It did indeed make for relentless hardship as he fought a never-ending battle to keep *Suhaili* sailing in the right direction and in one piece. However, that calculated risk, that seizing of the moment, was at the heart of what made the Golden Globe such an adventure. Knox-Johnston and *Suhaili* made it round without stopping, and they did it first.

Knox-Johnston now lives in a village near the waters of the Solent. He was knighted in 1995. He still owns and sails *Suhaili*. Even in the hard times of financial debt, he could not bring himself to sell her. He jokes she will be his coffin.

It is often said the *Sunday Times* Golden Globe race was a reckless stunt, but that is arguably to misunderstand a basic tenet of sailing. 'It is a skipper's decision whether to go to sea or not,' says Knox-Johnston. 'It is up to the individual. They have to decide if they want to do it.'

Undoubtedly, the judgement of many of the nine men was clouded from the moment the *Sunday Times* brought column inches, glamour and urgency to the challenge. Men dared to dream.

No one could have known then how the shattering of some of those dreams would have such a lasting impact, still felt with searing pain all these decades on. But history's first draft can be rewritten. It can be set straight.

Was Nigel Tetley worthy only of headlines like

'*Sinking feelings*'? In the two years between his boat breaking up and his death, he was hopelessly overshadowed by the two men he once, briefly, stood between at a press conference photo shoot; the sailing grandee Francis Chichester and the race winner, Robin Knox-Johnston. Tetley had carried on past Australia to sail, non-stop, almost twice as far as Chichester. He sailed only 1,100 miles fewer than Knox-Johnston – a shortfall of only three per cent. Yet, in a world in which the public likes its triumphs to be clearly defined, that meant little. As Knox-Johnston puts it now, Tetley's achievement has always been underestimated. The fact is that Lieutenant Commander Nigel Tetley, by crossing his outward track on the way home, before he sank, achieved the first circumnavigation of the globe in a trimaran. It was a feat the likes of Chichester had not thought possible.

Tetley's failure to finish in glory may have had nothing to do with his death. If Eve cannot be sure, no one else can. But if disappointment had any role, he would perhaps be comforted by the knowledge that his part in the race was vital to its enduring appeal.

Was Bernard Moitessier noble and magnificent or pretentious and self-important? He left behind a wife and children who have been scarred. Yet Francoise recognises that he was extraordinary, that he truly was a unique spirit. It is difficult to imagine a competitor in the modern era turning his back on society in such an uncompromising and heartfelt manner.

Was Donald Crowhurst a cheat and a liar, as many have described him, or is it more complicated? Even his harshest critics, the gentlemen sailors who for decades have felt their sport's image has been sullied, are now shifting uncomfortably and wondering if they judged him too harshly. The change in mood has been picked up by the magazine most popular with British cruising sailors, and which Donald Crowhurst would undoubtedly be reading if he was still alive, *Yachting Monthly*. On the 40th anniversary of Crowhurst setting sail from Teignmouth, the editor, Paul Gelder, addressed his readers through a page-one editorial. He wrote: 'How many sailors can honestly say that they have never talked themselves into a cruise or a project without having doubts about a successful outcome? Crowhurst was an ordinary man with a bold, brave dream that took him to his death. His is a moving story full of "what ifs". He could have thrown all his logbooks overboard and no one would ever have known what happened. Instead, he left behind the truth of his deception so we can better understand human frailty.

'There is a bit of Crowhurst in all of us.' Forty years on, judgements are softening, views are altering.

But perhaps it would have been better for everyone if the Golden Globe had not taken place?

'There was no stopping it,' says Knox-Johnston. 'It was going to happen anyway. We were there. It was the next thing to do. If the *Sunday Times* had not turned up I would have gone anyway. There were four of us already planning to go. They just saw a marketing opportunity, which is fair enough.

'We decided for various reasons. It was not about the money for me. The thought that I would be wealthy never crossed my mind, and I wasn't disappointed.

'Nor was it for fame. I had no plans other than to go

back to sea afterwards. What use is fame to me when I am on the bridge of a ship? I would have a little circle around my table at meal times. They think, "Wow." For how long do they think that? First couple of meals? I didn't do it for that. I just wanted to be the first to do something. That's all.'

The Golden Globe, with all of its charm, could not happen again; certainly not now. Even if a comparable challenge could be conjured up, it would have none of the innocence of these days gone by, when a group of men essentially fumbled around on their own, making it up as they went along.

They were undoubtedly pioneers: each of the nine sailing off into the unknown with courage and dreams, some without time to think fully of the consequences.

Little could they have realised then that they would alter lives as profoundly as they did and that, with the passing of the decades, they and their boats would become just a part of the whole, human story of the Golden Globe race.

October 31st 1968

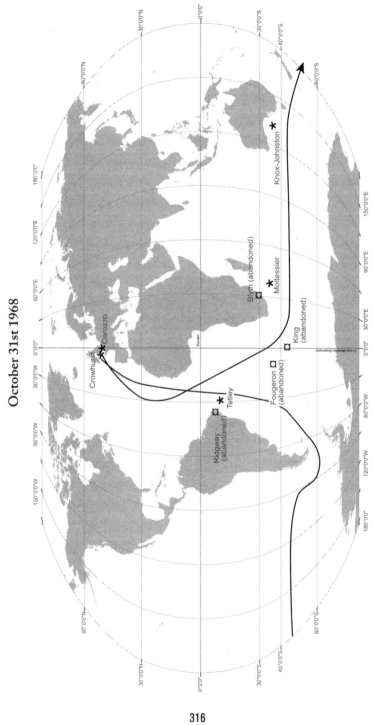

Christmas Day 1968

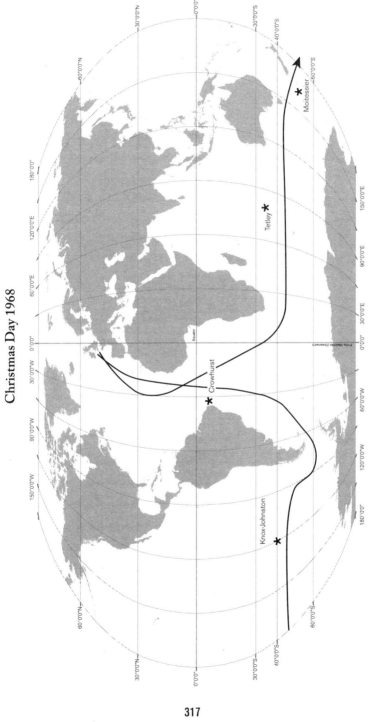

Moitessier sails on

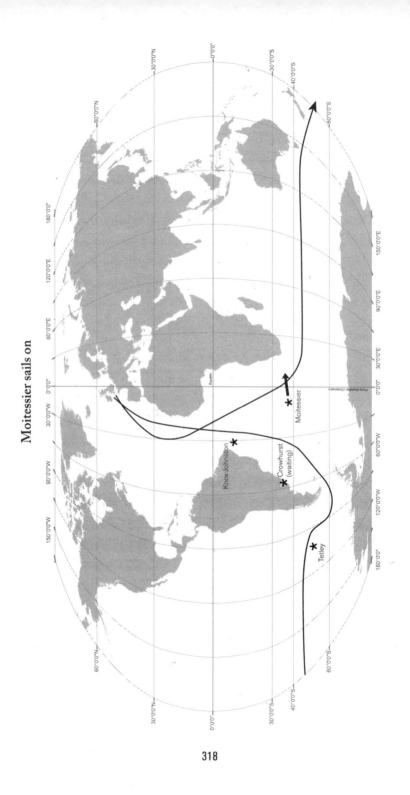

Crowhurst Route

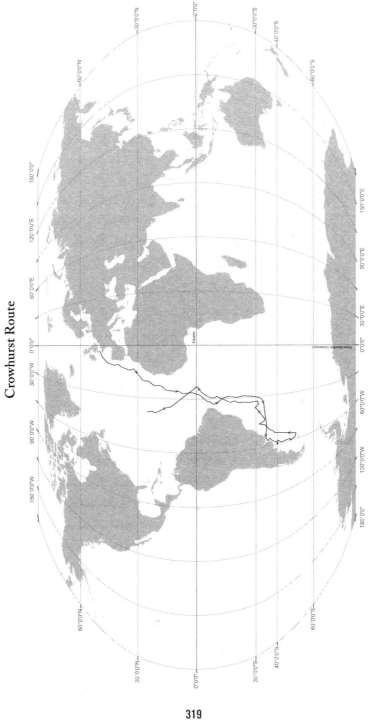

SOURCES

Along the Clipper Way, Francis Chichester, 1966, Hodder & Stoughton, London

Gipsy Moth Circles the World, Francis Chichester, 1968, McGraw-Hill, New York

A World of My Own, Robin Knox-Johnston, 2004, Adlard Coles, London

The Long Way, Bernard Moitessier, 1995, Sheridan House, New York

Trimaran Solo, Nigel Tetley, 1970, Nautical Publishing, Lymington

Capsize, Bill King, 1969, Nautical Publishing, Lymington

Innocent Aboard, Chay Blyth, 1970, Nautical Publishing, Lymington

Journey to Ardmore, John Ridgway, 1971, Hodder & Stoughton, London

The Strange Voyage of Donald Crowhurst, Tomalin & Hall, 1970, Hodder & Stoughton, London

Transformations, Glin Bennet, 2005, Broadcast Books, Bristol

60000 milles a la voile, Francoise Moitessier, 2004, L'Ancre de Marine, Louviers

MOITESSIER: A Sailing Legend, Jean-Michel Barrault, 2005, Sheridan House, New York

A Fighting Chance, Ridgway & Blyth, 1966, Paul Hamlyn, London

Force of Nature, Sir Robin Knox-Johnston, 2007, Michael Joseph Penguin, London

Celestial Navigation, Tom Cunliffe, 1989, Fenhurst, Arundel

Longitude, Dava Sobel, 1996, Fourth Estate, London

Donald Crowhurst logbooks courtesy of Clare Crowhurst

British Journal of Medical Psychology